ONE-ANOTHERING

DR. JIM HALLA

ONE-ANOTHERING

AN ASPECT OF PROGRESSIVE SANCTIFICATION

Ambassador International
GREENVILLE, SOUTH CAROLINA & BELFAST, NORTHERN IRELAND
www.ambassador-international.com

One-Anothering

An Aspect of Progressive Sanctification
© 2022 by Dr. Jim Halla
All rights reserved

ISBN: 978-1-64960-133-9
eISBN: 978-1-64960-183-4

THE HOLY BIBLE, NEW INTERNATIONAL VERSION®, NIV® Copyright © 1973, 1978, 1984, 2011 by Biblica, Inc.™ Used by permission. All rights reserved worldwide.

Cover Design by Hannah Linder Designs
Interior Typesetting by Dentelle Design

AMBASSADOR INTERNATIONAL
411 University Ridge Suite B14
Greenville, SC 29609, USA
www.ambassador-international.com

AMBASSADOR BOOKS
The Mount
2 Woodstock Link
Belfast, BT6 8DD, Northern Ireland, UK
www.ambassador-international.com

The colophon is a trademark of Ambassador

Contents

INTRODUCTION
One Anothering (OAN): A Function of the Ministry of the Word. 7

CHAPTER 1
OAN: A Function of the Ministry of the Word 11

CHAPTER 2
Fellowship and Relationships 23

CHAPTER 3
The Mind of Christ 51

CHAPTER 4
Submission and Putting up with One Another 107

CHAPTER 5
Love. 137

CHAPTER 6
Romans 14:1-15:7: Welcoming, Accepting, and Bearing With 163

CHAPTER 7
Family Affection 201

CHAPTER 8
Encouragement, Comfort, and OAN 209

CHAPTER 9
Encouragement through Exhortation 251

CHAPTER 10
  Encouragement through Comfort 257

CHAPTER 11
  OAN, Encouragement, and Stirring-up. 275

CHAPTER 12
  OAN, Encouragement, and Counseling. 281

CHAPTER 13
  OAN: Kindness, Compassion-Tenderhearted,
  and Forgiveness 285

CHAPTER 14
  OAN Hospitality 301

CHAPTER 15
  OAN and Intimacy 307

CHAPTER 16
  Passages addressing a negative aspect of
  One Anothering. 313

CHAPTER 17
  Summary and Questions. 321

INTRODUCTION

One Anothering (OAN): A Function of the Ministry of the Word

SEVERAL YEARS AGO, A SPEAKER at a counseling conference emphasized that discipleship is a ministry of the local church and a function of the ministry of the Word. Counseling was but one—although vital—aspect of the ministry of the Word. Intrigued, I began to catalogue passages in the New Testament that referred to OAN. The results of those efforts are recorded in this book before you.

In God's providence, He sent a pandemic. Christians are asking: what do we do about Church? What do we do about each other? In addition, America has changed radically. Some have said it is an unprecedented time. America is not one nation, and it is not one nation under God. His providence has brought to the forefront the issue of OAN and its importance for the Church and individual believers.

In response to, and as part of the above, people and churches have brought up cause after cause, issue after issue under such names such as social injustice, racial equality, Jesus as the Healer and Comforter, prosperity, and American values to mention a few. Causes and people are more important than Christ, His Person, message, and ministry. Now the message is *something more than Christ* rather *more of the something* which is Christ! Truth has become distorted. The Church is back in Galatia!

The change in landscape in America should remind us of the times in Rome. However, as then and now, the change has forced the Church to rethink its identity, purpose, and mission. One aspect of the change is a self-inventory—both individually and corporately. One result should be a renewal of what I call *"OAN strategies."*

One of my goals in writing is to convince others of the necessity and beauty of OAN God's way. God has not left His people and we are not to leave Him. OAN was essential for growth in Christ as a Church body and individually in apostolic times. The same urgency is applicable today.

Further, I wish to help others implement OAN principles personally and corporately. OAN is a vital aspect of progressive sanctification. To that end, I give God's rationale in commanding OAN. I show how His command fits into the context of the body of the Church as given in Ephesians 4:11-14: *It was he who gave some to be apostles, some to be prophets, some to be evangelists, and some to be pastors and teachers, to prepare God's people for works of service, so that the body of Christ may be built up until we all reach unity in the faith and in the knowledge of the Son of God, and become mature, attaining to the whole measure of fullness in Christ. Then we will no longer be infants, tossed back and forth by the waves, and blown here and there by every wind of teaching and by the cunning about and craftiness of men in their deceitful schemes.*

OAN is framed as an imperative, but it is not isolated or fragmented. It fits into the context of the whole of church life. The practice of OAN is intended by God to be part of solutions to problems that redeemed sinners encounters amongst themselves as they live and function together. Moreover, it is an integral part of the believer's progressive sanctification, both for the doer and receiver of OAN. Sadly, believers still often live and function in an ungodly manner within the body.

This book includes an examination of the biblical basis of OAN, the principles surrounding it, and various perspectives on how OAN is a necessary ingredient for a vital church. As you begin to read the material you may find it repetitious. Please note that repetition is a biblical construct. Specific passages are multifaceted; one passage serves multiple functions. As a result, a specific OAN activity may be covered in several passages with its own nuance.

The book of Deuteronomy is the book of "not forgetting" and "remembering." Psalm 105 and 106 give consequences of "forgetting" and 2 Peter is a letter of "remembering." In each case the life of God's covenant community and His name were at stake.

Moreover, I have found that for me, for patients in my rheumatology practice, and for fellow believers, repetition on several fronts is very instructive. Discernment is a gift and requires a delightful and fuller exposition of truth.

To that end Paul prayed for discernment for the saints in Philippi and Colossae (Philippians 1:9-11 and Colossians 1:9-12). Peter encouraged the people to grow in grace and knowledge of our Lord Jesus Christ (2 Peter 3:18). The ministry of the Word was to be alive and well.

People, including believers as evidenced by the disciples, have selective memories and are slow of heart (Luke 24:25-27, 32, 36-49). Any repetition in the book is intended to clarify and bless. May God bless us in the effort to OAN!

CHAPTER 1
OAN: A Function of the Ministry of the Word

OAN IS A FUNCTION OF the ministry of the Word. By the phrase *ministry of the Word*, I am referring to the presentation of God's truth. This presentation is both public and private. The ministry of the Word is public through preaching and teaching; it is also private through individual discipleship which includes OAN and evangelism.

One important purpose of the ministry of the Word is to impart knowledge and wisdom. Truth is understood and is to be applied to solve problems God's way. In that way, believers, individually and corporately, live in a manner that pleases Him.

Specifically, OAN is the ministry of fellowship within the body of Christ whereby believing members help one another to change and grow. It is an active ministry of the Word for and to those in God's family. On the other hand, evangelism is the ministry of the Word to the unbeliever.

More than fifty New Testament passages command various types of OAN activities thus emphasizing their importance for vital church life. The various passages use the expression *one another* or *each other* to illustrate and detail biblical fellowship. Some are supportive, others are confrontive, others are preventive, and some are illustrative of the outgrowth of the fruits of OAN. The ministry can be conducted properly or improperly.

OAN is a shepherding ministry by and of the members of the body. Certainly, God has called the elders and church leaders to a special ministry of shepherding that is distinctive, official, and exemplary. At the same time, most people would agree that the elders should not do all the praying, Bible studying, or evangelism for the congregation. It is in that same sense that the elders should not do all the shepherding. Indeed, the elders' shepherding is most effective when each member watches out for himself and other members of the flock.

Therefore, brothers and sisters as they grow in Christlikeness will develop an instinct for OAN which should be as instinctive as it was for Jesus and the apostles, post-Pentecost. Caring for the flock, both by the elders and members, is to be modeled after the great Shepherd (see Psalm 23 and John 6, 10, 15).

I. Jesus' Motivation, the Indwelling Holy Spirit, and OAN

Jesus came with one overriding desire: to please His Father, which included living a perfect life and dying a perfect death. He gave Himself to the Triune God and His life as a ransom for many (John 4:31-34; 5:19, 30; 6:38; 10:37-38; 14:31; 15:10; 17:4;

Matthew 20:20-28; Mark 10:35-45; 2 Corinthians 5:21). He is the Great One-Anotherer and the Church's model for OAN.

Moreover, the Holy Spirit indwells believers enabling them to grow and mature in Christlikeness and as an OAN-er (Romans 8:9-11; 1 Corinthians 3:16; 6:13-20;2 Corinthians 6:14-16; 2 Timothy 1:14). The Church and all believers are to be ready to be a blessing to fellow believers out of humble, joyful gratitude to the Triune God for Who He is and what He has done and is doing for them and the Church (2 Corinthians 4:1).

OAN, as does any aspect of progressive sanctification, reflects the Church's and the believer's view of God, Who He is, what the Triune God in Christ by the Holy Spirit has done, and what He is doing now for him and the Church. Gratefulness and joy for his salvation indicates a proper understanding of the following truths: the believer is released from debt, a ransom price has been paid, and the believer has been forgiven, comforted, and loved.

These truths properly understood and applied are vital for growth in Christlikeness which is the essence of life after salvation (Ephesians 4:11-14: footnote 2). A growing understanding and humble acceptance of God's forgiveness and love is a comfort; it motivates, even compels, the believer to confront himself (2 Corinthians 5:14-17; 13:5; Hebrews 3:12-13).

Progressive sanctification involves applying truths taught in such passages as Matthew 18:21-35, Luke 7:36-50, and Romans 5:6-

10. The forgiven one forgives; the comforted one comforts; and the loved loves others. The believer recognizes these gifts are by the Triune God through Christ by the Holy Spirit (Matthew 22:37-40; John 13:34-35; 1 John 3:23; 4:7-12, 19-21). The believer has been OAN and is to OAN. These truths are foundational for growth in Christ and OAN activities.

Please note the parallel between one's experience of God's love, comfort, and forgiveness (none of which are merited) and one's relationship with one another. The significance of a person's relationship with God controls his relationship with another believer. This is part of Jesus' message in the parable of the unmerciful servant and Jesus' words at the Last Supper (Matthew 18:21-35; Luke 7:36-50; John 13:34-35).

The unmerciful servant described in Matthew failed to grasp the two aspects of life: one, the magnitude—height and depth—of God's love and forgiveness of him (Ephesians 3:17-21); two, the enormity of his sinfulness, his ungodliness, his debt and indebtedness, and the magnitude of his position as a debtor.

He thought highly of himself and little of the master! *Just give me some time* he told the master! He followed the example of the Pharisee in Luke 18:9-14. Both men lived the lie. Neither understood and denied their debt and the depth and danger of their darkness and depravity. They failed to be humbled and wowed at the fullness of the dimensions—the depth, width, height, and length—of God's love.

The apostles were given an object lesson of servanthood and OAN when Jesus stooped, clothed Himself with a greater display of humility, and washed their feet (John 13:1ff). They did not understand—but they would (13:12-17)! A high view of self flows from a low view of God and vice versa. A high view of the cross results in a low view of self and vice versa. Interestingly, Jesus knew Who He was. Yet, He stooped to meet man.

The passages in Matthew and Luke indicate the link between being loved and forgiven and one's willingness to OAN, which includes loving and being loved and forgiving others and being forgiven. If a person is unwilling to OAN his brother and sister in Christ, then he must ask himself: Is he a true believer? Only the true believer has been OAN and understands and cherishes that fact.

II. Facts regarding OAN: Man's Fallenness

True biblical concern for the brethren is expressed as OAN; this is one important factor that separates God's people from the culture. It involves:

- watchfulness
- willingness to be a blessing to each other
- weighing in—active assistance in helping others grow in Christlikeness

Biblical OAN can be summarized as Christlikeness-in-action. It is an aspect of progressive sanctification. It is part of discipleship, but it can be done properly or improperly. It produces fruit, either good or bad.

Moreover, OAN is not natural or easy. After Adam's first sin, he, and his posterity, due to their union with Adam, entered Satan's family and kingdom. Man stopped functioning as God's sinless image bearer—and was motivated by the mantra of for self, by self, and to self.

Man, even though remaining as God's image, reflected Satan's character rather than God's (John 8:44). They distorted their dependence and creatureliness. Adam's and Eve's decision to sin was an attack on the pre-incarnate Christ Himself because Christ is the image of God (Hebrews 1:3; 2 Corinthians 4:4; Colossians 1:17).

Membership in Satan's kingdom is characterized by error, falsehood, ignorance, arrogance, orientation toward self, and unrighteousness. These are part of fallen mankind's deadness, darkness, and depravity. Theologians use various terms to describe this condition: *total* or *radical depravity*, and *total inability*.

These phrases express the truth that as a child and disciple of Satan, every person is anti-God and pro-self, seeking to serve his father and himself. There seems to be a certain enjoyment to this approach to life until the person "comes to his senses."

By following the serpent's original counsel in the Garden, man disobeys God and seeks to become more like Satan assuming this is best for him (Romans 1:18-23). He is an idolater—self-deluded and self-deceived—and he loves the darkness (John 3:17-

21). Using others for self gain is a patterned mindset and lifestyle that continues in varying forms unless something supernatural happens to the person.

III. OAN: Regeneration and Progressive Sanctification

A believer has been radically changed (regeneration: John 3:3-8; 6:60-64). But while he is considered perfect in Christ in terms of his standing (termed justification) and position (termed positional holiness) before God, the believer still retains characteristics of satanic thinking, desiring, and acting; he has remaining sinfulness and patterned habituation toward self-pleasing.

Even though salvation transfers the believer from Satan's family to God's, Satan's prior influence lingers and is strong (Colossians 1:13). Indeed, it intensifies as habits of pleasing self and pleasing Satan clash with the motivation to please God in any number of situations. The moral drama played out in the believer's heart is due to the believer's new orientation of pleasing God.

This is an aspect of the war within which occurs primarily in the believer's heart; it is a daily, moment-by-moment occurrence. It is characterized in such passages as Romans 6:12-14; 15-19; 7:14-25; 8:14; Galatians 5:13-18; and 1 Peter 4:1-3. Old habits of self-pleasing die hard.

Changing habituation is twofold (Romans 13:12-14; Ephesians 4:22-24; Colossians 3:8-10). Believers *put off* and replace sinful habits of thinking, wanting, and acting by putting on godly habits of thinking, wanting, and doing (Ephesians 4:22-24; Colossians 3:8-10).

This is done through what I call *radical replacement*; some theologians use the term *progressive sanctification*. A believer dies to self and is increasingly alive to God and the things of God. Changed thinking, wanting, and doing is evidence of this change. It is Holy Spirit birthed, motivated, energized, and actualized as the believer becomes more like Christ in daily life until Heaven. His growth in Christlikeness is tangible. OAN is one of the tangibles.

This is possible because the *old* is gone (what the believer was in Satan) and the new (what he is in Christ by the Holy Spirit) has come in principle. It is a reality! But the believer's practice of pleasing God is not perfected. He is to close the gap between what he is in Christ in principle and what he is in Christ in practice. The Holy Spirit works in and with the believer, but never for or against him as the believer changes thoughts, desires, and actions that are anti-God and pro-self.

Patterned and habituated self-pleasing (again these are thoughts, desires, and actions that are anti-God and pro-self in varying degrees) must and will be replaced with habits of pleasing God. This truth reflects the believer's confidence in the Triune's God word and work. OAN is one of those areas in which the believer moves from being a self-pleaser to a God-pleaser.

This change is necessary and evident, or the person is not a believer. It is also a blessing and a privilege. As a result, the believer grows in Christlikeness as he functions both as an OAN-er and an OAN-ee.

IV. General Passages that Help Establish OAN as Part of the Ministry of the Word

A. Acts 6:1-4: *In those days when the number of disciples was increasing, the Grecian Jews among them complained against the Hebraic Jews because their widows were being overlooked in the daily distribution of food. So the Twelve gathered all the disciples together and said, "It would not be right for us to neglect the ministry of the word of God in order to wait on tables. Brothers, choose seven men from among you who are known to be full of the Spirit and wisdom. We will turn this responsibility over to them and will give our attention to prayer and the ministry of the word.*

Early in the life of the Church, the apostles were faced with the issue of *how* to minister the Word of God. The issue concerned *serving up*. What was it that they were to *serve up*? It was the Word that Christ had called them to proclaim.

In verse 2, to *neglect the ministry of the word* meant to *stop preaching* or more literally to *leave the word of God*. This was not an option for the apostles. It was not an option for Christ! It is not an option for the Church or believers.

The issue was not whether they would serve.[1] Rather, the issue focused on the capacity of service and ministry of the Word in which the apostles were to be involved. Were they to minister by serving physical food or through preaching, serving spiritual food? They could not do both. Both services were important since both require good stewardship.

Moreover, all service to members of the church is service to God. The apostles had been called to serve the Word—to preach and teach the apostolic message. They had a responsibility to care for the flock—each person's body and soul, the whole person. In order to accomplish this, they ordained deacons to handle matters that would distract them from their primary calling—ministering the Word through preaching.

Meeting physical and spiritual needs is part of OAN whether through preaching, teaching, or taking care of widows. Diaconal ministry is part of OAN and is an official ministry of the Church.

B. Acts 20:20-21, 24, 27: *You know that I have not hesitated to preach anything that would be helpful to you but have taught you publicly and from house to house. I have declared to both Jews and Greeks that they must turn to God in repentance and have faith in our Lord Jesus . . . However, I consider my life nothing to me if only I may finish the race and complete the task the Lord Jesus has given me—the task of testifying to the gospel of God's grace . . . For I have*

---

1 The word translated as serving, to serve, and ministry is *diakonia*: verses 1-2, 4; the word minister comes from this root.

not hesitated to proclaim to you the whole will of God. So then be on your guard! Remember that for three years I never stopped warning each of you night and day with tears.

In his final address to the elders at Ephesus, Paul clarified what the ministry of the Word is and his involvement in it. The official ministry of the Word includes preaching, counseling, and teaching (also see Acts 19:9). The ministry of the Word is tethered to the proclamation of the Word publicly, but it is broader than preaching. Always and everywhere Paul ministered the Word both publicly and privately, he also OAN-ered!

Therefore, I consider that the ministry of the Word includes:

1. Preaching (v. 20): Paul made known, announced, declared, showed forth, and/or explained the gospel message and God's truth.
2. Teaching (v. 21): he purposed to teach by word of mouth in order to influence the understanding of the sheep—their thoughts, desires, and actions.
3. Declaring (v. 21): he bore witness and testified earnestly and solemnly in word and deed which included evangelism (outside the Church) and OAN (within the Church).
4. Testifying and declaring the whole counsel (purpose or will) of God (v. 24, 27): Paul defined the content of the Word which was and is to be the whole counsel or will of God.
5. One-on-one discipleship (OAN) which includes counseling

(v. 31): Paul describes the method and manner of this aspect of his ministry in terms of constancy and boldness. He was interested out of concern and care for the people to bring change in thought, desire, and action to the sheep individually and corporately. Paul knew that biblically-derived OAN was one of God's answers for His Church. It is one way to preserve His Church (Matthew 16:17-19).

CHAPTER 2
Fellowship and Relationships

WHY BEGIN HERE IN A study of One-anothering? Inherent in the meaning of the words *fellowship* and *OAN* is the idea of partnering together and companionship. Both involve people getting together individually and collectively. Both are based on interpersonal relationships.

The concept of OAN has taken on a new dimension because of the pandemic. In many churches, OAN seems less urgent and has taken a back seat. This seems strange. Reasons given include isolations, some of which are personally-imposed, medically-imposed, and/or governmentally-imposed. America and the world have experienced effects of the Covid-19 virus pandemic. Civil authorities have acted, people and churches have responded, and separation and even isolation has been promoted and practiced.

The Church cannot lose sight of one of its God-given tasks expressed in Ephesians 4:11-14: maturity of the body in Christlikeness.[2] How does OAN fit into this picture of a

---

[2] Ephesians 4:11-14: *It was he who gave some to be apostles, some to be prophets, some to be evangelists, and some to pastors and teachers to prepare God's people for works of service, so that the body of Christ may be built up until we all reach unity in the faith and knowledge of the Son of God and become mature, attaining the full measure of the fullness of Christ.*

pandemic? Careful thought, teaching, learning, and planning must occur in order for the Church to be a faithful steward of the Word and a light to the nations beginning with America.

God is a relational Being—with Himself via the Trinity and with His creatures. Do not miss the point: the eternal God focuses on Himself because He was before every other self! His Being is necessary. If there is no God, there is no being! If He is not Triune, there would be no OAN! Further, He is *sui generis*: He is totally other. Yet God has always been in perfect relationship to Himself.

Moreover, man is created a relational being, a covenant, dependent being, and the image bearer of God. He was created for fellowship with people (Genesis 2:18-23). Therefore, life is characterized by and flows from relationships: God to Himself within the Trinity and to the believer and the believer to God and to others. God is a relational Being and man is the image of God; as such he is a relational being created for fellowship. Man's being is derived from God as Creator.

First-century society was violent, ignorant, and arrogant, much as America is today. Life could be abruptly changed or shortened depending on one's relationships. Being a Christian often cost one his life. America is headed in this direction. The life and culture that characterized early Rome seems right around the corner or maybe even already here for America. How will the Church respond?

During the Roman era, slaves and children were objects of cruelty and mistreatment. It was in this type of world that Jesus planted Himself and His Church. His Church was to replace division with oneness and hostility and enmity with care and concern. Relationships mattered—they made a difference! Therefore, if we are to understand OAN, we must understand the Bible's teaching about relationships.

I. Relationships: The Triune God and Man

We begin with the Triune God. The term Trinity expresses the relationship of the three-in-one God existing in perfect harmony eternally. There has always been complete unity within the Godhead.

This unity is demonstrated in the work of creation and in the work of salvation. Creation is the work of the Triune God. The Father is in the foreground in the work of creation: Genesis 1:1; 1 Corinthians 8:6. But the Son (John 1:3; Colossians 1:15-17) and the Holy Spirit (Genesis 1:2; Job 33:4; Psalm 104:28-30; Isaiah 40:12-13) are active as well.

The work of salvation is also Intratrinitarian. It can be summarized as to God, through the Son, by the Holy Spirit (1 Corinthians 12:12-13; Ephesians 2:18; 3:12; 4:4-6). Some people express the truth as the Father planned, the Son purchased and accomplished, and the Spirit applied the Christ's earthly redemptive work.

Salvation is relational in two ways. One, there is perfect agreement between the Father Who planned; the Son Who accomplished, purchased, and secured; and the Holy Spirit Who applied and is applying the effects of the Son's atoning work in salvation (John 6:37-43). Because of the relationship within the Godhead, being saved and living as one saved (sanctification including OAN) is a blessed reality for believers.

Salvation is relational because God established a relationship between Himself and His children individually and the Church by placing them in Christ and indwelling them with the Holy Spirit (John 3:3-8; 6:60-64; Romans 8:9, 11; 1 Corinthians 3:16-17; 6:19-20; 2 Corinthians 6;14-17; 2 Timothy 1:14). Keeping His covenant promise, the Triune God draws individuals one by one into a relationship with Him (John 6:35ff).

Life after salvation involves the believer's growth in Christlikeness owing to his relationship to God, in Christ, through the indwelling Holy Spirit. The Holy Spirit is given to every Christian when God pours out His love into his heart (Romans 5:5). And because the believer is a new creature, he cherishes the privilege and blessing of maturing in Christlikeness (2 Corinthians 5:14-17).

In Philippians 3:7-11, Paul emphasized that the greatest privilege this side of Heaven is a vital and growing relationship with Christ through the Holy Spirit. The Spirit enables the believer to engage in true biblical fellowship and OAN thereby developing Christlikeness which is one goal of life after salvation.

Man was created for fellowship—not to be alone; he was created a social being (Genesis 2:18-23). Animals were not God's answer for man's fellowship issue. Moreover, the fact that Jesus Christ founded His Church demonstrates that "people need people." The Church is where brothers and sisters can know more and more God's love and fellowship with other Christians. It is within the body that God's love is made complete (John 13:34-35; 15:12-13; 1 John 4:7-12, 19).

It is in this context of biblical truth that we observe the pandemic and the seeming dissolution of America. Violence is an ever-present danger and people are dying "in isolation." However, no believer is truly forsaken although he may be placed in isolation. The Church must think through biblical truth in order to rightly function as an OAN Church.

II. The Book of 1 John and Relationships

Having laid the foundation that OAN and fellowship involve relationships, and which motivate and characterize living, we turn to several passages from the book of 1 John. In writing about fellowship, John refers to two sorts of relationships—a vertical relationship between God and the believer, and a horizontal one between believers.

One theme and purpose of John's first letter is the believer's assurance (5:13). How can one know if he is a child of God or of Satan? One way is via relationships and the activity between believers which is based on proper theology, specifically Who Jesus is.

In this regard, he followed the teaching of Jesus Who referred to the two great commandments: love of God and of neighbor (Matthew 22:37-40). Consider the following passages of 1 John 1:3-7: *We proclaim to you what we have seen and heard so that you also may have fellowship with us; and our fellowship is with the Father and with His Son Jesus Christ. We write this to make our joy complete. This is the message that we have heard from him and declare to you: God is Light. In Him there is no darkness at all. If we claim to have fellowship with him, yet walk in the darkness, we lie and do not live by truth. But if we walk in the Light as he is in the light, we have fellowship with one another and the blood of Jesus his Son purifies us from all sin.*

In this letter, John was combating false teaching regarding the Person of Christ—Who is He—and the believer's relationship to Him. He begins by emphasizing that doctrine affects life vertically (to God) and horizontally (to neighbor). Moreover, he states that the apostles had a sensual experience.

They saw and heard Christ—His Person and His message. They witnessed Truth (Jesus Christ) and truth applied daily—moment by moment. They were able to interpret what they saw and heard from God's perspective because they had the

Holy Spirit and truth. As a result, they lived in proper relation to God and to each other.

In these opening verses of 1 John (1:3-7), John stresses the link between a believer's relationship to Christ and to fellow members. John knew that a growing loving fellowship with God and between believers was one goal of sanctification. It fulfilled Matthew 22:37-40 and John 13:34-35. This fellowship is a gift from God in which He draws individuals, not only to Himself, but to one another (John 6:44).

In these opening verses (verses 3-7) John proposes a developing maturity, marked by joy and grandeur, for members of the kingdom of light. This is one aspect of a true circle of life. First, there is truth about God and self which leads to light and fellowship with God (verse 5).

Second, the changed life of a believer affects other believers (verses 6-7). The believer is linked to the Light via the Holy Spirit. This demonstrates at least two truths: the believer is light not simply in it (Matthew 5:14-16; Ephesians 5:8-14), and the believer is the light so that his way is lighted toward pleasing God (Psalm 119:104-105, 130; Proverbs 4:18-19).

Finally, truth, love, and life lead to ministry especially within the body which includes OAN (verse 7). John builds on the tetrad of truth, light, love, and life when he speaks of ministry.

God placed each Christian in proper relationship to Himself, and with the capacity to be in proper relationship to one another.

Fellowship with God results in fellowship with other brothers and sisters. Fellowship should result in OAN among God's people.

John uses the Greek word *koinoia* that is translated fellowship which means sharing together, communion with, and participating in something with another such as a common experience. *Koinoia* is pregnant with meaning; it emphasizes the reality of God's fellowship with man and man's relationship with fellow believers (Acts 2:42; 1 Corinthians 1:9; 10:16; 2 Corinthians 6:14; 8:4; 13:14; Galatians 2:9; Ephesians 3:9; 1 John 1:3,6-7).[3]

III. John and Paul Teach the Same Truth

Ephesians 3:6-9 epitomizes the underlying message of fellowship: oneness and intimacy where there was enmity (v. 6: *This mystery is that through the gospel the Gentiles are heirs together with Israel, members together of one body, and sharers together in the promise in Christ Jesus*).

---

[3] Each of the following verses describes various aspects of the term (koinonia): Acts 2:42 speaks of fellowship as an activity of the church in apostolic times. In 1 Corinthians 1:9, Paul sets the tone for God's solution for the embattled Corinthian Church. God is faithful and has provided the believer's union with Him through Christ. Since there is fellowship with God in Christ, true fellowship with each other another must follow (verse 10). And in 10:16, Paul uses the metaphor of the oneness of the body to encourage true OAN. In 2 Corinthians, Paul prohibits unequal fellowship (6:14); is thankful for generous giving for the work of ministry (8:4); and closes his letter with a benediction in a Trinitarian formula (13:14). In it he refers to the fellowship of the Holy Spirit meaning the union and relationship created by the Spirit first between God and a believer, and secondly between individual believers. Galatians 2:9 speaks of the right hand of fellowship offered to Paul and Barnabas by James, John, and Peter. Paul used *koinoia* to indicate their mutual agreement and acknowledgment of a common purpose, the solidarity between them, and the confirmation of their mutual interest in the spread of the gospel of Christ.

These verses emphasize God's overarching plan of salvation by bringing Jew and Gentile together as one. Paul spoke of the mystery of unity when there was only separation, enmity, and strife. God brought together two groups of people seemingly destined to be separated forever (3:3, 9).

Since God has broken down all barriers and hindrances, there must be and will be true biblical fellowship within the body. This is accomplished through the ministry of OAN. As a result, there is participation in another's life for the sake of growing the individual and the body of Christ in Christlikeness (Ephesians 4:11-14: see footnote 2). OAN is instrumental for the Church to complete its mission.

There are many wrong ideas regarding Christian fellowship and OAN. Many think of it as mild, light, inoffensive, and non-intrusive "getting together" or just "being a good old boy." Doing good deeds or simply being nice also fit the popular idea of Christian fellowship.

Others think of it as a time simply to "share stories," sing songs, or play games. Others may think of it as a time to unwind by simply unloading their burdens and problems on someone who is a "good listener." And still others may think of getting together to tell "my story" or bask in his victories.

While all of these descriptions may contain some element of truth, they fail to capture the essence of biblical fellowship. At its core, Christian fellowship means being a friend. True fellowship and friendship are quite similar; both refer to "sharing" one's concern with another for the purpose of solving problems God's ways and being a catalyst for another's growth in Christlikeness (John 15:13-15).

This may result in giving up one's life, literally or figuratively! Sharing with another may include confessing sin each to another, bringing comfort, or simply enjoying the company of fellow believers (1 John 1:9; James 5:16; 2 Corinthians 1:3-11; Galatians 6;1-5. See Acts 2:46-47).

IV. Walking in the Light

Since all of God's children have the mind of Christ and are the most loved, forgiven, comforted, and welcomed people in the universe, they should think God's thoughts and desire what God desires. As a result, believers engage in OAN which includes loving, submitting, forgiving, comforting, and welcoming another out of gratitude for what God in Christ has done for them.

These activities are evidence of *walking in the Light*. Paul comments on this fact in Ephesians 5:8-14. Believers are light as well as in the light. They are children of light, of truth. They are in fellowship with Truth; they have truth; and they think, desire, and act accordingly. They are a witness both within and outside the Church.

Fellowship and OAN must be grounded in God's Word (1 John 1: 3). The important issue is biblical truth and its specific application in daily life. Therefore, a person who emphasizes how well he is doing to the exclusion of his failures is fellowshipping with the wrong emphasis and the wrong motivation.

True fellowship centers on God's truth as found in the Bible and His grace in applying it. OAN is a major vehicle by which God's children apply truth (Psalm 119:9-11, 24, 99, 105). Fellowship with God is *walking in the Light*. The believer is a member in the kingdom of light and truth because he is a disciple of Christ (verse 7).

True fellowship is displayed by speaking the truth in love, and by engaging in the ministry of OAN both as one who has received OAN and the one who engages in it. If one is genuinely *walking in the Light*, he will demonstrate fellowship with others by being a *OAN-er* and a *OAN-ee*.

Fellowship with Christ always leads to a deepening relationship with the Triune God and others. This is manifested by learning Truth, learning greater truth about Him, and developing greater love for God and others. These result in greater service and ministry. Love, truth, light, and life are linked.

John taught that a by-product of ministry undergirded by truth, light, love, and life was joy (verse 4; also see John 15:11; 16:24; 17:13). This in turn leads to a greater understanding of Who God is, what He has done, and to a deepening of the believer's relationship with God and others expressed, in part, as OAN (John 3:30; 13:34-35; Philippians 2:3-4; 3:3-11).

Peter expresses this same truth in 2 Peter 1:4: *Through these he has given us his very great and precious promises, so through them you may participate in the divine nature and escape the corruption in the world caused by evil desires.*

He uses the phrase *participate in the divine nature* (also translated: *becoming partakers of a divine nature*) to indicate salvation which can be explained by the terms fellowship and intimacy between God and man.

Those *in Christ* have been released from the bondage of a feeling and impulse-oriented and driven lifestyle which is characterized by *I wants* and *me first* mantras. Fundamentally, a *me-first* approach to life is what characterizes membership in Satan's kingdom and family. Old habits change slowly. Such is the beauty of OAN: there is help and hope in changing.

Self-pleasing is at the core of the serpent's counsel in the Garden. It is what Satan's disciples do. When believers function this way, biblical OAN is hindered and even non-existent. When self takes center stage, getting along is made harder. Often strife, envy, slander, and unreconciled relationships occur resulting in chaos and disunity (James 3:13-4:3). God is greatly dishonored!

In contrast, according to John, Peter, and Paul, fellowship with Christ equates with *walking in the Light*. It is a relational term. Pleasing God is paramount in a believer's thinking and motivation. Humbled people are God-pleasers (consider Jesus), and proud people are self-pleasers (see Luke 18:9-14; James 3:13-18).

Therefore, in relation to God and others, pride—thinking and acting more highly than he ought about himself according to a self-proclaimed standard—is to be laid aside, put off, and replaced. The believer has a new lighting system: truth and the Holy Spirit!

The believer is light and therefore he is to be *walking in the light*. Only the saved sinner can do this because he is a child of the light, and the light has been turned on by the Holy Spirit (Ephesians 1:16-19). Therefore, the believer considers the other person and his needs before himself thereby imitating Christ Who is Light (Philippians 2:3-4; John 8:12; 9:5).

How he does depends on his relationship with the person and the situation. He may pray with and for that person; he may offer encouragement and biblical hope. Or, if confession of sin is needed, he will encourage it (1 John 1:9; James 5:16).

Relationships are strengthened as each person participates in the OAN activities we will be discussing. The point here is that one's relationship to God in Christ is at the core of one's relationship to his brothers and sisters in Christ. Relationships matter!

V. People *Come to Know* Christ: 1 John 2:3-5

In other places in his letter John describes a believer's relationship with Christ. We now look at those to further appreciate the impact of relationships on ministry: life, love, light, and truth.

John calls the people to *come to know him* and he explains what it means: 1 John 2:3-5: *We know that we have come to know him if we obey his commands. The man who says, "I know him," but does not do what he commands is a liar and the truth is not in him. This is how we know we are in him: whoever claims to live in him must walk as Jesus did.*

John declares an absolute truth: knowing and obeying. He uses the phrase, *come to know*, to communicate the truth that the Christian has more than a mere acquaintance with or simply knowing facts about Christ. Saving faith involves knowledge but also conviction and commitment. Paul clarifies the truth in Galatians 4:8-9. Knowing Christ flows from and is impossible unless the believer is known by God—he is regenerated!

John uses the phrase (*come to know him—Christ*) to mean a personal, intimate relationship with Him. As a result, the person grows his trust and reliance upon the Triune God. There is a familiarity with and more: an exploding interest in Jesus Christ as a Person and His work and biblical truth (Psalm 34:8; Philippians 3:7-11). The believer enjoys family life! In that way, he is anticipating heaven (Romans 6:9-11; 1 John 3:1-3).

The believer knows Christ as a Person. Therefore, he knows facts about Him; importantly, he knows that Christ knows him (Galatians 4:3, 8-9). Therefore, Christ is a genuine reality to the believer, and therefore, his relationship with Christ influences and directs his life. In that way, love, truth, light, life, and ministry meet in Christ by the Holy Spirit.

Therefore, the believer no longer wants to live—conduct himself—for self but for Christ (2 Corinthians 5:9, 14-15; Galatians 2:20). The love of Christ compels—strongly and passionately motivates—believers to live no longer for self but for Him. This change is expressed by changed thoughts, desires, and actions regarding self, God, and others. This is the process of progressive sanctification—growth in Christlikeness.

Moreover, the phrase *I know him* does not mean simply to know facts about Him obtained by purely sensual means. Everyone saw and heard Jesus. But only some had eyes to see and ears to hear. The phrase focuses on the use and results of using another interpretative standard.

The phrase—*I know him*—refers to the person interpreting information obtained through the senses by the use of a suprasensual interpretative grid. It means looking beyond that which is mere physical and seeing with the eyes of saving faith and true hope informed by biblical truth (Matthew 16:1-4; John 7:24; 8:15; 2 Corinthians 5:7; 10:7).

Knowledge of Christ and one's relationship with Him impacts the believer. It is relational. This knowledge is supernaturally-given and understood. The believer relates to the Triune God and to others in mutual fellowship with one another. Once brothers and sisters are motivated to think, to desire, and to act based on this dynamic, service to others through OAN will become instinctive, habitual, joyful, and a way of life. It was for

Christ! As a result, God is praised, and His people are comforted and energized.

Through the gift of saving faith and true hope and its use, the Christian knows he has fellowship with God. John says that this fact leads to obedience, which is evidence of a growing relationship with Christ (1 John 5:3-4).

The desire and quest to *know Christ* is what Paul sought in Philippians 3:7-11 and is what encouraged him in his daily life (1 Timothy 1:12). Paul taught that knowing Christ is incomparably superior to any achievement and success he had had in his life (Philippians 3:3-11).

At least, the phrase (*know him—Christ*) implies that the believer acts upon facts one of which is expressed in Romans 8:35-39: nothing can separate God from the believer or the believer from God. Saving faith is based on knowledge and a correct understanding of the facts. Fellow believers need help via OAN to accomplish this privilege!

Moreover, saving faith does not jettison reason. Reason does not divorce itself from the grid of saving faith and true hope. Faith seeks understanding and understanding seeks faith! The two are linked. Further, the believer is a winner-victor in Christ! OAN is designed to help the brethren understand and apply these truths.

In Galatians 4:8-9, Paul wrote that the Galatians knew God and then clarified himself by saying that each one of them is known by God. He referred to their saving relationship to God based on Christ's work applied by the Holy Spirit. They were united to Christ by saving faith, which is God's unmerited gift freely given, no strings attached.

Its exercise—the believer's faithfulness as one saved in life—is demonstrated as the believer receives and rests upon Christ alone for salvation and for growth in grace. His knowledge grows and he becomes a wise person!

What do the words in paragraph above really mean? In verses six and seven, John explained the phrase as obedience. The terms: *walking in darkness* and *walking in light* contrasts two patterned lifestyles—pleasing self and Satan versus pleasing God (Proverbs 4:18-19).

As mentioned Paul also uses the concept and the phrase *walking in the Light* in Ephesians 5:8-14 and in Galatians (1:9; 3:1-5). He asked the Galatians how they could return to a life of darkness that was characterized by the wrong use of the Law and personal lawkeeping such as taught by the Pharisees.

John and Paul taught the same message! *Walking in the Light* (John's term) is in agreement with Paul's admonition in Ephesians 5:8-14. As children of light, believers are light and will walk accordingly.

The Galatians had been saved and OAN through Paul's ongoing ministry. They had the true gospel and had embraced it. But now they were returning to the vomit of a false gospel (Galatians 1:8-10; 3:1-4; 4:3, 8-9; see the book of Hebrews).

Paul had learned that personal lawkeeping had no place for salvation. Reliance on one's own lawkeeping results from a false view of Christ, the law, and self. Knowing these basic facts means that the believer cannot and will not return to personal lawkeeping as a patterned way of life to earn and to get. Rather obedience is an act of gratitude for salvation and is part of the gift of life after salvation.

Knowing Christ is a relational term. The phrases *being in Christ* and *knowing Christ* both refer to the believer's relationship with Christ. As a result, the believer bears fruit in keeping with and in evidence of that relationship. What is that fruit? It is developing Christlikeness, at least in part, by and through OAN.

Peter taught the same truth. He calls the believer to grow in grace through the full knowledge of God (2 Peter 3:18). Knowing facts about God—His person, His goodness and wisdom, and His work as Creator and Sustainer—and relying on them are indispensable for growing relationships.

VI: *Live in Him*

John also calls the people to *live in Him*. Moreover, he explains what it means and how to do it: 1 John 2:6; 3:24; 4:13, 15: 2:6: *Whoever claims to live in him must walk as Jesus did . . . 3:24: Those who obey his commands live in him, and he in them . . . 4:13, 15: We know that we live in him and he in us, because he has given us of his Spirit; If anyone acknowledges that Jesus is the Son of God, God lives in him and he in God.*

The phrase *live, remain,* or *abide in Him* expresses the truth that the believer grows in Christlikeness so that he does not leave Jesus Christ either professedly or functionally. Rather, the believer matures in his ability and joy to apply biblical truth daily. His motivation is to please God. Relationships matter! The believer stays the course, endures God's way, and holds fast to his true anchor—Jesus Christ—and for His sake (Hebrews 12:1-3).

Previously, the now-believer failed to live a God-honoring life. He endured his way in his own strength thus living the lie. But there is *but now* for every believer (Romans 3:21; Ephesians 2:4; Titus 3:4)! A radical, divine change has occurred in and to him! As a result, the believer recognizes he has been living the lie! He is now in the light as light!

As result, he is alive as a child of God. He lives God's way (he knows how!) because of Christ's relationship with him and his relationship with Christ. Fellowship with Christ affects a person's attitude—thoughts and desires—and actions. It motivates and energizes OAN that is expressed in terms of friendship as given in the book of *Proverbs* (see 12:26; 17:17; 18:24; 27:6).

The OAN-er *hangs in there* with his brother even when it may be hard. Judas was one of the apostles and yet he went out from them and never returned because he was never of them (1 John 2:19).

Peter was a true disciple but functioned for a time as Satan's disciple when he denied the cross and Christ, the Person (Matthew 16:22-23; 26:69-75). Yet, because he was a true disciple the Triune God held him fast (John 10:28-30). Christ restored and commissioned him to strengthen his brothers through the ministry of OAN which he did (Luke 22:31-34; John 21:15-17).

The word *abide* has often been misunderstood. Rather, it means *remaining* or *staying in*; it refers to the perseverance of the saints as evidenced by fruit bearing. Perseverance of the saints is not simply moving along but it is characterized by godly fruit-bearing. Jesus is speaking of His union or relationship with the believer and the believer's to Christ and the effect of that relationship. It is the result of the indwelling of the Holy Spirit (1 John 3:24).

Jesus is the True Vine and apart from union with Him the believer can do nothing to please God (John 15:1-8). The believer develops and demonstrates the fruit of the Spirit. The unbeliever's fruit is always self and Satan-pleasing while masquerading as godliness, which it is not! Sadly, believers still function in this way. Such was the case with Judas. His fruit was ungodly. He attached himself to Jesus, but Jesus did not attach Himself to him in saving way. He bore satanic fruit because he was not of Jesus. He was never truly linked to Christ (Hebrews 6:4-56; 1 John 2:19).

As a result, the believer imitates Christ's love and obedience. John is teaching the doctrine of the perseverance of the saints. True disciples do not leave Christ or fellow brothers and sisters (John 8:31-36). Relationships and truth do matter. It is one's relationship with Christ that so impacts a person's life that he develops a pattern of trusting obedience and obedient trust. Jesus made this point in John 14:9-21.

Obedience is a fruit of a Christian's vital, growing relationship with Christ just as it was a sign of Christ's relationship with His Father (John 14:15, 21, 23, 31). Love and obedience are twin pillars for *and* of a relationship with the Triune God.

Perseverance of the saints and obedience are testimony to God's perseverance; they show the believer's assurance of his salvation (Hebrews 12:1-3). Believers persevere because God does! God perseveres and pursues all believers as they develop in Christlikeness. Again, OAN is evidence of the Christian's saving relationship with God through Christ.

The fruits of love, loving, trusting, and obedience are a result of and proof of Christ's relationship with His Father (John 4:34; 5:19, 30; 6:38; 12:49-50; 14:31; 15:10); so too, they are a sign of the believer's relationship with the Triune God (John 14:15, 21, 23). Love for God is an obedient love and a loving obedience. As we will see in the section entitled Love, biblical love is OAN love.

The biblical concept of love is so misunderstood in our culture and its understanding is important that I briefly characterize it now and discuss it more fully in chapter four. Biblical OAN love is giving (John 3:16; Galatians 2:20; Ephesians 5:2, 25). It is an action not dependent on feelings although it may be associated with them.

Consider the Bible's teaching that God is love (1 John 4:8). God not only loves but He is love. It is of His essence. Therefore, to love is a whole-person activity involving knowledge, thoughts, affections and desires, and willful actions. As such believers are to love wholeheartedly. Love must characterize them as it does their God. OAN is one means for doing it.

Love is purposeful and constructive. It meets needs: Isaiah 59:1-2; John 9:31; Colossians 1:21; 1 John 2:2; 4:10. It is not arbitrary; it uses the correct standard: Isaiah 59:1-2; Ephesians 5:25. Love is expensive, takes risks, and requires a personal investment no matter the cost: 2 Corinthians 5:21; Galatians 3:10-13; 4:4-6. It cost God His Son, Jesus His place in heaven for a time, and the Holy Spirit indwelling imperfect creatures.

Love is obligatory; it is a testimony of one's love for God but, moreover, of God's love for Himself and the individual. It functions out of the right motive: John 14:15, 21, 23; 1 Corinthians 13:3; 1 John 4:10; Romans 5:6-10. It is expressed in several forms.

The command to love God and neighbor wholeheartedly is universal and non-negotiable, but its expression is varied. Love is to be demonstrated in the proper way and manner: John 10:11, 15, 17; Romans 5:6-10.

VII. *Love Occurs in the Light*

John then moves to the truth that *love occurs in the light*. In John 2:9-11, he says:

> Anyone who claims to be in the light but hates his brother is still in the darkness. Whoever loves his brother lives in the light, and there is nothing in him to make him stumble. But whoever hates his brother is in the darkness and walks around in the darkness; he does not where he is going, because the darkness has blinded him.

The phrase, *being in the light,* focuses on the believer's relationship with God which is initiated in and by God's love. As I have said, Paul teaches that the believer is light not simply in it. As a result of being light and in the light, the believer thinks, desire, and does truth! It is a manifestation of loving the brethren (1 John 4:7-12, 18-19). Again, Paul and John have the same message!

OAN love may be expressed in a variety of ways. Those ways depend on each person and their relationship. Some may simply enjoy praying together, while others enjoy working together. In some way fellowship is developed and nourished.

Light has a twofold significance: truth-knowledge and purity-righteousness, whereas darkness represents falsehood-ignorance and impurity-evil. *Being in the light* is best defined as knowing truth—about God, self, and others—*and* doing that which pleases God. Hatred is a result of being in the darkness both in terms of error and acting on that error. Love is displayed in obedience: obedient love and loving obedience. Such was Christ's life!

Hatred includes bitterness, resentment, grudges, and hostility toward another. Darkness is the opposite of light. The hater, which may be a believer, responds to presumed or actual being sinned against in an unbiblical manner—darkness, which includes the concept of the presence of evil. The result is furthering of unreconciled relationships within the body of Christ. This hinders OAN. Hatred is opposed to fellowship and OAN (James 3:13-4:3).

VIII. Regeneration, Love, and OAN

John explains the meaning and significance of *the one born of God loves*: 3:9, 4:7, 5:4: *3:9: No one who is born of God will continue to sin, because God's seed remains in him; he cannot go on sinning, because he has been born of God . . . 4:7: Dear friends, let us love one another, for love comes from God. Everyone who loves has been born of God and knows God . . . 5:4: for everyone born of God overcomes the world. This is the victory that has overcome the world, even our faith.*

Born of God is John's term for regeneration. Regenerated people have been acted upon by the Holy Spirit (John 3:3-8; 6:60-64). As a result, the believer has a new heart and motivation center. Thus, he begins to put off and replace old lifestyle patterns of thoughts, desires, and actions that are anti-God and pro-self with those that please God (Romans 6:6; Galatians 2:20; 5:24).

In 3:9, John speaks of *putting off* habit patterns and lifestyle of self-pleasing and *self-love*. John knows that the Christian has been transferred to a new family and kingdom (Colossians 1:13). The believer is now God's son and Jesus' disciple and brother. As such, there is active and purposeful *purification of self* in terms of loving others and God, especially when it is hard to do (4:7-12).

John pictured the person who says or acts as if self is number one as living the lie. The person relies on feelings, sin-tainted reasoning, and he interprets the circumstances as bigger than God. The person believes God should treat him better than He did Jesus. He has inverted the world order and functions as if he is God in his world. He is living the lie.

In 1 John 5:4, John speaks of victory and overcoming the world. The world is not the physical world because this is our Father's world who is Creator and Controller (Acts 17:24-28). The term world refers to a system that opposes God. Its beliefs and actions focus on getting and being number one! The term refers to people and a system that opposes God.

Victory comes only to the believer. It is by and through the exercise of God's gifts: saving faith and true hope through the use of enabling grace. The believer is able to embrace, heed, and apply Christ's and Paul's teaching (Matthew 5:43-48; Romans 12:17-21). Love is God's firepower for gaining the ultimate victory over evil!

Throughout his letters, John views the believer's relationship with Christ from the standpoint of regeneration which is the result of the redemptive activity of the Holy Spirit in the believer. John emphasized that the regenerate person is to view himself, others, and God through the reality of his changed relationship—he is *in Christ*. The believer has a changed interpretative grid.

Effects of this relationship are observable as he grows in Christlikeness. The believer will produce the fruit of the Holy Spirit thereby developing Christlikeness as manifested through and by OAN. This fruit-bearing is part of progressive sanctification which is partial and incomplete in this life but is a foretaste of heaven (Romans 6:9-11; 1 John 3:1-3).

IX. Love, Knowledge, and OAN

John gets relational. Love involves knowing God. First John 4:8 says, *Whoever does not love does not know God because God is love.*

The love of God and being known by God (Galatians 4:8-9) are related. Both originate with and by God. Because of His love, the believer is united to God through the gift of saving faith and is united to fellow believers.

Faithfulness—fruit bearing—is the evidence of union with Christ. One result of this union is the believer's love of the brethren and the practice of OAN.

OAN love is a testimony of God's love of the believer, the presence of the indwelling of the Holy Spirit in him, and the believer's testimony that he loves God. The believer is the most loved person in the world and, therefore, should be the most loving person. OAN should become second nature as it was for Christ.

Loving one another must take concrete form (see 1 John 3:11, 14, 18). The situation and the personal relationship direct and even dictate how brotherly love manifests itself in OAN activities. It may be a prayer, a text message, a phone call, or actual time spent with the person. The possibilities are endless, but they must be actual and visible!

The believer's relationship is first and foremost vertical—it is with God through Christ by the Holy Spirit. Fellowship with Christ results in a way of life that is modeled after Jesus' way of life (2:6). A proper relationship with Christ always bears fruit that is reflected in one's horizontal relationship with others.

One's vertical relationship controls horizontal relationships. A person's relationship with others reflects the significance he puts on living out his relationship with the Triune God. Loving God produces and displays itself as love for others (Matthew 22:37-40).

The believer's relationship with Christ should and will produce a growing, vital, vibrant, and living relationship with other believers. It is never silent; it is an expression of being one of Christ's disciples (John 15:8). Discipleship is seen in deeds and service as a reflection of changed thoughts and desires (1 John 3:16-18).

Satan has his disciples and Christ has His (John 8:42-47). As a disciple of Christ, the believer loves God and others even the enemy. That love is active, aggressive, contagious, observable, and objectifiable. It is God's love that changes the believer from a rebellious self-lover to a lover of God and others. God's love and the radical change in the believer make OAN and fellowship a reality and a blessing (Romans 5:6-10). A pandemic and a radically-changing culture are no match for God's truth!

CHAPTER 3

The Mind of Christ

YOU MAY WONDER WHY I am continuing our study of OAN by moving to the topic of the mind of Christ. First, it is not easy to fellowship with those who are different from you, who disagree with you, who are humanly unlovable, or who have sinned against you.

Second, fellowshipping may be a burden simply because you do not *feel* like it for whatever reason. Third, the fact of the matter is that growth in the Christian life which includes OAN requires the mind of Christ. Feelings are linked to and follow thoughts and desire; feelings are faulty taskmasters. One goal of the believer is to desire and to think about God, self, others, life, and situations as Christ did.[4]

Since OAN is an aspect of Christian growth, both the OAN-er and OAN-ee must think and desire as Jesus did. He functioned out of an identity. Knowing Who He was and His purpose influenced His thinking, desires, motivation, and actions.

---

[4] Isaiah 40:13; Romans 11:34; 1 Corinthians 2:16; 2 Corinthians 4:1; 10:3-5; Philippians 2:3-8; 3:3-7; 1 Timothy 1:12-16.

I. Paul and the Mind of Christ: The Letter to the Philippians

Paul presents one of the clearest descriptions of the mind of Christ in his letter to the Philippians. One reason he does so is to bring about unity within the congregation. There was a lack of OAN in the congregation and the result was disunity; moreover, two ladies failed to reconcile one to another. They had not demonstrated the mind of Christ (4:2: *"I plead with Euodia and I plead with Syntyche to agree with each other in the Lord."*).

Elsewhere Paul taught that agreeing with one another meant to think as Christ did. For instance, the Corinthian church had picked sides separating into factions (1 Corinthians 1:10-17). They were a divided bunch. They did not function as a unit. The factionalism was not related to differences in foundational doctrinal truths. Rather, it was related to such issues as entitlement, position, personal connections, and personal and group advancement.

Having the mind of Christ includes thinking about self, others, God, and circumstances as Christ did. This requires a change in one's thinking about God, self, and others. It includes the desire to please God in lieu of self. As believers the Corinthian congregation as a whole and the two ladies in the Philippian church had the mind of Christ but they functioned as if they did not! They lived the lie!

OAN grows out of proper thinking about self and others which springs and flows from proper thinking about God. James made the same point in James 3:13-4:3. When self takes center stage it reflects satanic thinking. There is pride, strife, and chaos (Proverbs 11:2; 13:10; 16:18; 18:12). Pride breeds quarrels. OAN is missing or ineffective; disunity is the result.

OAN reflects the mind of Christ which promotes unity; the only possible way to OAN is to think and desire like Christ. Christ considered pleasing His Father and the interest of others more important than pleasing Himself (John 4:31-34).

One of Paul's themes in his letter to the Philippians was unity through humility. Humility and humiliation differ. Humility is the result of a self-judgment; the conclusion is based on a standard other than a self-generated one.

It is the esteeming of oneself correctly using the proper standard. It occurs in a person as a result of a changed heart and results in changed thinking and wanting. As a result, the humble person brings himself low in regard to God and others.

He takes off the mindset characterized by pride and replaces it with the mindset of Christ. The terms for pride in the Old and Testaments carry the idea of high and lofty and a lifting up of self. Their necks are stretched out so that they are in the clouds as an untouched one. The person looks over and down at people.

Sinful pride is an inner-man activity, a self-evaluation and thinking in which a person places self as the lawmaker and lawgiver (standard maker and keeper) in relation to God and others. He expects a certain response from others and has various tactics to obtain it.

Humiliation refers to the situation itself—the context the person is in—and often the accompanying feelings. It involves disgrace and even shame. Jesus was humiliated but His circumstances did not humble Him. He humbled Himself thus demonstrating His heart.

Humiliation always generates a response which may be one of anger, bitter, and resentment or Christlikeness. Humility is active and is a result of thinking like Jesus. Jesus knew Himself and His mission. He knew His relationship with the Father. These three ingredients were essential for Jesus humbling Himself.

II. The Mind of Christ, OAN, and Philippians

Philippians 2:3-4: *Do nothing out of selfish ambition or vain conceit, but in humility consider others better than yourselves. Each of you should look not only to your own interests, but also to the interests of others.*

Paul had called the congregation to think as one in verse 2: *. . . then make my joy complete by being like-minded, having the same love, being one in spirit and purpose.* He explained what he meant in verses three and four. He set forth two fundamental principles of Church unity which reflect a foretaste of heaven. Both were based on Christ's mindset which leads to OAN.

The first principle is given in verse 3: that action proceeds from attitude—thoughts and desires are expressed in and by the whole person (inner—heart, and outer man—especially the brain).

Christ did nothing out of selfish self-interest. His self-interest was the Triune God's interest! Members of the congregation were to do (think, desire, and act) nothing out of self-interest, self-dependence, self-exaltation, and self-motivation. Rather each believer was to think differently about Christ, himself, others, and the body of Christ.[5]

Each member was to do everything from with a learner's spirit and a servant's heart.[6] Salvation does not automatically give the believer humility. Humility strikes at the heart of pride, which is defined as *self first, second, and third.*

Basically, each person must stop putting himself first which puts Satan first. He must stop living the satanic lie! The believer has died to himself, sin, and Satan in principle. Therefore, instead of returning to and following the serpent's original counsel in the Garden, the believer must die to self functionally and daily.

---

[5] The word *phroneo* is translated as "to think, have a mindset, be minded involving the whole person" and is found in Philippians 2:2,5; 3:15,19; 4:2; Matthew 16:23; Mark 8:33; Romans 8:5; Colossians 3:2.

[6] The word translated "humility" means "lowliness of mind, esteeming oneself small, in as much as he is": Acts 20:19; Ephesians 4:2; Colossians 2:18, 23; 3:12; 1 Peter 5:5.

He must think and desire about self and others in a radically different manner—as Jesus did about Himself (Matthew 10:32-38; 16:24-28; Mark 8:33-34; Luke 9:23; 14:25; John 12:25). The believer is to earnestly seek to promote the good of others so as to achieve and maintain unity. It sounds easy but it is radically counterintuitive and countercultural!

A second principle of OAN is described in verse 4. In verse 3, Paul taught that humility involves considering others more important than a self and is the replacement for selfishness. He adds another dimension in verse 4. Putting another's interest above one's own is how one actively considers another more important than self.

Looking out for one's own interest is not necessarily wrong, but other-orientation, rather than self-orientation, is what Paul had in mind. When concern for self—*I had it first, my rights, my way, my toy, my view, or opinion, my time, and my money*—takes center stage, there is disunity; the believer is functioning as if this is his world and people, and things exist for him. He lives the lie!

Paul is speaking of service: first to Christ and then love to neighbor (Matthew 22:37-40). The word translated as *look out* carries the idea of an extreme and diligent focus. [7] Jesus set His face toward Jerusalem (Luke 9:51). By that phrase, Luke meant

---

[7] The word translated "looking out" is *skopeo*. It means a "marking of something"; "to spy out, look toward an object paying attention to it" (Luke 11:35; Romans 16:17; 2 Corinthians 4:18; Galatians 6:1; Philippians 2:4; 3:14,17).

that Jesus "locked onto" His mission much as a pilot would lock onto his target. So, too, is a believer "to lock onto" another by putting that person's interest above his own.

III. The Mind of Christ, OAN, and Philippians

Philippians 2:5-8: *Your attitude should be same as that of Christ Jesus Who: being in very nature God did not consider equality with God something to be grasped, but made himself nothing, taking the very nature of a servant being made in human likeness. And being found in appearance as a man, he humbled himself and became obedient to death—even death on a cross.*

Paul furthers his description of the mind of Christ. He exhorted each believer to think about himself in the same manner as Christ thought about Himself. To think the way Jesus did is to have the mind of Christ. The Philippians were to think in such a way that their thoughts, desires, and actions imitated Jesus.

How did Christ think about Himself? Paul described Jesus' thinking in verse 6 through 8, which is to be the believer's pattern. Jesus set aside His right and privilege of being recognized and honored as God. He elected to not exercise this right.

He *elected* to not exercise His right and privilege of being recognized and worshipped as God. Amazing! Paul knew who Christ was—the Godman: very God and very man. He wanted his people to know Christ. As a result, they would put on truth, thinking more like Christ and less like Satan. They would put off living the lie!

Paul expressed the reality that Christ did not *hold onto His Godness with a tight grip*! Otherwise, He would not have left heaven! Being recognized as, treated as, and worshipped as God while on earth was not as important to Him as was pleasing the Father. Amazing! Jesus was God in all the fullness of deity, yet He laid aside the rights and privileges of deity in order to please His Father as Messiah.

The Incarnation is the application of verse 4. Verse 7 explains the willing submission of Christ: as the God-man, Jesus laid aside the fact that He was God; He was willing to be considered and treated as a loser by man and a sinner by God. He did this for the sake of the Triune God and His people who rejected Him (John 1:5-11).

Paul wrote that Jesus *made himself nothing*; others translate the words as *He emptied Himself*. Paul did not mean that Jesus ceased being God. Rather, He laid aside the manifestation of His deity and the right to be worshipped as God for a season—a time. His time! It is impossible to ignore God eternally. Heaven and hell confirm that fact.

Ask yourself how it is possible for the sun to come down to earth and hide its power and heat. It is impossible. We marvel at an eclipse which is high in the heavens and lasts for a truly short time. However, an eclipse gives a picture of what the Son of God did. The sun does not stop being the sun and neither did Jesus stop being God. He came down from heaven and laid aside the fullness of Who He was in order to please the Father.

Verse 8 further explains that Jesus' actions flowed from the mindset described in verses six and seven. Jesus was truly God and a watchful, willing, and faithful Son of God Who thought like His Father and acted on behalf of the Triune God. He looked forward to hearing the Father say, "Well done, Son. Mission accomplished" (Hebrews 12:1-3; Matthew 25:21, 23; Luke 19:17, 19).

IV. Paul's Personal Experience: Philippians 3:3-6

Next, consider the mind of Christ from another vantage point. Paul gave some details of his past life in Philippians 3:3-6. As a young man, Paul thought of himself as a person with rights, privileges, and achievement. He prided himself on his pedigree, performance, position, and personal lawkeeping. At a young age, he lived as he wanted by his own rules and standards as if this was his world. He lived the lie!

At his conversion he began to think and desire differently. He no longer lived the lie in terms of thinking and wanting. In verses seven and eight, he recorded the results of his change of heart. As a believer, he thought differently: he counted or considered those things that he had held dear and important as "manure" (useless and worthless; inferior is too mild a translation!). His desire followed his thinking: *life is not about me!*

He embraced his union with Christ or better, Christ's union with him! Being united with Christ was far superior to any experience he had had (3:8). He realized that because of his relationship with Christ through the Holy Spirit and His indwelling, he now had the mind of Christ. Changed thinking and wanting led to changed actions and a patterned lifestyle.

He now desired a more intimate (close, personal) relationship with his Savior. He longed to fully develop the mindset of Christ (3:8-11). He calls for believers to do the same based on Christ's example and his own experience (Philippians 2:5; 3:15).

V. OAN: *Putting On* Christ: Progressive sanctification.

The call for believers to *put on Christ* grows out of the fact that Christ united Himself to them, forming a personal relationship with each one (Romans 13:14; Galatians 2:20; 3:26-27; 5:24; Ephesians 4:22-24; Colossians 3:8-12). In a sense, Christ has put on the believer! *Putting on Christ* embraces several implies truths:
- The believer desires what Christ desired, thinks the way Christ thought, and does the Father's will—not perfectly but he is growing as a child of the King.
- The believer invests in Christ thus imitating Christ who gave Himself to the Triune God and to each believer.

- The believer functions as a true disciple which requires and results in thinking and desiring differently about God, self, and others (Philippians 2:5).
- The believer will no longer live the lie that this is his world, to be lived his way, and for his glory; he will begin to put off this anti-Roman 11:36 approach to life.

Further, the believer was put in Christ so that he has *put on Christ*. This was done to and for him by the Holy Spirit (Ephesians 4:22-24; Colossians 3:8-10). Paul summarizes this transition in Galatians 2:20: *I have been crucified with Christ and I no longer live, but Christ lives in me. The life I live in the body I live by faith in the Son of God, who loved me and gave himself for me.*

VI. Contrasts between the Old and New Man

Paul identified the old man, the old person—what the person was an unbeliever—as being crucified in Christ. The old person, a patterned way of thinking, wanting, and acting, had died with Christ. Union with Satan and his old lifestyle was broken. Christ was the believer's substitute and when He died physically, the believer died spiritually. He died in Christ and the believer is in Christ—united to him! This was a one-time event.

The old man no longer exists or lives. A word of caution is in order. The believer does not function in practice as he is in principle and fact. There is a disconnection between what a believer is in Christ and how he lives daily. Becoming more

Christ is accomplished as the believer closes the gap between what he was in self and Satan and what he is in Christ!

The believer was put in Christ, and he has put on Christ because Christ lived and died in his place as the perfect man. Not only that, God counted Christ's perfect life and death as the believer's! OAN is one means that enables believers to grow in Christlikeness.

As a result, he is a new creature in Christ and only in Christ (2 Corinthians 5:17). In Christ, the now-believer died in principle and is dying in practice to his old ways of self-pleasing: thoughts, desires, and actions. The *already* has come: the believer is a new creature! But the fullness of that change—the *not yet*—awaits heaven!

Now the believer enjoys being in Christ more than he enjoys being in self and Satan. As one *in Christ* indwelt by the Holy Spirit, the believer *puts on Christ* or he imitates and patterns his thoughts, desires, and action after Christ and biblical truth. The believer revamps his thoughts, desires, and actions so that they are more God-centered as opposed to self-centered. The believer grows in Christlikeness!

Therefore, the believer does not satisfy and gratify selfish desires which had been learned so well as an unbeliever. The mindset of *I wants* and *I deserves* are less of a driving force! Rather, the believer is motivated to please God out of gratitude, privilege, and blessing for what Christ has done (Romans 13:14; Ephesians 2:1-3; Galatians 5:16-18; 1 John 5:3-4).

OAN grows out of having the mind of Christ and applying it. A person cannot put on what He doesn't have (1 Corinthians 2:16; Ephesians 6:10-18). All those saved have been given the mind of Christ in principle.

Therefore, Christians can think God's thoughts and desire what God desires. The reason: they have been rescued from and removed out of the kingdom of darkness and placed into the kingdom of light (Acts 26:18; Colossians 1:13). Falsehood and ignorance have been replaced by wisdom and knowledge.

Further, the believer is indwelt by the Holy Spirit Who works primarily in the inner man. His effect on the body, specifically the brain, is predominately mediated by inner-man changes (Romans 6:6). However, both the heart (inner man) and the body including the brain have been programmed to please self. Physical, material, and neurochemical changes occur in the body.

However, as a result of salvation, habituation of the whole person must and will occur. Theologians call this activity progressive sanctification. The change process is through *putting on Christ* and Christlikeness as a response to being in Christ and being indwelt by the Holy Spirit. The person puts off self and self interest in order to please God. Changes in thinking and wanting occur in both the heart and the brain, the body.

The Holy Spirit illumines the believer as a whole person—inner and outer man. The Spirit specifically illumines the heart and enlightens the mind—both are terms for the inner man (John 14:17; 16:13; 2 Corinthians 4:6; Ephesians 1:14-19; 3:14-21). Thinking and wanting occur in the material aspect of man (the body), and in the inner man, the heart (Romans 6:6). The brain is connected to the heart non-anatomically.

Through Scripture the believer has access to divine thinking and by the Spirit he is given the capacity and ability to think God's thoughts and desire what pleases Him. This is the essence of putting on Christ! Paul called the Philippians to demonstrate the mindset of Christ through OAN. How were the Philippians to do that?

Self must be in its proper place. How did it get "out of place?" In the Garden, Adam and Eve received God's counsel and then the serpent's counsel. Adam decided that he would serve as the final arbiter of that which both he and Eve would follow. Faced with two counsels, he bought the lie of Satan. Eve was deceived but not Adam (2 Corinthians 11:3; 1 Timothy 2:14).

Adam and Eve believed the way to get ahead in *their* world was to compete with God in His. They reversed the Creator-creature distinction. They became a *God-want-a-be*. They exchanged the truth of God for a lie (Romans 1:18-25).

Self—for me, by me, to me—took preeminence in their thinking and wanting; as a result, they failed to submit to God.

Disobedience followed because Adam and Eve bought the lie that God could not be trusted but self and Satan could. Placing self at the center of life is what Satan advocated as preferable for Adam and Eve.

Accepting this counsel led to disobedience of God's good command. They lived the lie. As a result of God's judgment, all mankind was plunged into deadness, darkness, and depravity. Such is the result of living the lie.

VII. Jesus, the Gospels, the Mind of Christ, and OAN

One aspect of the truth embodied in the phrase *mind of Christ* can be summarized as true wisdom manifested as self-renunciation which was taught and demonstrated by Christ (Matthew 10:32-38; 16:24-25; Mark 8:33; Luke 9:26-27; 14:24-25; John 12:25). He set aside self-pleasing for the superior goal of pleasing His Father (John 4:31-34).

How did this look in His life? You could begin anywhere: in the stable, on the run from Herod, at home with parents, mingling with friends and foes alike, at His *trial* and on the cross, and post-resurrection. First and foremost, He was a servant of God to mankind. As such, He washed the feet of His disciples (Matthew 20:20-28; Mark 10:35-45; John 13:2-17).

Following close is the fact that He was a Lover par excellence Who loved the unlovely (Romans 5:6-10). We have already defined love as looking away from self to God and others. The highest *looking away* is toward God, the believer's Father, and toward Jesus, his brother. When one's focus is properly upward, he will minister to God's people rather than satisfying self (Colossians 3:1-3). He will be of earthly good!

Consider OAN and the mind of Christ based on Jesus' teaching from the Gospels: *Who is the Greatest?* Jesus revealed His mindset in response to the question of the disciples who asked: *Who is the greatest?* Consider the following passages: Mark 9:33-37; Matthew 18:1-5; Luke 9:46-48: *They came to Capernaum. When he was in the house, he asked them, "What were you arguing about on the road?" But they kept quiet because on the way they had argued about who was the greatest. Sitting down, Jesus called the Twelve and said: "If anyone wants to be first, he must be the very last and the servant of all." He took a little child and had him stand among them. Taking him in his arms he said to them, "Whoever welcomes one of these little children in my name welcomes me; and whoever welcomes me does not welcome me but the One who sent me."*

Jesus questioned the disciples' inter-relational activity. He was concerned because the disciples were missing the mark! Their concern—*who is the greatest?*—is far too common among God's people (see Matthew 20:20-28; Mark 10:35-45; Luke 22:24-25). The disciples were arguing about rank, position, preeminence, prominence, approval, acceptance, and status. This is contrary to Jesus' mindset as given in Philippians 2:3-4.

Any one of the above is a common motivation that may be enthroned in the human heart. When that happens, a person is a functioning idolater and living the lie. Something more important than God and pleasing Him has taken center stage in the person's thinking and wanting (Exodus 20:1-7). God is dishonored and the Church fails God and His people.

Arguing one's status or rank is viewing life as *I must have and win* and is opposed to Jesus' example and teaching. Childlike-dependence and trusting was the key to pleasing God. In his gospel, John recounts that Jesus displayed absolute and total trust and dependence on the Father (John 4:31-34; 5:19, 30). He expected this same orientation from His disciples then and now.

Concern for self in place of concern for God and others discourages OAN; it is counterproductive to it, and it is living the lie. Jesus never lived the lie! Winning for the sake of *me* reflects sinful pride. It says that what I want is more important than what God wants.

It is no mere accident that each of the Synoptic Gospels records the account of *who is the greatest?* The writers place it after Jesus predicted His death and resurrection. The contrast between Jesus' focus and that of the disciples is monumental.

Jesus focused on pleasing His Father as the Substitute Suffering hard-working Servant; in contrast, the disciples lived the satanic lie and focused on their own glory—what they wanted and thought they deserved. They considered self as the object of another's notice and perhaps worship.

Based on their mindset, they would not be a servant of others; rather, they would function as a king waiting to be served. Jesus knew that their focus was egocentric; OAN will not take place. The apostolic ministry would fail, and Jesus' ministry would fail if the apostles continued with their present mindset. Matthew 18:1-5: *At that time the disciples came to Jesus and asked, "Who is the greatest in the kingdom of heaven?" He called a little child and had him stand among them. And he said, "I tell you the truth, unless you change and become like little children, you will never enter the kingdom of heaven. Therefore, whoever humbles himself like this child is the greatest in the kingdom of heaven. And whoever welcomes a little child like this in my name welcomes me."*

Similarly, Matthew recorded Jesus' prediction of His death and resurrection (17:22-23) and then came His question for the disciples: *Who is the greatest in the kingdom of heaven?* The disciples had not heard Jesus with *spiritual ears*—their hearts were not fully bathed in the balm of saving faith and true hope. They heard words physically—with physical ears—but there was no correct interpretation of what they heard.

They had had a sensual experience only; they didn't understand His words. They had a wrong interpretative grid. Their interpretative grid was feelings and thinking and wanting divorced from biblical truth. The disciples, not just Judas, lived the lie at Jesus' expense!

The use of saving faith and true hope was not yet fully developed but they had the core of the gospel message much like the saints of the Old Testament (Luke 24:25ff; Romans 4:1-3; Galatians 3:8; Hebrews 11:26). They also interacted with Jesus face to face. Consequently, Jesus held them responsible for their thoughts, desires, and actions.

Jesus knew that they did not have the fullness of the Holy Spirit and His whole armor which came at Pentecost! However, He must have expected much more spiritual maturity from them! Yet He did not leave or forsake them. He gave them peace, not as the world does, and the Holy Spirit (John 14:25-27). That is true OAN!

Believers today live on the resurrection side of the cross and have the fullness of the Holy Spirit in them and in the Church. We have no excuse for failing to OAN by misunderstanding the concept of the greatest. Pandemics are one of God's tools to sharpen His people and Church.

Imagine: the "Greatest" was standing before the disciples. He defined "the greatest" in word and deed. Throughout His ministry, Jesus had been describing Himself—His Person and mission (Philippians 2:5-8).

At this point in His life, Jesus predicted His death and resurrection; He told them Who and what was great in His kingdom. Please note: the kingdom came in Christ because in part, He is the Kingdom. He ushered in a new reality. In order to do that, Jesus set aside Himself!

He was motivated by His relationship with the Father and His overriding desire to please Him (John 6:37-43). He did by living perfectly and dying perfectly in the place of undeserving sinners who considered themselves the *greatest* (Romans 5:6-10). Yet He calls those He died for, His children, His brothers, and His sisters (John 4:31-34).

He placed a little child in their midst and had the disciples gaze upon him (also Mark 9:35-37 and Luke 9:46-48). A child is a sinner—that was not the issue. The child was considered least in Jewish society. He held one of the lowest stations. He was considered and treated as insignificant. A child is generally helpless devoid of power, but he is trusting and quick to show his dependence. The disciples' concern contrasted with these truths.

Unlike a child, the disciples were concerned about their status, rank, position, and welfare (see Paul's concern in Philippians 3:3-6). Jesus called them to repentance—they had not humbled themselves but sought to be number one. They trusted themselves and their own accomplishments. They did not exercise the mind of Christ. They had no interest in OAN. They were living the lie.

Unlike the child who had no status and did not seek one, the disciples were intent on securing a place in the kingdom which they did not understand. Previous membership in Satan's kingdom and remaining sinfulness warped their spiritual vision. Their thoughts, desires, and action were still influenced more by satanic orientation than by biblical truth.

Jesus who is Light, Truth and Life, came to give light, truth, and life (John 14:6). He demonstrated and taught that the greatest is the least and acts like it (John 13:1-17). He is not *pushy* for self but properly *pushy* for God and others.

The apostles needed to properly exercise what they were in Christ by the Holy Spirit. His coming occurred at Pentecost and the fullness of His presence, reign, and rule awaits consummation. The disciples' hearts were renewed but they were slow to exercise saving faith and true hope (Luke 24:25-27, 44-49; Romans 8:24-25; 2 Corinthians 5:7, 9; 1 Corinthians 13:11). Christ continued to teach, an aspect of OAN.

The disciples asked a question concerning one's position in the kingdom but in contrast, Jesus taught that the fundamental issue was entrance into the kingdom and life afterwards. He referred to His teaching in Matthew 5:3 (*"Blessed are the poor in spirit . . ."*) where He taught that members of the kingdom of God must be like a little child to enter into God's kingdom and family. Moreover, and emphatically, they must become like Christ: total dependence on the Father and the Spirit divesting themselves of self!

The scene in Mark 9, Matthew 18, and Luke 9 is a reminder of Nicodemus' encounter with Christ (John 3). Initially Nicodemus did not get it either (John 19:39 indicates that Nicodemus accompanied Joseph in the burial of Jesus. This suggested that he was a believer—he did get some of it!). Before Jesus, Nicodemus acknowledged only that God was with Jesus as evidenced by the signs Jesus was doing (John 3:2).

Jesus then opened the discussion to membership in the kingdom—*you must be born again* or *from above* (3:3). Nicodemus understood *born again* (*born from above*) to be another physical birth. He knew this was impossible. But he went no farther. Jesus rebuked him because as a spiritual leader of Israel he was ignorant of truth (John 3:10-11).

Similarly, the mindset of a child does not refer to age as such. Rather, Jesus is speaking of dependence and trust that is childlike in nature. As the child steps out toward his parents, so believers are to step out to the Triune God by denying self. This stepping out is part of *putting on Christ* and *putting off self*. The two are linked. The believer denies himself that which has been most important to him—himself!

One manifestation of self-renunciation is God-centered service—the greatest was the one who served God and others rather than himself. Jesus modeled that truth in John 13:1-17. One is not born a OAN-er—it is not a natural inclination. It is a result of a supernatural activity of the Spirit in the believer. Consider Luke 9:46-48. In verse 44 Jesus predicts His death and in verse 45, the disciples did not understand and were afraid to ask. *An argument started among the disciples as to which of them would be the greatest.*

Jesus, knowing their thoughts, took a little child and had him stand beside him. Then he said to them, "Whoever welcomes this little child in my name welcomes me, and whoever welcomes me welcomes the one who sent me. For he who is the least among you all—he is the greatest."

The greatest is defined in two ways. First, the disciples are to become as little children—not little children—described in Matthew 18:1-5: dependent and trusting acknowledge their helpless estate or condition.

Second, being *poor in spirit* is the only way to receive and enter the kingdom (Matthew 5:3). *Poor in spirit* is something that is given. It is something you are and something you do. Jesus turned the tables on the arguing disciples when He said that the humble will be exalted but the proud will be humbled (Matthew 18:4; 20:27; 23:11).

The proud are those who first seek their own place—they will not give or receive OAN! The humble are those who are growing in their dependence on God and will OAN. As are children, they are dependent and trusting in God and not in self. They believe in a Person—not in themselves (Proverbs 3:5-8)! Their strength and confidence is based on fact: they are *in Christ* indwelt by the Holy Spirit (Galatians 2:20; Romans 8:9, 11).

Those who display proper concern for others (they are OAN!) are those who are *putting off self* by *putting on Christ*. This honors God as each person puts on Christlikeness (Matthew 5:3; 2 Corinthians 5:9-15; 12:7-10; Philippians 2:3-4; Proverbs 13:15; 26:11).

VIII. The Mind of Christ, OAN, and 1 Corinthians

Consider the mind of Christ as taught in the first letter to the Corinthians. Paul also emphasized the mind of Christ in other churches and always for the purpose of bringing about change in individuals and in the body of Christ. He taught that OAN reflects the mind of Christ.

The Corinthian Church was beset with a myriad of problems that Paul addressed in his first letter to the Corinthians (see pages 35, 81, 124). These included division (chapters 1, 3); a misunderstanding of wisdom and its source (chapter 2); a lack of church discipline and sexual sin (chapter 5); lawsuits (chapter 6); and failing to properly understand marriage and divorce (chapter 7).

There were wrong views of knowledge and Christian liberty (chapters 8, 10); misuse of the Lord's Supper (chapter 11); and misunderstandings of gifts (chapter 12), love (chapter 13), the resurrection (chapter 15), and perhaps Christian giving (chapter 16).

A central flaw and theme in all these problems could be traced to a lack of true biblical fellowship and OAN. These people had the mind of Christ (1 Corinthians 2:16: *For who has known the mind of the Lord that he may instruct Him? But we have the mind of Christ*). Yet they were functioning as though they did not (1 Corinthians 3:3: *You are still worldly. For since there is jealousy and quarreling among you, are not you worldly? Are you not acting like mere men?*). They were living the lie!

Worldly is sometimes translated as *flesh*. It refers to what believers were as unbelievers. Ephesians 2:1-3: believers were dead and disobedient in their sins; according to James 3:13-4:3, they were fools. Even though the Corinthians possessed the Spirit, there was none of His fruit in their lives. Instead of oneness and unity, there was factionalism, schism and disunity. Pride was the manner of the day.

The Corinthians had failed to OAN: to receive it and give it. They desperately needed to understand that having the mind of Christ meant understanding and acting upon the facts that self in not number one—God is; and one part of the body of Christ is not more important than another.

Paul used the metaphor of the human body and its members to illustrate important facts about the Church: its unity, the purposeful diversity within it (differing functions), and the interdependence of all the parts (1 Corinthians 12 and 14). Care and concern for self at the expense of others divides the body. In contrast and a corollary truth is this: care and concern of others motivated by a desire to please the Father brings about oneness.

First, consider how Paul relates the mind of Christ to OAN in the following passages. 1 Corinthians 1:10: *I appeal to you, brothers, in the name of our Lord Jesus Christ, that all of you agree with one another so that there may be no divisions among you and that you will be perfectly united in mind and thought.*

As mentioned, the Corinthian Church was beset with internal problems. Following his greeting and opening remarks (v.1-9), Paul continued his letter by getting to the heart of the matter: the people's heart as manifested by thoughts, desires, and actions. People were not getting along; there was division, factions, and strife: pride! Paul pictured the Church at Corinth as one ripped open and needing mending.

In verse ten, Paul urged his brothers to act as though they had the mind of Christ because they did! They were united to Christ (He took them in) and the Holy Spirit indwelt them (Galatians 2:20)!

Paul called on them to agree on what they think which will affect their actions (see section: Romans 14:1-15:6 where Paul gives direction regarding the weaker and stronger brother). A proper view of God will facilitate a proper view of self and others and OAN.

Paul urged—exhorted—them to imitate Christ (to *put on Christ*) who put God and His ways first and set self and *I wants* aside. Thinking and desiring like Christ leads to true biblical OAN which leads to the breaking down of walls that separate people.

Relationships are to be restored which is evidence of and encourages growth in grace (John 13:34-35; 2 Peter 3:18). In this way, division and strife are minimized and even abolished. Differences of opinion may persist, but they will not lead to strife and division (James 4:1-3).

Verses ten through seventeen of 1 Corinthians explained what was happening—factionalism and me-ism. Proper doctrine was less an issue. The Corinthians drew sides and lines in the sand. They had set up their own turf; they set men on pedestals; and they committed themselves to men and positions rather than to the Way, the Truth, and the Life (John 14:6). Self was truly on the throne! Again, they were living the lie.

The Corinthians had taken up the serpent's counsel given in the Garden. The people protected and defended their person and their positions. Therefore, there was a cacophony of sounds within the body of Christ calling out *for me* and *for us*. There was no OAN. People were too busy looking after their own interests.

Paul emphasized the way to unity is by speaking all together as one—agree with one another in the Lord (verse 11). He uses an idiom drawn from Greek political life which meant to "pull together for a common purpose." The people were to be bound together by the same attitude and motivation as was Christ's—pleasing the Father. This requires OAN.

Differing opinions (diversity) are not necessarily wrong. It is the source of those opinions and what one does with them that reflects their status in one's heart. When *having what I want* becomes the driving force in one's life, he is a functioning idolater serving self. OAN and biblical fellowship is hindered which brings division and disunity.

I have heard it said in some Christian circles that we need to *agree to disagree*. I find nothing in Scripture that fosters this view. Rather, Paul teaches believers to be of one mind—not yours or anyone else's, but Christ's. We must all agree to aggressively OAN. OAN not only requires the mind of Christ, but it is a tool in developing it.

Second, consider 1 Corinthians 10:16-17: *Is not the cup of thanksgiving for which we give thanks a participation in the blood of Christ? And is not the bread that we break a participation in the body of Christ? Because there is one loaf of bread we who are many are one body, for we all partake of the one loaf.*

Paul had closed a section addressing Israel's past (verses 1-14). He began chapter 10 by stating that he did not want the brothers to be ignorant about their forefathers (verse 1). Paul as did John (see chapter 2: Fellowship and Relationships) knew that knowledge, life, and truth are vital to and for ministry.

Further, in the opening verses of chapter ten, Paul warned against idolatry (verse 7), by appealing to a main message emphasized in the Old Testament (verses 6, 11), and concluded the section by urging the Corinthians to flee idolatry (verse 14). Paul knew Israel was the forerunner of the Church and that idolatry at its core was self-worship (Galatians 6:16: the Church is the New Israel; see Exodus 32 regarding idolatry).

Seeking the place of preeminence is an expression of sinful pride and self-worship and always leads to division and disunity in the body. If the members of the Corinthian congregation persisted in their failure to flee idolatry, serious consequences would continue. They would function as a disruptive, disunified body grieving God, slandering His name, and harming His Church and themselves.

As an aside, so often we think of idolatry as making and worshipping some physical object. The physical activity of making the idol begins in the heart such that idolatry is an inner-man activity with visible manifestations. The person has inverted the Creator-creature distinction rejecting his creature status (Romans 1:18-23). He has exchanged the truth of God and of himself for a lie.

Every person is a religious worshipping being by God's creative design. Moreover, God has determined who and how to worship. God is the true God who deserves loyalty, devotion, and affection (Exodus 20:1-11, 17, 22-23).

The idolater attempts to push God off His throne and worships himself through people or objects. The New Testament widens the concept of idolatry in such passages as Romans 1:18-25; Ephesians 5:5; Colossians 3:5; and 1 John 5:21. It emphasizes the believer's heart activity of *me first* that is and further promotes idolatry. It is an expression of the fundamental satanic lie.

Paul encouraged the Corinthians. The command to flee idolatry was doable and would come via OAN. Paul was not referring to some physical object that a person appointed it to be a god. The person fashions that which he worships for his own glory. He is the idol and the idol-maker! Even if it was a physical object, the action of the person's hands who carved the object flowed from a heart that said: I am the god-maker!

OAN is one antidote for idolatry. Paul intended to give hope through these truths. In verse 15-17, he adds to that hope by emphasizing the unity of the body. The body of Christ is one as Paul taught here and in Ephesians 4:1-16.

Moreover, the Christian life is not a solitary, isolated one. There are no "Lone Ranger" Christians on earth or in heaven. God intended Christians to function as a unit thus reflecting the Trinity. One means of doing so is through OAN.

Third, consider 1 Corinthians 11:33: *So then, my brothers, when you come together to eat, wait for each other.*

Paul in chapter 11 teaches that the abuse of the Lord's Supper was an abuse of the body of Christ and of Christ Himself. The abuse had come about due to a lack of self-judgment and appropriate self-discipline (verses 27-32). OAN was non-existent.

Not only did Paul encourage eating together as a body, but also waiting on each other. The word translated "wait" is a simple term for displaying common courtesy to another. [8] Paul exhorted the brothers to be considerate of one another which

---

8 The word translated "wait" is *ekdechomai* which occurs six times in the New Testament all of which refer to simple common courtesy: Acts 17:16; 1 Corinthians 11:3; 16:11; Hebrews 10:13; 11:10; James 5:7—and perhaps John 5:3

could be displayed in several ways such as waiting one's turn, letting another go first, speaking to another before spoken to, and providing physically for another.

This seems such a simple command. However, in chapter 11 the stakes were high. God chastised some of the congregation and others died because they had abused the taking of the Lord's Supper (lack of simple courtesies, gluttony, and favoritism-discrimination). That abuse resulted from and led to the mindset that produced factions and divisions within the Church (verses 17-21 and 1:10-17).

Self ruled in the Corinthian congregation; some placed their own interests over the interests of the body and one another. Functionally, they rejected Christ's words and Christ Himself (verses 23-26). Their sinful behavior brought God's judgment. Such it is when OAN is not in place.

Next consider 1 Corinthians 12:25-27: *so that there should be no division in the body, but that its parts should have equal concern for each other. If one part suffers, every part suffers with it; if one part is honored, every part rejoices with it. Now you are the body of Christ and each of you is part of it.* (See 12:22-27).

In this chapter Paul addressed the problem of the misuse of gifts which was one cause of strife in the congregation. Verse 1 opened with a call for the Corinthians not to be ignorant of spiritual gifts. Knowledge and understanding is linked to OAN. The misuse of gifts promoted disunity. Throughout the chapter, especially verses four through twenty-seven, Paul emphasized that each member was a vital part of the whole and needed the rest of the body.

All parts of the body are essential for proper functioning of it. Therefore, the correct understanding and use of gifts is one means of caring for each other. This promotes and maintains unity in the body.

Paul emphasized concern and care for one another such that there should be no division within the body (verse 25). The root of the word translated concern (*merizo*) means "to divide, part, or share."

Sometimes the word is translated "to be anxious, troubled, and to take thought." It is generally translated as "to worry" and "to be anxious," activities which are prohibited in Scripture.[9] The word refers to thinking and wanting. It is a cognitive and desire-oriented activity. Worry results from and produces division within a person's heart which is often manifested outwardly toward others.

However, there is also a "good" side to the word as here and 2 Corinthians 11:28. In both verses, Paul emphasized proper concern—thoughts, desires, and actions—toward and for each other and the unity of the body. Proper concern is not simply being kind or sweet. Rather it refers to one brother showing an interest in, giving thought to, caring for, paying attention to, looking out for, and checking up on another brother and sister.

---

9   Matthew 6:25, 27-28, 31, 34; 10:19; Luke 10:41; 12:11, 22, 25-26.

The concern is to be mutually edifying and can be demonstrated in any number of ways. One of those is given in 2 Corinthians 2:7-8 and includes forgiveness, help, and reaffirmation of one's love to the man who was disciplined out of the church but returned as a member.

IX. The Mind of Christ, OAN, and the Book of Romans

Paul also described the mind of Christ in the Book of Romans. But his use of it differed when compared to his letters to the Philippians and Corinthians. The book of Romans was less a letter and more a treatise on systematic theology.

Apparently, there were few problems in the church at Rome (an exception is expressed in Romans 14-15). Yet, throughout the book of Romans, he exhorts his readers many times to OAN.

What he says about OAN, in principle, can be applied to any situation in every age. The New Testament was written for the Church's instructions for all ages until Christ returns (Romans 4:23-24; 15:1-6; 1 Corinthians 9:8-10; 10:6, 11; 2 Timothy 3:15-17).

A. Romans 12:1-2, 3-8

Beginning with Chapter 12, Paul began a concerted effort to apply the truths taught in chapters 1-11. First, Paul urged each believer to present himself as a whole person (body including the brain in verse 1 and the inner man/heart in verse 2) to God as the believer's most logical and worthwhile endeavor: 12:1-2 *Therefore, I urge you, brothers, in view of God's mercies, to offer your bodies as living sacrifices, holy and pleasing to God—this is your spiritual act of worship. Do not be conformed any longer to the pattern of this world, but be transformed by the renewing of your mind. Then you will be able to test and approve what God's will is—his good, pleasing and perfect will.*

He then followed the call in verses one and two by explaining the *how to* in the rest of the chapter. He exhorted each person to engage in the whole-person activity of thinking and wanting that would result in OAN (12:3-8, 9-13). They are to think correctly about themselves. No one is to think too highly of self but soberly. He is to be *right minded* which is to be *Christ-minded* as he taught in Philippians 2:3-4: *For by the grace given to me, I say to every one of you: Do not think of yourself more highly than you ought, but rather think of yourself with sober judgment, in accordance with the measure of faith God has given you*, and in Romans 12:4-5: *Just as each of us has one body with many members and these members do not all have the same function, so in Christ we who are many form one body and each member belongs to all the others.*

To facilitate this Christlike activity of proper thinking and wanting, Paul encouraged the believer to make a self-inventory: Romans 12:6-8 (see 2 Corinthians 13:5): *We have different gifts according to the grace given to us. If a man's gift is prophecy, let him use it in proportion to his faith; if it is serving, let him serve; if it is teaching, let him teach; if it is encouraging, let him encourage; if it is contributing to the needs of others, let him give generously; if it is leadership let him govern in diligently; if it is showing mercy, let him do it cheerfully.*

The goal of self-inventory is to determine one's gifts (verse 6), to evaluate their proper use (verses 6-8), and discover the purpose for which they were given (verses 7-8). Paul emphasized that one's gifts are for service to and for the benefit of the body. Thus, gifts are given for OAN which is to be for the glory of God.

B. Romans 12:9-13

Paul then began a series of exhortations that addressed various types of relationships. *Love must be sincere. Hate what is evil; cling to what is good. Be devoted to one another in brotherly love. Honor one another above yourselves. Never be lacking in zeal, but keep your spiritual fervor, serving the Lord. Be joyful in hope, patient in affliction, faithful in prayer. Share with God's people who are in need. Practice hospitality* (Romans 12:9-13).

In verse 9, Paul gave a three-fold exhortation that covers all human relationships but especially those involving believers: love, hate, and cling. He urged genuine love (*agape*) in contrast to "counterfeit" love. True love is without hypocrisy, pretense, or insincerity.

Paul also urged a right hate: abhor or loathe that which is evil. He is to love what God loves and hate what He hates. The one who loves develops an intense dislike for doing evil to another and grieves over his evil and the evil of others (Psalm 34:14; 37:27; 45:7; 97:10; 119:104, 113, 136, 139-140, 163; 139:21).

The true lover clings or adheres (stays glued) to that which is good—namely the Triune God and His truth. But he moves out to others. Love motivates a person to remove himself from himself and from doing evil; he relates to another by OAN. In this way, he remembers Christ the OAN-er and how others OAN him.

The truth conveyed in verses 10-13 strikes at the heart of OAN. Specifically, members of God's family are to manage the Church unlike the world. In verse 10, Paul urged warmth rather than coldness (even coolness!) towards one's brother. The word honor has the idea of preferring another. Both words carry the idea of showing mutual respect in thought and action.

Instead of being preoccupied with one's own agenda in terms of *my ideas, my needs, my wants, my plans,* and *my goals,* the OAN-er properly turns his attention to the other person. Truth, light, and life replace falsehood, darkness, and deadness. Paul urged members of God's family to be so inclined to each other that in every legitimate situation credit is given where credit is due.

For example, defer to the person who can sing or play an instrument more effectively than you. When the other person has something to contribute prefer his thoughts and words to your own. Let him have your chair or your area at the table, and certainly your appreciation.

Moreover, members of the body of Christ are not to be *turf hogs* as was the case with the apostles and the Corinthians (Matthew 20:20-28; Mark 10:35-45; Luke 22:24-27; 1 Corinthians 1:10-17). No one is to stake a claim on things, areas, people, or God for their own benefit.

Paul, as Jesus did, emphasized the giving of honor over against seeking to gain it (John 5:41-44; 8:54). It is far better to give than to receive (Acts 20:35). The way to honor another is by applying Philippians 2:3-4 and 1 Corinthians 1:10 (see those verses in this section).

In addition, the idea of *honoring* and *preferring another in honor* may mean to remain devoted to the other person in spite of the circumstances. OAN-love is wise, and it enables the believer to give others the benefit of the doubt; it hopes all things and endures all things (1 Corinthians 13). This devotion is expressed by coming alongside of another even when it may be hard to do.

Verses 11-13 of Romans 13 continue Paul's exhortations on how to get along within the body of Christ and include zeal, joy, hope, patient, prayerful, and share. These can be summarized under the term *endurance*. Believers are to *keep on keeping on* because God is pleased, and the body of Christ and individuals are blessed.

Paul calls believers to have fellowship with one another for the benefit of everyone in the body (John 13:34-35). The motive is love for the Triune God and the brothers (Matthew 22:37-40). The person will gain from OAN but that can't be the believer's motivation for giving and receiving it. The same principle applies to evangelizing unbelievers. Everyone gains!

As an aside, Paul addressed the issue of favoritism in the Church in 1 Corinthians 11 (also in Romans 2:11; James also warned against favoritism: 2:1-7). Jesus did not play favorites, and neither should His people.

Favoritism can be displayed anywhere including in one's own church family. It is favoring self and one's own importance rather than God and one's neighbor. Simply not taking time to say hello, or failing to inquire about someone, or failing to encourage and pray for others especially those with whom you disagree can be forms of favoritism.

I once asked a person how he was doing and then must have scooted on by him. He brought me to an abrupt halt by asking me if I really wanted to hear his answer. Asking the question of how a person is doing should never be routine or done in a flippant manner.

Sadly, there are many opportunities and reasons given for discouragement and broken relationships within the body. Paul said these should not be. But they do. Fellow members sin against one another.

In response, it is easy to give up, draw away from other members, or even leave the church. The reasons given are often the sinfulness and hypocrisy of the present members. Functionally, those leaving the church consider themselves better than others and those staying may have the same thought about themselves. In both cases, the Triune God is dishonored, and the body is harmed.

Paul urged his readers not to be slow and hesitant when it comes to endurance. Believers are to continue in the race of maturing in Christlikeness (Hebrews 11:39-12:3). OAN is instrumental in developing endurance and Christlike maturity.

The word translated endurance means to stand up under for the purpose of pushing forward (see my book: *Endurance: What it is and How it Looks in the Believer's Life*). Biblical endurance is never passive, static, or defensive. It is not simply coping, accepting, or tolerating. It is not being under the circumstances.

Rather, the endurer uses circumstances as God's instrument to grow in Christlikeness. This is part of the process of *putting on Christ*. The goal is victory, not simply putting up with or getting by.[10] The person is on fire—aglow, burning, boiling,

---

[10] Victory is defined as overcoming. The once-for-all victory for every believer came as Jesus lived perfectly, died as the perfect Sacrifice, and rose as the victorious Son. He paid the debt owed God in full. As a result, the hostility between God and man has been replaced by Fatherly concern. Victory for the Christian occurs daily as he becomes more like Christ in thoughts, desires, and actions. OAN—giving it and receiving it—one way to gain victory daily and eternally (1 John 3:1-3)!

and fervent—for the honor of God, the beauty of the Church, and the welfare of individual saints.

OAN is one of God's tools to accomplish victory. This mindset flows from the reality of who the Triune God and what He has done, is doing, and will do for the Church and individual believers. Resurrection life and an eternal perspective begins at salvation; therefore, the believer can be of earthly good (1 John 3:1-3).

One's love is to be warm because one's heart has been warmed by God's love (verse 10 and Romans 5:5). This innerman change will be expressed in boundless but controlled enthusiasm suited for the person and the situation. Serving the Lord and serving others is a package-deal!

Serving the Lord is motivated by truth and thankfulness for God and for salvation. Moreover, it produces and encourages joy and hope enabling believers to endure hard times by using God's providence, whatever it may be, to grow and change. Serving the Lord is a function of perseverance, and it produces perseverance. Therefore, believers don't live the lie by giving up and giving in to feelings.

Circumstances are viewed through the "eyes"—the grid, the standard—of saving faith and true hope. The truth that God is in the problem, up to something, up to something good now and eternally becomes a rallying cry for all believers. Praying then becomes a regular activity.

God may seem far away, but He isn't. Recalling the truth of God's presence and covenantal faithfulness enables the believer to rightly respond to God's answer of "no" or "wait." All of life takes on a different perspective as it did for Christ and the saints of old!

The biblical endurer refuses to live the lie! He knows that God is good, wise, and powerful even if circumstances and feelings say differently. In verses 13, Paul calls for sharing and hospitality as a means of meeting the needs of the saints in good and hard times. All of these are examples of OAN.

C. Romans 12:14-21

Bless those who persecute you; bless and do not curse. Rejoice with those who rejoice; mourn with those who mourn. Live in harmony with one another. Do not be proud, but be willing to associate with people of low position. Do not be conceited. Do not repay evil for evil. Be careful to do what is right in the eyes of everybody. If it is possible, as far as it depends on you, live at peace with everyone. Do not take revenge, my friends, but leave room for God's wrath, for it is written: "It is mine to avenge; I will repay;" says the Lord. On the contrary: "If your enemy is hungry, feed him; if he is thirsty, give him something to drink. In doing this, you will heap burning coals on his head." Do not be overcome by evil, but overcome evil with good.

Verses fourteen through twenty-one of chapter twelve are dedicated to the believer's attitude—thoughts and desires—

and action predominantly toward those outside the Church including enemies. The principles are similar to those related to the Church family. If God treated His enemies—believers had been His enemies—as described in Romans 12:14-21, then how much more should believers act toward their enemies.

Moreover, God directs believers to act toward unbelievers as He did to them. How much more should believers act to fellow believers! They are in the same family and love begins in the household of God (John 13:34-35). God in Christ and the Holy Spirit has given the Church quite a wake-up call for OAN! The unbeliever does not have the mind of Christ but through the application of OAN principles he can be properly evangelized. That is true love!

Verse 16 occurs in the middle of the section (*Live in harmony with one another. Do not be proud, but be willing to associate with people of low position. Do not be conceited*). It sounds much like Paul's words in Philippians 2:3-4. In both places, Paul called believers to live and think as Christ did!

There can be harmony and agreement between one another even those outside the Church. Paul is not speaking of capitulation and compromise; he is not advocating peace loving—peace at any cost. Jesus came and He brought a sword and division (Matthew 10:34). But Paul is against making trouble. It will come (John 16:33)! Paul told the people to think, desire, and act as Jesus did toward believers and unbelievers. He ministered! He wanted the people to be God's kind of trouble-maker!

Paul told his readers: don't be haughty by setting your thinking on high things. Haughty and arrogant have to do with height, the idea being that a proud person is one who attempts to stand above others with them looking up at self and he down with contempt on others (See Luke 18:9-14; Colossians 3:1-3).

Pride opposes OAN which requires humility—a lowering of self in one's own eyes by considering others and their concerns more important than self (Philippians 2:3-4; Ephesians 4:1-3).

The phrase in verse 16: *live in harmony* reflects the person's thinking and wanting from which actions flow. It does not necessarily mean that everyone should or will agree on everything. Differences of opinion are not necessarily sinful or unhealthy (1 Corinthians 11:19). Rather it is how one responds to those differences (Romans 14:1-15:6; James 4:1-3).

Disagreement does not lead to conflict unless the differences of opinion are handled in a manner that displeases God. Disagreeableness is sin when it is fostered by *I must win* attitude rather than *God must get the glory* attitude of Jesus Christ (James 4:1-3).

Living and thinking in harmony with each other and God must be understood in terms of thinking and desiring as Christ did 24/7. Jesus set the bar at perfection. Otherwise, He would not have been Perfect Lamb of God. Believers are to imitate Him. In that way, the Triune God is honor, and the Church and individual believers grow.

D. The Mind of Christ, OAN, and Favoritism

As an aside, Paul addressed the issue of favoritism in the Church in 1 Corinthians 11 (also in Romans 2:11; James also warned against favoritism: 2:1-7). Jesus did not play favorites, and neither should His people.

Favoritism can be displayed anywhere including in one's own church family. It is favoring self and one's own importance rather than God and one's neighbor. Simply not taking time to say hello, or failing to inquire about someone, or failing to encourage and pray for others especially those with whom you disagree can be forms of favoritism.

I once asked a person how he was doing and then must have scooted on by him. He brought me to an abrupt halt by asking me if I really wanted to hear his answer. Asking the question of how a person is doing should never be routine or done in a flippant manner.

Sadly, there are many opportunities and reasons given for discouragement and broken relationships within the body. Paul said these should not be. But they do. Fellow members sin against one another.

In response, it is easy to give up, draw away from other members, or even leave the church. The reasons given are often the sinfulness and hypocrisy of the present members. Functionally, those leaving the church consider themselves better than others and those staying may have the same thought about themselves. In both cases, the Triune God is dishonored, and the body is harmed.

E. Lack of the Display of the Mind of Christ: The Church at Galatia

The Bible warns people to be aware when the mind of Christ is not evident in the church. When that happens, believers are functioning as unbelievers (1 Corinthians 3:3). This failure seems to be demonstrated all too frequently in our churches.

The Church at Galatia was tearing each other part! Galatians 5:15: *If you keep on biting and devouring each other, watch out or you will be destroyed by each other.* In this verse, Paul is speaking of *verbal cannibalism* and its consequences. The acceptance of false teaching and a false gospel led to destructive attitudes—thoughts and desires—and actions in the Galatian Church. Strife and dissension were the result.

Paul is describing a whole-person activity from the inside-out. People live out of their hearts which is linked to the body and results in thoughts, desires, and actions which are visible outwardly. The actions are the fruit produced by the person's heart activity (root). Fruit is testimony of inner-man activity (Matthew 15:1-20; Mark 7:1-23).

The context of our verse in Galatians 5 is given in verses 13-18: *You, my brothers, were called to be free. But do not use your freedom to indulge the sinful nature; rather, serve one another in love. The entire law is summed up in a single command: "Love your neighbor as yourself. If you keep on biting and devouring each other, watch out or you will be destroyed by each other. So I say live by the Spirit, and you will not gratify the desires of the sinful nature. For the sinful nature desires what is contrary to the Spirit and the Spirit what is contrary to the sinful nature. They are in conflict with each other, so that you do not do what you want. But if you are led by the Spirit, you are not under law.*

Verses 16-18 bring to the fore the tension between two ways of living: what the believer was when he was a member of Satan's family and kingdom in contrast to what he is now in Christ. Direction, influence, and motivation will either be Holy Spirit-initiated and energized or self-generated: *for me, to me, by me for my gratification.*

The believer has habit patterns of thinking; wanting; and doing that still resembles his former way of life. These are opposed to a Holy-Spirit influenced, motivated, energized, and guided life.

Biting and devouring one another is the result of putting self before God and others. It is devoid of OAN. Paul pictures another person as a meal. In fact, the two verbs are often used of animals at mealtime. First comes the chewing—perhaps just little pieces at a time and then the eating—larger pieces and maybe even chunks are torn from the bone. The meal is consumed so that nothing is left! What a sad picture of God's Church!

In verses 13-14, Paul calls his readers to serve one another in love because love sums up the law (Romans 13:8-10). Biblical love looks away from self to God and others. The Christian is motivated to please God. Freedom from self-service is manifested as personal lawkeeping to get: salvation and earn "brownie points" with God. This freedom leads to freedom to serve God and others. The reverse is also true. OAN expresses these truths!

It is vital that the believer and the Church have a proper understanding of salvation and life after salvation. Paul addresses these two points in the book of Galatians. Proper OAN was desperately needed in the Church.

F. Freedom, Law, and Law-keeping: Their Relation to OAN

The Christian is free from personal lawkeeping for salvation (Romans 8:1-2 Corinthians 5:21). The law properly demands perfect, perpetual, personal obedience for salvation and sanctification. But at salvation, the burden of personal lawkeeping for being saved has been removed.

How can that be (see footnote 20)? God provided the perfect Lawkeeper! Christ lived and obeyed perfectly, and He died perfectly. God then counted (the term is a courtroom and accounting term) Christ's perfect obedience in His life and in His death as if the now-believer had kept the law perfectly. Jesus did what the first Adam did not do.

Therefore, personal lawkeeping is no longer necessary for salvation; it is no longer a burden for the one saved; rather lawkeeping is now part of the fruit of salvation; it is a blessing and privilege (1 John 5:3). Paul is never against law-keeping, but he is against the wrong use of the law, that being to earn or keep salvation (Galatians 3:10-13). OAN is of means of helping the believer put the law and lawkeeping in proper perspective.

Paul always pointed to the perfect Lawkeeper: His Person and work. The believer's personal lawkeeping is a testimony to Christ's perfect lawkeeping and of God's gift of the law which points to Christ's perfect lawkeeping (Psalm 119:16, 72, 97, 104-105).

Moreover, OAN is more than personal lawkeeping to get. While it is commanded, OAN is a privilege and a thank offering for what Christ did for His people collectively and individually (Ephesians 4:1-3; 5:1-2). OAN and lawkeeping are not to be motivated by a desire to earn points with others or God. If it is, it is an attempt to use God. He will not be mocked or used (Galatians 6:7)!

Paul was concerned that the people would misuse their Christian freedom. In verses 13-14, he emphasized the horizontal relationship of the two great commandments (Matthew 22:37-40). Christian freedom (verse 13) is freedom *in* Christ; it is freedom from self-gratification; and it is freedom to please the Triune God (2 Peter 1:3-4, 5-10).

The habit patterns and tendencies developed while an unbeliever are by nature self-focused. In contrast, the now-believer lives in the new creation as a new creation and new creature. The license and desire for selfishness is removed and being replaced (Romans 14:1-15:6; 2 Corinthians 5:14-17).

God and other-centeredness characterizes the believer wholly in principle but not in practice. However, the believer is becoming more like Christ in practice. However, old habits of pleasing self die hard; believers do continue to function as if they were unbelievers.

Therefore, biting and devouring each other are satanic activities. They are unbecoming, unnecessary, unproductive, and unfaithful to God's work in His children. They are the opposite of OAN! James speaks to this same subject and draws the same conclusion: self is the problem; not God and not others (James 3:13-4:3)!

In Galatians 5:16-18, Paul calls for believers to live a patterned life (*peripateo* translated to *walk* is one of the New Testament words used to indicate a habitual way of living—thinking, wanting, and doing).

Indwelt by the Holy Spirit, the believer is motivated and enabled to please God rather than to please self. He begins more and more to recognize, resist, and replace patterned thoughts and desires learned and developed as an unbeliever; the Bible often refers to the person and patterned living as the *old man*.

Paul teaches that the orientation and influence of the Spirit and the flesh are diametrically opposed. Principle (the believer is in Christ—and practice (Christlikeness is not there yet) clash. Satan does not indwell the believer, but the believer has remaining sinfulness and powerful, remaining habituation of self-pleasing (1 John 5:18).

These habit patterns were developed while in Satan's family and under his influence. Paul uses the concept: *but now* (Romans 3:21; Ephesians 2:4; Titus 3:4)! A radical, supernatural change occurred in the believer. In principle, not in practice, the believer is freed from self, sin and Satan. He is freed to and is desirous of loving God and neighbor. The believer produces fruits of the Spirit including OAN (5:22-23).

G. Put off the Fruit of Self and Satan and Put on the Fruit of the Spirit

Paul closes chapter 5 after he has listed the fruits of the Spirit (5:22-23). In verse 25 (*Since we live by the Spirit, let us keep in step with the Spirit*), Paul referred to the truth contained in verses 16-18. These refer to a believer's motivational system—what he wants—and the believer's belief system—what he thinks.

The believer is indwelt by the Holy Spirit (Romans 8:9, 11; 1 Corinthians 6:19-20; 2 Timothy 1:14). Under the direction of the indwelling Holy Spirit, the believer uses biblical principles to do two things:

- *Put off* or replace a self-centered lifestyle which promotes self and results in the practice of and deeds of the flesh (5:19-21); these are more than actions. They include thoughts and desires that promote those actions.
- *Put on* Christlikeness in thought, desire, and action which results in the fruit of the Spirit (5:22-23). Every person is a fruit-bearer. The issue is which kind? Putting on Christ is a result of being in Christ—united to Him by the Holy Spirit. Fruit-bearing is relational!

In verses twenty-four and twenty-five (*Those who belong to Christ Jesus have crucified the sinful nature with its passions and desires. Since we live by the Spirit let us keep in step with the Spirit*), Paul reminded his readers who they were. They were united to Christ in the Holy Spirit. They were in Christ because Christ was in them by the Holy Spirit. This union was done to them and for them. The Holy Spirit indwelt them. These are facts! OAN is built these and other facts!

Paul gave an indicative statement of a completed fact: the Galatians *belong to Christ*. As a result, he gives an imperative (a command): they are to *live by the Spirit*. They no longer belong to self or to Satan! The Holy Spirit's pervading and pervasive influence sets the believer apart from his old self and the unbeliever. They are alive spiritually because of the new birth (John 3:3-8; 6:60-64; Titus 3:5).

Believers are no longer in Satan's family! Something supernatural had happened to them and in them. They were recipients of the Holy Spirit's work of regeneration! This is a non-negotiable fact. They are ready for OAN!

Based on what they are, Paul gave them another imperative which follows from *live by the Spirit*: *walk by the Spirit*. They were made alive—regenerated—by the Spirit (John 3:3-8; 6:60-64). They were saved; they did not save themselves. Therefore, they are to live as one indwelt by the Spirit—because they are—which is the most logical and reasonable thing for a believer to do (Romans 12:1-2).

In verse 26 (*Let us not become conceited, provoking and envying one another*), Paul followed with a negative command again highlighting the necessity of avoiding selfishness and pride and its destruction.

Salvation is of the Lord. It is a gift that must be nurtured and watered. Paul gave wrong ways of interacting with one another. Self-focus is a function of sinful pride and results in division and murder (Also see James 3:13-4:1-3; Galatians 5:15).

The word translated "conceited" (*kenodoxia*) means "empty, vain, or futile glory" (Philippians 2:3; Galatians 5:26). The idea is that one desires to be considered worthy, but he has no worth intrinsic and innate to himself. This is true for every person!

However, man remains the image of God. He is God's image bearer, by God's creational design. In that sense any worth and dignity he has is derived. As such, he is set apart from nature (Genesis 2:18-20; Psalm 8). All people are responsible to God as a covenant, dependent being to function as a truth receiver, teller, and implementer as God's vice-regent.

But salvation lifts the believer and sets him apart from using others, from pleasing self, from hell, and from Satan. He is able to function as the true image bearer! The unbeliever, and too often a believer, is an empty, vain, and foolish person but due to self-deception he fails to acknowledge it. *In self*, he is an unsaved sinner, an enemy of God, a rebel, and a friend of the world. He denies those facts. The concept of sin and sinner has no place in his vocabulary.

In contrast, the believer is something *in Christ*, but in himself he is an arrogant, ignorant rebel. *In Christ*, the believer is a child of God and of the King; he is a victor in Christ but a loser apart from Him (1 Corinthians 1:30; Galatians 2:20; Romans 8:35-39).

The only lasting worth anyone has is one that is derived from what he is in Christ. Yet the sinfully proud person presses his point and is unable to minister to others through OAN. Rather, he needs OAN!

The word translated "challenging" (*prokaleo*) is only used here in the New Testament and means "to call forward or before oneself" or "to challenge, provoke, irritate." Believers are to be challengers but not for their own sakes; rather it is for the sake of Christ, the body, and the individual. The same concept is expressed in Hebrews 10:24-25. There is a correct manner and place for stirring each other up—being a good burr under another person's saddle.

The word translated envying (*phthonos*) means to covet. It is an inordinate wanting and desire (Galatians 5:21; 1 Peter 2:11; Titus 3:3; James 4:5). Paul is invoking the Tenth Commandment and with it the First and Second Commandment. Idolatry was and is alive and well. Coveting is an attempt to steal from God. It carries grave consequences. God will not give or share His glory to or with another (Isaiah 42:8; 48:9-11).

There is correct desiring; *epithumeo* is the usual word for desire in the New Testament. It can be good (1 Timothy 3:1) or it can be sinful (Matthew 5:28; Romans 7:7; 13:9; Galatians 5:17). Consider that God is a jealous, zealous God desiring to keep His glory and His people for Himself.[11]

God deserves undivided and exclusive loyalty, affection, and devotion. Therefore, believers must be jealous and zealous God's way for His honor and glory. Self-focus is competition

---

11 Exodus 19:5-6; 20:5; 34:14; Deuteronomy 4:24; 6:15; Joel 2:18; Nahum 1:2; Zechariah 1:14; 8:12; Isaiah 42:8; 48:9-11; 49:6; 1 Peter 2:9-10.

with God. The giving and the receiving of OAN is one way for believers to put to death idolatry.

A desire can be wrong simply because God says it is (it is forbidden) or a "good" desire can be elevated to the status of God in one's heart. Self is on the throne competing with God. A simple test is to find out the position of a desire in your heart—its status and position—is to ask by what means you seek to gain it and what happens when you don't receive what you want. The person is a functioning idolater when he sins to get it or when he uses sinful means to get it or to avoid it.

When self is enthroned, pleasing God and satisfying Him are replaced with getting what I want—the "I *wants*." If a desire has this place in one's heart, the person will either sin to have the desire fulfilled or he will sin in response to not getting what he wants.

When that happens pursuing those desires is sinful and damaging to the body—both one's physical body and the body of Christ. Consequently, OAN will not occur or at least will be hindered, and the individual will not mature.

CHAPTER 4
Submission and Putting up with One Another

WE COME TO A THIRD topic in our study of OAN: submission and putting up with one another. I have chosen to study submission because OAN involves submission which leads to a proper understanding of putting up with. Submission is a major pillar of the Christian life in general and OAN specifically.

To review: OAN is ministering God's truth to another believer as part of the life of the church. It requires fellowship with God in Christ and the mind of Christ. It flows from the believer's relationship with Christ and is anchored in God's love of His former enemies.

In Ephesians 5:21 (*Submit to one another out of reverence for Christ*), Paul called for submission to one to another as part of body life out of honor, respect, and reverence for Christ; as a result, the family of God is blessed! What is Paul's purpose for the call? One theologian comments on this verse: *God has bound us so strongly to each other, that no man ought to endeavor to avoid subjection; and where love reigns, mutual services will be rendered. I do not except even kings and governors, whose very authority is held for the service of the community. It is highly proper that all should be exhorted to be subject to each other in their own turn.*[12]

Paul intertwined God's authority and His grace. Submission to God always results in a radically different way that a believer relates to one another and to authority—the home, the church, the workplace, and the state. Therein is the key to Paul's call of submission.

The believer has been radically changed by God's power working through grace by the Holy Spirit. Within the body of Christ, submission to each other is antithetical to one's former habit patterns developed while under Satan's mastery and tutelage. Relating to one another as a fellow sinner saved by grace is what I am referring to as *OAN submission*. One manifestation of this activity is putting up with one another God's way.

Paul followed with three examples of the authority-submission motif given in Scripture: husband-wife in the home (5:22-33), parent-child in the home (6:1-4), and boss-worker in the workplace (6:5-9) to demonstrate the beauty and benefits of godly submission. Peter used a similar motif (1 Peter 2:13-3:6)

Submission is a cornerstone for unity within the church, home, and workplace; Paul used these examples to highlight its importance of submission for all of life because life is relational! Again, authority and submission are linked.

---

12 *Calvin's Commentaries XXI: The Epistles to the Galatians and Ephesians*, page 317

Paul knew that submission leads to order within the Church (as well as the home and workplace) which leads to a proper teaching milieu. This leads to truth. As a result of teaching truth, there is life for the growing believer which then moves to ministry including OAN.

I. Submission: a Proper Understanding

The word translated submission means to subject oneself to; to stand up under; to place for orderly function. Submission to authority is submission to God and to each other. Fear of the Lord motivates the believer to properly submit. Since fear of the Lord is the beginning of wisdom, a submissive person is wise (Proverbs 1:7; 9:10).

Submission is demonstrated as the person actively places himself under the authority of another to preserve function. It flows out of a right view of God, self, and others which produces and facilitates OAN.

OAN requires submission because proud people do not submit. They fail to OAN and to be OAN-ed. Submission to fellow believers occurs only after one has submitted to God. Paul's examples highlight the importance of submission for proper function in the Church, the home, and the workplace.

OAN is commanded (Ephesians 5:21; Galatians 5:13-15; Colossians 3:18; 1 Peter 2:13; 2:18; 3:1, 5. Titus 2:5). Therefore, every member of the church is to be a OAN-er and OAN-ee.

However, let's be clear: the command to OAN does not give official authority to the OAN-er over the OAN-ee. That authority is reserved for the church's leadership. However, even that authority must be used to imitate Christ in feeding and caring for the flock (1 Peter 5:1-4).

Otherwise, chaos and disunity will result as each one takes to himself—steals—that which is not his. This is what happened in Corinth. Different groups attempted to establish themselves as the authority for the congregation (1 Corinthians 1:10-17). OAN did not exist, and disunity was the result.

This same principle is true for counseling which is a one-on-one discipling ministry under OAN. The leadership is to counsel in an official capacity mandated in Scripture while every believer is to counsel in an unofficial capacity (see section on counseling and footnote 41; Colossians 1:28; 1 Thessalonians 5:12-14; Galatians 6:1-5; Romans 15:14).

Here is an important consideration. There is submission within the Godhead. I avoid the term subordination and the subsequent debate. The Trinity is expressed as God who is three-in-One and One-in-Three. The Trinity is a functional unit and an ontological oneness. Proper Intratrinitarian function was required for creation and redemption: salvation and growth after salvation.

The single most important example of submission is the Son coming to earth. His motivation was to please the Triune God. He accomplished the Father's will through the fullness of the indwelling Holy Spirit (Isaiah 11:1-5). Salvation was and is Intratrinitarian through and through (Ephesians 2:18, 3:12)!

A proper understanding of submission pushes the Church and individual believers into heavenly realms! It is humbling and exciting. It is an expression of the mind of the Triune God. The present life seems so *unlivable* for some! They can't wait for heaven, but they say they can't continue the race (Hebrews 12:1-3). They view circumstances and themselves apart from their good God who has His glory and their good as His only goal.

There are many OAN activities described in Scripture such as welcoming, accepting, and bearing with (Romans 14-15); restoring (Galatians 6:1-5); stirring up (Hebrews 10:24-25); and encouragement and comforting (2 Corinthians 1:3-4).

These activities are needed because it is easy for the believer to live the lie that God has *missed the boat* or that He does not care or is impotent. Functioning as a biblical OAN-er and OAN-ee requires submission to God and respect for and gratitude for God's family of brothers and sisters. These two are linked.

II. A Working Definition of Submission

Consider this definition of submission. Since submission is fundamental to growth in the Christian life including OAN, it is important to know what it means. Adding to what I wrote earlier, the word translated submission means "to arrange in rank order for the purpose of function." It is a military concept involving authority, a hierarchy of authority, and a response to that authority.

Submission recognizes the fact that the structure of any authority is for the purpose of the maximum function of an organization, institution, or body of people. It places the rights, privileges, and obligations of people in the context of the whole.

It includes respect for, paying attention to, and obedience to authority. God's plan for unity and order in His church, and for growth, both individually and corporately, is for believers to submit to their leaders and to one another (Hebrews 13:7, 17). The Christian is to be willing to correctly define and be the least.[13]

Biblical submission is an internal activity as well as an external one. So, too, is OAN. Both are first and foremost an attitude towards God that says God is God—not me or another person. Therefore, submission's focus and concern is on God's person and position rather than on self.

By analogy, biblical submission results from a proper concern of another person and his position and rights as much as a person is about his own (Romans 14:1-15:6; 1 Corinthians 1:10-17; James 4:1-3). Remember: submission has both a vertical and horizontal

---

[13] Similarly, consider God's plan for function in the home, state, and workplace. God's plan for the home is headship by the husband. All others must fall in line for the home to function as God intended. The purpose of the civil government is to protect the righteous and punish the evil doer by making laws, enforcing justice, and maintaining law and order even to the use of force for these purposes. God's people are called to submit in order for the state to carry out its proper function. The same principle holds true for the workplace.

reference. Unless that fact is foremost in the believer's thinking and wanting, he will fail to please God and bless his brother.

OAN easily flows from this double focus and concern. OAN and biblical submission are motivated by the desire for and the purpose of glorifying God. When all parties are involved in building up the body, God is glorified which is one of the results of OAN.

III. OAN and Submission: The Letter to the Ephesians

OAN, both giving and receiving it, requires the courage of honest humility and open approachability. It requires a learner's spirit and a servant's heart. Listening to learn to love to lead is a key to OAN. You must listen to learn from and about others. Listen for another's victories, their failures, and the tension between pleasing God and pleasing self.

True OAN-ers will take the information as a springboard for applying God's truth to help the person become more like Christ. OAN is submission in action. It has a vertical and horizontal reference. It is submission to God, and it is submission to one another.

In his letter to the *Ephesians*, Paul lays out theological truths in chapters 1-3. These are the so-called doctrinal chapters. But Paul knew correct doctrine is meant to be properly applied (Titus 1:1-2; 2 Peter 1:5-10; 3:18). Therefore, in chapters four through six, he gave direction on how to apply these truths. He began with the subject of unity within the body because unity within the individual and within the Church is God's way to please Him. Don't miss that point!

Paul reminded the Ephesians that they were not alone: there were no "Lone Ranger" believers. This fact was established by God in the Garden. Man was created a social being. He was not created an animal or to be isolated. In response to the pandemic, many isolate themselves with sad results. People die alone and others live alone.

Further, Cain asked God if he was Abel's keeper, apparently hoping for a "no" (Genesis 4:9). The word for "keeper" (*shamar*) is used of God as the Keeper of Israel.[14] Cain was asking a OAN question: "Should I OAN my brother as God does to His people?"

God's answer, even in this pre-Church age, makes it clear that each person has OAN responsibility for members of the covenant community. The OAN-er and OAN-ee recognizes and acts on the fact of man's original design. God created His people to be in relationship to Him and to each other. Relationships matter!

The emphasis on OAN in Ephesians is for the purpose of unity and order which facilitates teaching God's truth, applying that truth daily, and ministering to one another. The

---

14   *Shamar* is translated watch, guard, protect, keep, and exercise great care over. It is found in Genesis 2:15; 3:24; 4:9 and in the Psalms: 16:1; 17:8; 34:20; 86:2; 121:3-5, 7; 141:9, all referring to God as the Keeper and Protector of His people.

same truth taught here is taught in 1 John 1:3-7. There is unity throughout Scripture!

Paul began the practical section (4:1-6) with a call to think, desire, and act according to biblical truth. The believer is united to Christ and therefore he is united to other Christians.

IV. OAN and Submission: Ephesians 4:1-3

Paul began chapter 4 with a fundamental OAN principle: in humility, meekness, longsuffering, and endurance make every effort to preserve the unity and peace of God's people (4:1-3).

Unity among Christians is the result of walking—living together—properly (4:4-6). A function of the church is to develop the maturity of Christ in its members (4:8-14: see footnote two). Paul then gave direction for walking and living together (4:15-6:9). Much of that direction included talking to one another—the ministry of OAN.

Paul highlighted the fact and importance of relationships as did Christ. One's duty to God and his obligation to another are never set over and against each other (Matthew 22:37-40). Rather living out one's relationship to God involves interacting with people. How one responds to others reflects the significance he gives to his relationship with Christ for daily life.

Properly done, OAN promotes the growth of the one OAN-er and one OAN-ee. It maintains peace, purity, and unity within the Church, all of which are necessary for proper functioning of the whole. Without submission, the Church would be marked by chaos and anarchy as demonstrated in Israel during the period of the Judges: *In those days Israel had no king; everyone did as he saw fit* (17:6; 21:25).

The same inclination to waywardness is seen individually as noted in the book of Proverbs (12:15; 14:12; 16:2, 25). As I have said: both OAN and submission look away from self to God and others to reverence and reflect Christ.

Consider Ephesians 4:1-3: *As a prisoner for the Lord, then, I urge you to live a life worthy of the calling you have received. Be completely humble and gentle; be patient bearing with one another in love. Make every effort to keep the unity of the Spirit through the bond of peace.*

In these verses, Paul gives a description of the believer's "walk" (a characteristic, patterned lifestyle consisting of patterned thoughts, desires, and actions) to which he is called:

1. Humility is the estimation and esteeming of oneself small, inasmuch as one is and acting accordingly.[15] Humility is not an attribute of the eternal Godhead. Rather, Jesus, the Godman, humbled Himself as He left heaven.

He stepped into humiliation and practiced humility. Jesus, as the Godman, did not consider Himself above pleasing the Father (Philippians 2:5-8). Even though Jesus was God, He humbled Himself to serve the Triune God.

---

15   Acts 20:19; Ephesians 4:2; Philippians 2:3; Colossians 2:18, 23; 3:12; 1 Peter 5:5.

As I have written, humility and humiliation are not synonymous. Jesus humbled Himself as the Godman. His humiliation consisted of changing conditions and His environment: He was born; in a low condition; made under the law; undergoing miseries of this life, the wrath of God, and death of the cross; in being buried and continuing under the power of death for a time (see the Westminster Shorter Catechism Question #27).

Humility is an essential fact of Jesus' Being as the Godman. God is not humble—Christ is! Humiliation is the context that a person is placed by God's providence. In a real sense, Christ humiliated Himself! He came to earth just as another male Jew.

A person can be humiliated, but not humbled! God humbles you as you humble yourself. Jesus did both: He humbled Himself as He stepped into humiliation. A believer is in Christ and therefore is able to humble himself and engage in OAN.

2. Meekness is calmness within a person. The person accepts the fact that he stands first and foremost before God. Eternally, no other eyes matter. The person is present before God without anyone to blame for his sins. Meekness was expressed by Christ regularly. Meekness is expressed by the person as slowness or restraint in insisting on one's rights and what he wants and thinks he deserves. OAN requires this fruit.

The meek person knows and acts upon the truth that everything is derived from God's eternal decree; "life" and people are held together by God's providential control; and nothing is original with the person. Therefore, it is not his world; the believer lives less as if it is his. The meek person is set free from self. Life is simplified.

The meek person has a soothing disposition.[16] Meekness is demonstrated. The meek person is active and provides solutions when none seem possible rather than being the problem or adding to it.

3. Long-suffering is defined as enduring patiently with self-restraint in contrast to losing faith, giving up, demonstrating sinful anger, and or retaliating. [17] God is long-suffering; it is to the believer's benefit that He is.

The Triune God has a "long fuse" in that He holds His anger in check. He is angry every day as He should because He is the just Judge of the world (Psalm 5:5; 7:11; Genesis 18:25). The final justice of the Triune God awaits Christ's return (2 Thessalonians 1:5-10; Revelation 6:9-11; 19:11-21; 20:7-15)

Yet the full display of His anger was seen at the cross but in terms of our time, it was only for *moment*. Darkness covered the land for three hours—a return to pre-creation chaos, the darkness of false gods, and sin-darkened hearts (Matthew 27:45; Mark 15:33; Luke 23:44; Genesis 1:1-2; Exodus 10:21-23; Corinthians 4:6)!

---

16 Matthew 5:5; 21:5; James 3:13; 2 Corinthians 10:1; Galatians 5:23; 6:1; Colossians 3:12; 1 Timothy 6:11; 2 Timothy 2:25; Titus 3:2.

17 Romans 2:4; 9:22; Galatians 5:22; Ephesians 4:2; Colossians 1:11; 3:12; 1 Timothy 1:16; 2 Timothy 4:2; Hebrews 6:12; James 5:10; 2 Peter 3:15.

God unleashed the fullness of His wrath on Christ at the cross! The world had a glimpse of His fury and wrath as Jesus bore God's full unmitigated judgment. The world including the disciples missed it! Yet God is holding back the full and eternal display of it until Christ returns (Romans 2:4; 9:22-23).

Suffering-long is one of the fruits of the Spirit. It is what the believer does in imitating Christ. The believer develops Christlikeness and as a result, he puts on meekness and long-suffering. He practices putting up with another! OAN requires long suffering. As one whom God treated with self-restraint, so God's child will be long suffering especially toward others in God's family (Matthew 18:21-35; John 13:34-35; Romans 5:6-10).

4. Patient forbearing and putting up with is tolerance when it is not easy to do so and when you have the power and perhaps authority to retaliate and hurt another. The word translated "put up with" also means "to hold up or back." It is a stronger term than long-suffering.[18]

V. Putting Up with Another: a Function of OAN

Putting up with somebody is an aspect of OAN and it works both ways: putting up with another and being "put up with." OAN is a two-way street that requires humility, meekness, and long suffering!

---

18 The word translated "to forbear" is *anechomai*. See Matthew 17:17; Mark 9:19; Luke 9:41; 2 Corinthians 11:1, 19.

Paul called for putting up with each other here (Ephesians 4:2) and in Colossians 3:13. What does it mean to put up with another? Look at what Jesus said and did as recorded in Matthew 17:17: In response to the father of the unhealed son, Jesus said: *"You unbelieving and perverse generation . . . how long shall I stay with you? How long shall I put up with you? Bring the boy here to me."*

Jesus "put up with the people." Putting up with people is characterized at least by these and perhaps more descriptions: withholding sinful retaliation especially when it is not easy and you have power to retaliate; withholding that which is due another; demanding to hear someone else's viewpoints and rights rather than your own; and making sure you do not give more credibility to your viewpoint before you have understood the other person.

The concept is summarized as *having a learner's spirit and a servant's heart* as the believer puts on meekness, long-suffering and putting up with one another. All of these are subsumed under the concept of humility. Jesus learned obedience (Hebrews 5:8). He was the Suffering Servant (Matthew 12:15-21). The phrase underscores the heart of OAN and those activities that fit under it.

Consider that Jesus the Creator came to His own, but they rejected Him (John 1:10-11). But He had His people—His remnant—and He did not forsake them. You also read about

God's long-suffering with Israel during the wilderness march to the Promised Land (Exodus 15:22-17:7; 32-33; Numbers 11, 13-14, 17, 20-21, 25). The Triune God OAN His people throughout redemptive history! He will continue unto Christ returns.

In verse 2 of Ephesians 4, Paul combines long suffering and enduring one another in love. Humility and meekness are inner-person dispositions directed primarily at God that produce the fruit of the Spirit including patient endurance and OAN love. This promotes the unity of the body. OAN is something every believer is called to do. It is not an option. It is to be part of every believer's walk or way of life.

In contrast is the secular mindset which is bent on pragmatism and self-preservation. The culture may advise to "put up" with someone and his behavior but it is not for the purpose of OAN and it is not for the purpose of honoring God. Rather self takes center stage.

Sadly, secular counsel has invaded the Church. That *advice* calls for the person to resist showing open hostility or resentment, but the goal is not to honor God or OAN. Rather, "things would only get worse for you." That counsel and its implementation are not biblical "putting up" with one another.

Secular counsel is counterfeit. It is based on the teachings of relative truth, no absolute truth (except the statement!), no ultimate reality, and unity at all costs for "peace." However, peace-loving is antithetical to biblical truth. Moreover, it only promotes trouble: division. God calls His people to be peacemakers not troublemakers or peace lovers (Matthew 5:9; John 14:27; Romans 12:17-21; James 3:17-4:3).

Jesus was the Ultimate Peacemaker but one way He did was to produce division (Matthew 10:34; John 14:27; 16:33). Peace costs. Peace comes through the way of the cross and embracing Christ for who He is by the Holy Spirit.

In marked contrast, Paul emphasized OAN love which as I have said, looks away from self and toward God and others. As children of God, Christians are called to "put up with one another." This call is countercultural and counterintuitive: it is radical, pervasive, and non-discriminatory.

Believers accomplish OAN by focusing on God's love of them and His "putting up" with them (Matthew 18:21-35; Luke 7:36-50; Romans 5:6-10). This focus flows from and leads to a desire to reflect God's *putting-up-with love* in daily life out of reverence for the Triune God and for gratitude for what Christ and the Holy Spirit has done and are doing. God put up with you believer. You are called to *put up* as God did to you!

The command to submit (Ephesians 5:21) closed the general section begun in 4:1. Submission underlies all OAN because it reflects one's view of God, his view of God's relationship to him, and his relationship to other believers. Paul called each believer to submit to promote his own godliness, the unity of the body, the benefit of each believer, and the glory of God.

VI. Submission and OAN Glorify God and Solidify the Church

Consider the reasons that submission glorifies God. Submission is what Christ did. Without it, He would not have been the Perfect, Sinless, and Substitute Sin-bearer. Believers are to imitate Christ. Submission is one of God's ordained ways for the believer to imitate Christ. It is God's way for the believer to function within the body of Christ for God's glory, the Church's growth, and the believer's good.

Further it is part of God's divine plan for order and function within the following:

- The Godhead: Submission for the purpose of proper function is an Intratrinitarian activity. Moreover, it is what Jesus as the Godman did to and for the Father and the Godhead (John 4:31-34; 5:19-20, 30; 6:38).
- The Church: It is a picture of the Church obeying Christ who obeyed the Father; further, it is what the Church was called to do: Ephesians 5:22-24.

Consider the book of Hebrews. The author was concerned about his discouraged, fearful flock, many who were considering apostatizing and returning to Judaism. He knew the importance of order and function and the role of submission in the life of his church.

In chapters ten and thirteen of the book of Hebrews, he calls his wavering flock to OAN: Submission leads to OAN which holds the body together. *And let us consider how we may spur one another on toward love and good deeds* (10:24). Later the author of the book of Hebrews continues to exhort his people to stay together—hold fast to each other as they hold fast to the triune God. *Keep on loving each other as brothers. Do not forget to entertain strangers, for by so doing some people have entertained angels without knowing it. Remember those in prison as if you were fellow prisoners, and those who are mistreated as if you yourselves were suffering* (13:1-3).

Uncertainty and confusion were present in the congregation. Persecution from within and from outside the congregation was ongoing and increasing. Relationships were broken and being broken. The solution for some was a return to Judaism and a false gospel.

The author calls the people to OAN as they had done in earlier times (10:32-34; also see 1 Corinthians 12:26: *If one part suffers, every part suffers with it; if one part is honored, every part rejoices with it*).

The people were in hopes of avoiding being sinned against, trouble, and the hurts of broken relationships. It would be easy for each member to withdraw to himself by taking a self-centered approach to the current situation.

However, God's people and Christ's name and Church were at stake. The author of Hebrews was a caring and knowledgeable servant of God. Therefore, he called his people to consider others and their needs more important than self and to get busy with OAN. We are not told the results of this exhortation. Some of the members returned to Judaism. One can only speculate the degree to which God blessed and protected His people through OAN.

In verses seven and seventeen of Hebrews 13, the writer urged the people to remember, to look at, to obey, and to submit to their leaders by following their example. He was encouraging OAN.

The leaders were to be engaged in OAN and the people were to heed and imitate them. In this way, the pastor beckoned the people to stay united to and with the sufficient Christ. He is better than anything Judaism had to offer including angels, Moses, and the priestly system of sacrifices (Hebrews 1-3, 6, 8-10). Submission and OAN are God's ordained means to maintain unity which will preserve God's people especially during hard times.

Moreover, OAN was and is to be part of church life in every age (Ephesians 5:21; Hebrews 12:9; James 4:7). Walking and talking together paves the way for a growing OAN ministry and vice versa. Paul, knowing that submission was essential for OAN, gave the general call to submit in Ephesians 5:21 which facilitated walking and talking together in the body.

VII. Submission, OAN, and God's Providence

Not only did the author of the book of Hebrews call for OAN and submission as discussed above, he added a Fatherly note.

In Hebrews 12:4-11, the pastor reminded the people of the true Fatherhood of God. Hardships come for God's hand for various reasons. Sometimes the person sins or is sinned against. At other times we know that God is working godliness in believers.

Situations do not change people. Rather, the believer uses tough providence (and even easier times: Proverbs 30:7-9) to become more Christ. That concept is based on truth about God: He takes care of His children, and He is interested in Christlikeness in His people. It is also based on knowledge that every believer must and will grow in godliness and faithfulness; every believer must be refined (Romans 5:1-5; 1 Peter 1:6-7; James 1:2-4). This is heavy theology!

Discipline—corrective and instructive—is part of the loving Father's activities. The writer of the book of Hebrews was given the people a true, godly perspective of the circumstances. Submission was required: first to God and then to others. The body needed to stay together (Hebrews 10:24-25).

Hard times are part of God's discipling activities and part of living in a sin-cursed world of sinners with a sin-cursed body. The general purpose and goal for all things is given in Romans 8:28-29: for the believer to become more like Christ. Pain is not the key. Pain tells you something is amiss. It alerts the person.

Several courses of action are available to the believer. One may be called to remain in the situation God's way for His glory. Another course of action may be to remove the cause of the pain through an operation (to remove an unwanted growth) or through labor. Either activity may be painful itself. Its purpose is for the gain which is Christlikeness in or out of the situation.

In Hebrews 12:9, the author points out the common understanding that disciplining from the hand of a human father was respected. Based on the argument from the lesser to the greater, the child of God should embrace the Father's love by submitting to His heavenly-derived discipline. Becoming more like Christ is the one truth that godly submitters must hold to tightly. God is purposeful in how He runs His world—for His glory and the benefit of believers.

All the writers of the New Testament emphasize God's providence. God's control includes being sinned against by fellow countrymen and even family. The tendency is for us to proclaim: what a bummer! However, the road to glory is via the cross. But the road is never to be walked alone. OAN is one of God's tools to be used to run the race as a victor in Christ (Hebrews 12:1-3)!

God's discipline in whatever form is fair, correct, and beneficial for His child and His Church. He will not exceed the believer's capacity to respond in a godly way. The believer's faith and faithfulness are being tested, pruned, and refined (John 15:1-8; Romans 8:28-29; 5:1-5; James 1:2-4; 1 Peter 1:6-7). All believers are to be Christian oysters—making the pearl of Christlikeness from God's providential irritation in the believer's life (2 Corinthians 5:9, 14-17).

The Bible highlights God's good purposes for His providence which are growth in holiness, fear of the Lord, and the development of Christlikeness. It is the way of the cross brought home to the believer by the Holy Spirit (Hebrews 2:14-18; 4:15-16; 5:7-8). OAN helps these truths impact the believer's life especially during hard times. Individuals grow and the body of Christ grows as they mature in Christlikeness together.

VIII. Submission and OAN: Two Lifestyles

In addition, submission to God results in OAN and vice versa. James wrote that God opposes the proud; proud people do not submit to God or to others because submission requires God's grace (4:6-7). Enabling and sanctifying grace results in honest humility and open approachability which produces repentance (4:7-10). Submission is a fruit and evidence of a humble heart. All biblical submitters are OAN-ers and all OAN-ers are submitters.

Individually, the believer submits as he takes captive every thought and desire to the Lord (2 Corinthians 10:3-5). There is a wrong kind of submission. One can submit to falsehood and ignorance which are marks of the kingdom of darkness.

Paul focused on this theme in Romans 6:12, 16: *Therefore, do not to let sin reign in your mortal bodies so that you obey its evil desires; Don't you know that when you offer yourselves to someone to obey him as slaves, you are slaves to the one whom you obey—whether you are slaves to sin which leads to death or to obedience, which leads to righteousness?*

Feeling orientation flows from and leads to thoughts and desires focused on self. Every person is on unstable footing when there is feeling-orientation and motivation. Moreover, feelings come and go and are malleable. The believer is not to submit to a desire, feeling-oriented lifestyle. Rather, he disciplines his thoughts and desires to put on a lifestyle that motivated by the Spirit through His Word.

How does one know the difference between the two lifestyles? When self is center stage, the Holy Spirit is offended and opposed (1 Thessalonians 5:19). Galatians 5:13-18 and James 3:13-4:3 give vivid descriptions of *me-first* approach to life. These passages picture a complicated life of misery and confusion (see Proverbs 5:21-22; 13:15; 26:11)! Relationships are stale or in flames. Control is an issue. Every person is for himself. Hearts are sinfully inflamed. It is not a pretty sight.

When pleasing God is center state, life is simplified. Joy in one's salvation and confidence in pleasing God became more tangible. David and Paul captured the beauty of pleasing God (Psalm 34:8; Philippians 3:7-11). It is as if both of these men were truly intoxicated with their God. They could not get enough of Him. Knowing Him, intimacy with Him, and being familiar with Him as a person enabled them to stay the course.

The orientation and mindset characterized as pleasing God flows from a right view of self, God, others, and circumstances. David and Paul did not live the lie. They wanted more of the truth—God Himself. Times were still unpleasant and hard for both of these men, but their God was and is theirs and they were His! Moreover, this mindset characterized Jesus' approach to life (John 4:31-34). What is good for Christ is good for His children!

John under the banner of love and adoption captured this mindset in 1 John 3:1-3: *How great is the love that the Father has lavished on us, that we should be called children of God! And that is what we are! The reason that world does not know us is that it did not know him. Dear friends, now we are children of God, and what we will be has not yet been made known. But we know that when he appears we shall be like him, for we shall see him as he is. Everyone who has this hope in him purifies himself just as he is pure!*

John, the last living apostle and an old man, could not get enough of the love of God and the God of love! Here he emphasized adoption as the greatest display of God's love! Therefore, as God's child, he urged a proper eternal perspective in this life. Salvation was now! Being saved is stupendous. But there is more! The believer is to be motivated in this life toward the *not yet*: heaven and the eternal presence of God.

In verse 3, John wrote that the believer in this life prepares for the great day of Christ's return by purifying-cleansing-sanctifying himself. These are John's term for putting on Christlikeness and growth in Christ. That is victory, daily and ultimately!

Self-gratification and following feelings (*my wants*) breeds strife and confusion in God's family and erect a barrier to OAN. On the other hand, OAN moves away from self and to God and others. The believer is practicing and developing a lifestyle of pleasing God which tears down the walls of separation between God's children.

IX. Submission, OAN, and the Home

Earlier, I mentioned that submission is part of God's divine plan for order and function within the Godhead and the Church. The home has also been targeted by God to be a place characterized by submission. That is denied today but sinful man's denial does not change God's eternal design and decree.

Husbands are to lovingly manage their households as good stewards. This requires a servant's heart that is demonstrated by submission to God and to others. Submission begins with the husband as it did with Christ! Therefore, a correct view and definition of submission is vital for a God-honoring Church and home. Where there is submission there is OAN and vice versa. If there is an absence of one, the other is absent.

The importance of the role of submission is highlighted by the fact that Paul required an elder to be a good family manager. This ability was a testimony to the prospective elder's understanding and application of the fullness of the concept of submission (1 Timothy 3:4-5).

A manager is one who knows his people, who has developed a relationship with them, and who uses the resources of each person for the good of the household. He does not try to do everything himself and understands that another person may be gifted in an area that he is not.

Moreover, he desires to develop the abilities of each person for the good of the body. A husband who is managing his household well models submission and teaches by word and example its benefits for the family and each family member.

So, too, is the elder within the Church. The manager-elder will try to build up the entire body through OAN whether at home or at church. OAN is "other person-oriented" because it is God-oriented; it results in the development of an individual's gifts and skills for the good of the body.

X. More on Submission and OAN

Submission, as is OAN, is an act of the will motivated by a desire to please God; the blessing comes in the doing (John 13:17; James 1:25; Luke 11:28). There will be blessing for both the OAN-er and the OAN-ee. Both are proof of the love of God and are testimonies of that love and the desire to imitate Christ (John 14:15, 21, 23, 31).

Submission and OAN are not natural or easy. Because of the curse of sin and every person's union with the first Adam who sinned and Satan, all are born self-pleasers and self-protectors. They are like their father the devil (John 8:44).

Self-protection and self-pleasing are what people do, naturally, best, and with ease; these facts are true even for believers because of their previous membership in Satan's family, remaining sinfulness even as a new creation in the new creation, and habituation as a self-pleaser. This orientation toward and even preoccupation with self is a destroyer of OAN.

In the Garden and post-fall, Adam and Eve began modeling a *fig-leaf function* of life. They covered themselves to hide their guilt and shame, to *protect* themselves from the gaze of each other, and to hide from God (Genesis 3:7-11). They refused to relate to each other as OAN-er and OAN-ee.

They began living another aspect of the lie. They knew God but not as they ought and did before the Fall. They thought God was not all-knowing and all-seeing and that they were not accountable to Him or dependent on Him.

Their relationship to each other was now characterized by thinking and wanting that is termed sinful fear. This results in fleeing and futility and no OAN (Proverbs 28:1). Adam failed his wife and Eve her husband. Both dishonored God.

Self-pleasers, including believers, function as if people, the world, institutions including the church, and even God Himself should work for them. They attempt to manipulate others and even God. When self takes center stage, there is no OAN.

OAN and submission boil down to one major mindset summarized by the question: Whose world do you think it is? The issue is one of control and allegiance: yours or God's? (Joshua 24:14-15: who will you serve?).

Moreover, submission and OAN to the Lord are non-negotiable. Both are the desired response to loving God and others out of gratitude for God's Person and His love. If a person refuses to submit to God by failing or refusing to be an OAN-er or OAN-ee, he should question his status as a believer.

XI. Submission and OAN: True and False Views

There are many false views of submission and OAN which include:

One: passivity, *doormatism,* or inequality. Rather, submission and OAN is demonstrated actively and aggressively respecting one another as fellow heirs in God's kingdom by being OAN-er and OAN-ee for the Lord's sake and for His honor. A growing Church is a testimony of and to God's love (John 13:34-35).

Two: immobility demonstrated by the excuses of silence or the alleged inferiority of the OAN-er. Immobility can be demonstrated by such statements as "I can't be influential," or "I can't do anything to help," or "They don't need my help," or "Who am I?" Rather, the OAN-er is watchful, willing, and faithful in his concern for members of his church family.

Three: manipulation by the OAN-er to get what he wants or to earn brownie points.

Rather, OAN involves humility which demonstrates itself as submission. Humble people submit and are OAN-ers and OAN-ees. Proud people don't submit and cannot OAN or be a OAN-ee. Submission and OAN flow from a humble, contrite, and thankful heart (Psalms 15 and 24).

Humility is the mindset and the disposition which acknowledges and acts on the fact of the Creator—creature distinction. God is the Creator and man is a created being completely dependent on God. When this fact is denied, the creature arrogantly and ignorantly attempts to push God off His throne.

The creature is not equal to the Triune God. This truth is also expressed as: you are not God but a mere creature; this is not your world, and you are not in control. Therefore, a person will submit to God as the Creator and Ruler of His world at some point in his life.

Submission is one of the believer's most logical activities as part of growth in Christ (Romans 12:1-2). However, it is easily neglected. Submission is an absolute. It will occur at Christ's coming either via saving faith or the sheer force of God's majesty and justice (Philippians 2:9-11).

Submission to God will be demonstrated by OAN. God has commanded and equipped the Christian to be OAN-er and

OAN-ee. Biblical OAN is God's way for the Christian to model the Triune God. God takes care of His people. He expects His people to act accordingly toward every believer. Jesus Christ explained this and other truths because He explained the Triune God (John 1:14, 18).

CHAPTER 5
Love

WE COME TO THE FOURTH topic in our study. So far, we have learned that OAN is relational. Relationships matter! God loved Himself from all eternity because He is love (1 John 4:7-12). As a result, the Triune God loves Himself, loves His people, and He established fellowship with them (John 6:37-43).

Through the Holy Spirit, the Triune God gave the believer the mind of Christ who is now able to think and to desire as Christ did. One result of having the mind of Christ is submission which underlies all OAN. Failure to OAN is failure to submit to God.

Now we turn to the question, how are OAN and love connected? OAN is the result of being loved by God (1 John 4:19) and it expresses confidence in and gratitude for God and His love. Loving another is the deepest expression of OAN (John 13:34-35; 1 John 4:7-12). It is a sign to true friendship.

I. John, the Apostle of OAN-Love

There are many passages that call for OAN-love. John, the son of thunder who became the apostle of love, wrote more extensively about the subject of love than any other New Testament writer. In his gospel, John used the word love in some form seven times in chapters 1-12 and over 30 times in chapters 13-17 (also see 1 John 2:7-11; 3:11-18; 4:7-21; 5:1-5).

His gospel has been called the *gospel of love*. He continued to marvel at God's love even toward the end of his life (1 John 3:1-3). The incredibly old saying—*love makes the world go around*—is more theologically correct than the originator realized![19] However, the key is not love but God! If there is no Triune God, there is no life or love. Love is because God is and He is love! The statement: God is love must be understood through the lens of God's holiness. A holy (set apart from) God loved unholy people!

In our culture, the meaning of the word "love" is antithetical to the Bible's teaching. When the culture speaks of "love" and "lovers," it emphasizes self-centeredness, self-gratification, self-pleasure, and self-worship. It describes a person getting and using another person. Often, these facts are true for both people.

Moreover, too often, when churches say that *God is love*, they mean that God has warm, fuzzy feelings for everybody, His judgment and discipline are unloving activities, and that He accepts people just as they are apart from Christ, the cross, and change in them.

---

19 From the web: *"The statement "love makes the world go round" is an English idiom and proverb which means that love is very important and essential thing for this world and that life is more enjoyable when people love one another. In the absence of love, life is not pleasant."*

In stark contrast, the Bible teaches truth about the Triune God. One such truth: He is love eternally (1 John 4:7-20). The thrice holy God is Love and the Lover (Isaiah 6:3). There is no being like Him. Love then is eternal because the Triune God is eternal.

Moreover, love existed in the Garden before the fall only because God is love. In the fallen world, love exists only because God exists. If there is no God, there is no creation, no love, no salvation, and no OAN. *Love does not make the world go round—* God does as He loves people into His kingdom and cares even for His enemies!

God is the Initiator and Sustainer of love because He is love. As such, He goes to the uttermost to bless His people even giving Himself. He is the Fountainhead of all love so that all loving actions, such as OAN love, flow from Him (1 John 4:19).

Moreover, those loved by Him love others. It is a privilege and blessing to be loved by God. And because love is commanded it is an obligation as well as a privilege and blessing. So, too is OAN: it is love-in-action which is a blessing, privilege and a duty. A biblical lover is a OAN-er.

As I have said before, all men are created, dependent beings and are under obligation to submit to God, the Creator, Controller, Lawgiver, and Judge. Also, it bears repeating that all believers were at one time in Satan's culture (family and kingdom) of self-pleasers, self-worshippers, and God's enemies; but lovingly and supernaturally, they have been removed from bondage, deadness, and darkness. Now God is their Father and Jesus is their brother (Acts 26:18; Colossians 1:13).

Those loved (the "lovee") are transformed into lovers, albeit imperfectly and non-redemptively, of God and others. Only Christ loves redemptively? Those loved are believers and are under obligation to love because only believers have been loved by God (Matthew 22:37-40; 1 John 4:7-12).

Believers are the most loved people in the universe; therefore, they are called to be lovers. God saved them just as they were but with an agenda to change from self-lovers to lovers of God and others (Romans 5:6-10; 1 John 4:7-12).

Therefore, the command to OAN-love grows out of Who God is. In His very Being, He is love which is demonstrated in the Trinity in eternity past and by what He has done through His Son and by what He is doing and will do by His Spirit (John 3:16; Ephesians 5:2).

The command to OAN-love grows out of who the believer is or has become in Christ by the Holy Spirit. Loving one another is initiated and continued by God's love. Loving others is evidence of the continuation of God's love in and for us; it is due to the indwelling Spirit (Romans 5:5; 1 John 4:8, 12-13). Therefore, the command to love begins and continues with God. It will never end! Love is eternal as God is eternal.

In addition, Jesus taught by example that submission is love thus setting the stage for OAN. To please His Father, He humbled Himself, hid His glory for a time, and identified with His sheep as

He lived among them teaching, encouraging, and confronting. In other words, Jesus OAN-ed His people (John 15:13-15)! God expects each church member to imitate Jesus as an OAN-er.

Love is distinctly relational. In the Garden, God loved Adam and Eve pre-fall in a perfect earthly world. God was, and more accurately, is love. Love is Him, His very Being. Those facts are hard to grasp!

Pre-fall, God had no enemies among men. Post-fall, on earth, God loved His enemies, and He commands His people to do the same (Romans 5:6-10; 12:17-21; Matthew 5:48). God loved His enemies first and foremost as He loves Himself (Romans 5:6-10; 1 John 4:19). He is the Standard-Maker and Standard-Keeper regarding everything including love. These facts are simply mind-boggling.

Jesus broadened the command to love to the second great commandment: love your neighbor (Leviticus 19:18; Matthew 22:37-40; Mark 12:28-34). Your neighbor includes but is not limited to fellow believers (1 John 4:7-12). However, OAN focuses on the family of God.

Salvation brings one into God's family and within that family each member is to love as he has been loved (1 John 4:11-12). To the degree that one is moved by the fact of being loved by God is the degree that he displays OAN-love. OAN-ers are lovers for God's sake and glory! Loving another follows Christ.

The call to OAN is the call to love those who have been loved by God. As hard as it is at times to love spouses and fellow brothers and sisters, it pales when contrasted with God's love of His enemies, including you and every believer (Romans 5:6-10). Paul expressed this great truth in Ephesians 3:17-21. The height, width, depth, and length of man's sinfulness are no match for the height, width, depth, and length of God's love. OAN is the humble expression of this fact.

Loved out of Satan's family and into God's family, brothers and sisters are fellow-heirs in and with Christ. OAN assumes a kinship and calls upon each Christian to minister as one who has been OAN-ed. Scripture calls for a deep, genuine love among believers—love from the heart (Romans 6:17; 1 Peter 1:22).

However, the ultimate purpose of love and its fulfillment is *to love the Lord your God* (Matthew 22:37-40). The circle of love began with God and ends with Him (1 John 4:7-12). Saved people are changed from self-lovers to lovers of God and others. One expression of love and being loved is OAN. Believers love because they had been loved.

The unbeliever can't love or OAN because he has not been regenerated. Only believers can love and engage in OAN! The highest goal and expression of love is love of God. And one way love of God is expressed is by OAN.

II. Love Defined

Love is a whole-person activity. It involves thoughts, desires, and actions. As a Personal Being, God loves personally. Love involves at least these elements that I mentioned briefly earlier: One, love is giving: John 3:16; Galatians 2:20; Ephesians 5:2, 25. It is an action not dependent on feelings although it may be associated with them. Love is something one does based on thoughts and desires. It expresses the totality of the person in terms of changed thinking about himself, others, and God.

God is love and He is love. It is of His essence. With His whole Being He loves. Therefore, to love is a whole-person activity involving one's knowledge and thinking, affections and desires, and willful actions. It imitates the Triune God.

Therefore, believers are to love wholeheartedly—like God. Love must characterize the believer as it does his God. Love makes OAN possible and OAN is an expression of genuine, from the heart, love.

Two, there is the Giver and a giver. By defining what a lover is, God also defines what a OAN-er is. God gave Himself not simply of Himself. Love requires an investment by the giver who is a lover and OAN-er. God wholly gave His Son, and He gives His Spirit. Those loved by God are obligated as well as privileged and blessed to give (of) themselves (1 John 5:3). A believer gives of himself; otherwise, he is a self-pleaser.

The believer has not arrived as a lover while on this earth, but he is to be growing and changing as OAN lover. He is learning more and more how to and in what manner to give himself not simply of himself.

The question to be answered is this: What does it mean to give yourself and how does that look in OAN? As we study specific passages the call for specific OAN activities, you should be able to answer those two questions. As you read on, write out what you have learned and how you need to change in the area of OAN.

Three: consider the gift: The gift is God Himself. The believer has received that gift through the gift of saving faith and true hope because of the finished work of Christ and the Spirit's application of that work through the believer's growing relationship with Christ.

A person can give only what he has been given. The believer has the mind of Christ, the indwelling Holy Spirit, and the truth—the Person, Jesus Christ, and the Bible. Therefore, the OAN-er gives himself as a testimony to what he is and has; Who God is; and what God has done, is doing, and will do.

As a result, he ministers God's truth to himself and to another thereby giving testimony of God's love for and of him, his relationship with Christ, and the presence of the indwelling Holy Spirit. The believer gives himself not simply of himself in Christ by the Holy Spirit.

Four, there is the object of love—the one loved. The one loved is an OAN-ee. The receiver of God's love was His enemy—you and me when we were unbelievers (Romans 3:21-26; 5:6-10). As mentioned earlier, loving a humanly unlovable and unlovely person is one proof of the height, width, depth, and breadth of God's love (Ephesians 3:14-21). The OAN-ee acknowledges this truth when he OAN.

Fifth, OAN recognizes and responds to the fact that fellow heirs and siblings do not always get along and enmity may develop within the family of God. God's call is to love as OAN-re and OAN-ee because love is what God is, is what He does, and is what His children do for His glory and the benefit of His people (John 13:34-35; Galatians 5:13-15, 22-23; Ephesians 5:8-14).

III. Love is Demonstrated: Nine Considerations

First, consider the fact that love is demonstrated: OAN love is shown by deeds that flow from a changed heart. As a result, thoughts, desires, and actions are its fruit: 1 John 3:16-18. *This is how we know what love is: Jesus Christ laid down his life for us. And we ought to lay down our lives for our brothers. If anyone has material possessions and sees his brother in need but has no pity on him, how can the love of God be in him? Dear children, let us not love with words or tongue but with actions and in truth.*

Based on a proper understanding of biblical love, John called his people to forgo simply praying for another or saying nice things to him. Rather, John called them to engage in OAN. In verses 16-17, John described a type of "laying down one's life for another" using Jesus as the model and new standard of love.

John characterized the person with material things as cold-hearted and a self-lover because he failed to OAN. He recognized that his brother was in need but failed to give of himself by giving of his possessions (Romans 12:9-11).

Second, consider the fact that love meets a need. It is purposeful and constructive: Isaiah 59:1-2; John 9:31-33; Romans 5:6-10; Ephesians 5:27; Colossians 1:21; 1 John 2:2, 4; 4:10. Unlike God Who knows everything and everyone completely and perfectly, OAN requires getting to know a person.

Data gathering is needed to determine what a person needs and how to target God's truth appropriately to that individual. God's truth is vast and deep, and the Bible is a large book. However, there is always the basic need of fellowship with Christ (Luke 10:38-42). After salvation, the emphasis of OAN is on life after salvation. This includes developing the full influence of one's relationship with Christ in daily life.

OAN demonstrates the significance of and facilitates a growing relationship with Christ and helps in developing a deeper trusting faith and reliance on God and His provision. OAN may take the form of supplying material needs or simply fellowship by sharing good and hard times to grow together in Christ.

Third, consider the fact that OAN love requires the correct standard: Isaiah 59:1-2; Ephesians 5:25-33. Love is not arbitrary, a whim, or feeling although it may involve feelings. It begins with God and was modeled by Christ. Jesus Christ's self-giving is the standard for love. He understood the Ten Commandments as a reflection of the mind and will of the Triune God. He came to and did fill full the Law (Matthew 5:17-20). They were His standard by which to measure His obedience.

Sin is lawlessness and loveless-ness. It is not simply an action or inaction. Sin expresses one's sinfulness. If man did not have remaining sinfulness, he could not and would not sin. Sin and sinning involves being. Sin is not simply the absence of good, truth, and light; it is the presence of evil, lies, and darkness. It is anti-God-ness!

Fourth, consider the fact that love is lawful because love summarizes the Law and the prophets (Matthew 22:37-40; Romans 13:8-10; 1 John 3:4). Love brings the Triune God into the picture!

Fifth, consider the fact that love is giving no matter the cost: 2 Corinthians 5:21; Galatians 3:10-13; 4:4. Love is expensive and requires a personal investment. Unlike God, the believer's love takes risks; he does not know the final outcome.

Sixth, consider the cost. Love costs the Trinity, Jesus, and the believer. Love cost the Trinity. It cost the Father His Son; it costs Jesus His place in heaven for a time; and it costs the Holy Spirit to indwell initially unholy and post-regeneration imperfect creatures.

It cost Jesus such that He was not given His full due and His glory while on earth. Rather, the Son veiled His glory so that He was not recognized and appreciated for Who He was. Initially, He was "seen" only by and with physical eyes. It could only be appreciated by the *suprasensual*—the eyes of saving faith and true hope (2 Corinthians 5:7). Only the one loved by the Triune God has *eyes to see and ears to hear and a heart tuned into God.*

Love costs the believer. The believer must decrease (John 3:30). He must die to self (Matthew 10:32-38; Mark 8:34-38; Romans 6:6; Galatians 5:24). Giving oneself to God and others is part of OAN.

Seventh: consider the fact that true love functions out of a right motive: John 4:31-34; 14:15,21,23; 1 Corinthians 13:3; 2 Corinthians 5:9,14-15; 1 John 4:10. It also obligates the lover and is a testimony of one's love for God. Love is the essence of life because God claims to be and is Love and the Lover; and the believer has been loved into the kingdom.

Moreover, love and loving is testimony of God's love for the individual. If the one loved does not acknowledge that he was no prize for God, but His enemy, he will not think much of God—who He is—and His love. He will not be inclined to love others! Pleasing the Father motivated Jesus and should motivate the believer.

Eighth, love functions in the right way—in the proper manner (John 10:11, 15, 17; Romans 5:6-10; Ephesians 5:25-33). God's love is always successful. In the end so, too, is the believer's OAN-love. Being loved and loving reflects who you are—one loved by God and changed from an enemy and self-lover into a God-lover and lover of others. Love destroys enmity, falsehood, and arrogance.

The command to love God and neighbor wholeheartedly is universal and non-negotiable (Matthew 22:37-40); but its expression can be varied. OAN love is the essence of the many OAN activities described in the Bible.

Ninth, what love is not? What is the opposite of love? It is taking. It is self-exaltation and self-worship. It is esteeming of self worthy and deserving such that one's effort is directed toward achieving that end. It looks within and is focused on "me," "my good," "my rights," "my wants," and "what I deserve."

A selfish person uses others, including God, for his own gain and goal. *My sake* takes center stage which only breeds strife and chaos. When self reigns, OAN will be non-existent, and the Church will be no different than any secular organization. Selfishness eviscerates the Church and attempts to make a mockery of Jesus' self-giving life and death.

IV. John's Understanding of Love in His Gospels and Letters

Consider other verses in which John offers further teaching on OAN-love.

A. 1 John 4:7-12: *Dear friends, let us love one another, for love comes from God. Everyone who loves has been born of God and knows God. Whoever does not love does not know God because God* *is love. This is how God showed his love among us: He sent his one and only Son into the world that we might live through him. This is love; not that we loved God, but that he loved us and sent his Son as an atoning sacrifice for our sins. Dear friends, since God so loved us, we also ought to love one another. No one has ever seen God; but if we love one another, God lives in us and his love is made complete in us.*

Not only does love sum up OAN and is the reason for it, it is also part of the OAN. God OAN-ed His people: He established a personal relationship with each believer. In doing so, He saved and sanctified them (4:16). Believers enjoy fellowship with Him which is expressed in loving relationships with other believers.

It is in the context of God's relationship to believers that loving the brethren is commanded and is an obligation (1 John 4:7-12). Therefore, OAN love is not to be a burden but an expression of gratitude for what Christ has done for and in believers (1 John 4:19; 5:3; 2 Corinthians 4:1).

OAN grows out of the *family-fact* that believers are members of God's family and therefore brothers and sisters. God's family was created supernaturally—the Holy Spirit regenerated His people and enables them to call God their Father (Galatians 4:4-7)

If OAN is a vital part of a church, there will be no enemies within the body. That is a strong statement! God's way does not fail! However, some members within the congregation do function as enemies. The command to love one's enemy applies within the body as well as outside of it (Matthew 22:37-40; Romans 12:14-21).

Those within the body may or may be not believers. Unbelievers cannot love because they have not been loved by God. Ipso facto, an unbeliever is a self-lover. Therefore, when there is enmity within the body, it is because believers are functioning as unbelievers and self-lovers (James 3:13-4:3). It should be noted that OAN may be God's way of returning the believer who is functioning as an unbeliever.

The command and obligation to OAN love is reflected in Paul's description of how the husband is to love his wife: Ephesians 5:25-33. The husband is to love his wife sacrificially, purposefully, constructively, constantly, finally, and perfectly. The model for the husband is Christ's love for His Church. This same model applies to all believers as they relate to one another.

The format to love is the same as for submission. Submission is a privilege, duty, and obligation not just for the husband but for all believers to other believers (Ephesians 5:21-24). Loving and submitting are part of OAN. The question before each one of us is: How will my OAN love look at home and at church? The answer requires understanding OAN love and developing concrete means of being a lover, "lovee," OAN-er, and OAN-ee.

B. John 13:14-17 *"Now that I, your Teacher and Lord, have washed your feet, you should also wash one another's feet. I have set you an example that you also should do as I have done to you." I tell you the truth, no slave is greater than his master, nor is a messenger greater* *than the one who sent him. Now that you know these things, you will be blessed if you do them.*

Washing feet refers to the loving humility that Jesus demonstrated not only that night but throughout His life. Paul applied *washing feet* in Ephesians 4:1-3 and Philippians 2:3-4 as an expression of and a requirement for OAN.

In these verses, John recorded Jesus' illustration of OAN by demonstrating what lowliness of mind and putting others first is (Ephesians 4:1-3; Philippians 2:3-4, 5-8). *Washing feet* is best interpreted to mean to do whatever it takes, even a menial task, to help a brother or sister in need. The cross was God's answer for man's greatest need (Romans 1:16-17).

The apostles did not understand love, the cross, or Jesus. They were not fully aware of how much they needed to be loved; few do. Before the cross, lovingly Jesus washed their feet! They still did not get it. But they would!

Jesus, fully God and fully man, stooped to His knees (John 13) and then later went to the cross (John 19) to serve others putting them above His own concerns in submission to His Father. The apostles did not understand the feet washing or the cross. Knowledge puffs up when used wrongly but it is a weapon for righteousness, joy, and peace in the context of OAN (1 Corinthians 8:1-6; 1 John 4:7-12). Pentecost brought a fuller understanding and greater love. Luke 24:36-49 records an introduction to Pentecost.

Jesus' whole life was characterized by the *wearing of the apron* of humility for His Father's honor and the benefit of His people (John 13:1ff; 1 Peter 5:5-7). He did not assert His rights or claim He did not have time or the energy to be a blessing to His people.

In verse 17, John promises a blessing for serving God's people (Matthew 7:24-27; James 1:25). Doctrine is intended to be practiced. OAN is one means to accomplish that end. Jesus was the humble suffering Servant Who came to serve not to be served which is the essence of OAN love (Matthew 20:28; Mark 10:45).

C. 1 John 3:11-12, 23 *This is the message you heard from the beginning: we should love one another. Do not be like Cain, who belonged to the evil one and murdered his brother. And why did he murder him? Because his own actions were evil and his brother's were righteous. And this is his command: to believe in the name of his Son, Jesus Christ, and to love one another as he commanded us.*

The command to love one another is an old and new command—it is the same message that Jesus taught from the beginning of His ministry, and it is embedded in the Old Testament (Exodus 34:6-7; Numbers 14;18; Nehemiah 9:17; Psalms 86:15; 103:8; 145:8; Lamentations 3:22; Joel 2:13; Nahum 1:2-3; Jonah 4:2).

John explained the opposite of OAN love by pointing to Cain. Remember in Genesis 4:9, Cain asked God if he was his brother's keeper in response to God's question, "Where is your brother?" Cain had no use for his brother and the God who gave him Abel.

In response, he murdered Abel. He removed him from his presence. He lived as if this was his world, and all should serve him (James 4:1-3). Cain's unbelief and rebellion were directed against Abel and Abel's God (Hebrews 11:3-4). God asked Cain an OAN question. Cain's answer demonstrated he was a rebellious self-lover, the antithesis of OAN (Hebrews 11:4). Self-love destroys OAN (1 Peter 5:5-6; James 4:1-3).

Another aspect of John's teaching regarding love focuses on love as a new-old commandment.

D. John 13:34-35; 1 John 2:7-8; 2 John 1:5

John 13:34-35: *"A new command I give you: Love one another. As I loved you, so must love one another. By this all men will know that you are my disciples, if you have love for one another."*

1 John 2:7-8: *Dear friends, I am not writing you a new commandment but an old one which you have had since the beginning. This old command is the message you have heard. Yet I am writing you a new command; its truth is seen in him and you, because the darkness is passing and the true light is already shining.*

2 John 1:5: *And now, dear lady, I am not writing you a new command, but one we have had that from the beginning. I ask that we love one another.*

In this group of passages, John teaches that OAN love is for the glory of God and a testimony to His greatness (John 13:34-35). One must be a child of God to understand love, to appreciate being loved, and to grasp the quality of that love. A child of God loves; OAN love builds up Christ's body. Christ's command to love one another was a new, old teaching.

The newness or freshness of it was not in the command itself but in the method of how, the lover, and one who was to be loved. *Feet washing*—humble service and serving humbly—was the example Jesus used to demonstrate His point (John 13:1, 12-17). The command's newness rested in those loving: the lover must be regenerated to function just as the Beggar-Servant King did.

The newness of the command also resided in those receiving love: one's enemy, little children, and one's wife. These three groups were considered least in society and unworthy of concern. Jesus inverted the culture's foundation of self-centeredness and replaced it with the two Great Commandments (Matthew 22:37-40).

The "how to" of OAN love was taught but more: Jesus gave a concrete demonstration of what OAN-love is. Jesus was a living example, a walking sermon, a visible reality of what love is and therefore of Who God is: John 14:6-9; 15:12; 1 John 2:7-8: Jesus loved completely, sacrificially, constructively, purposefully, unmistakably, and finally. He lived among His people as the Great OAN-er.

V. Selective Writings of Paul and Love

We move to Paul's writings and see more examples of the subject of OAN-love.

1 Thessalonians 3:12: *May the Lord make your love increase and overflow for each other and for everyone else, just as ours does for you.*

Paul's concern for the church and its members was evident in this letter. In this verse, he draws the connection between the Fountainhead of all love and the obligation that the recipients of God's love have—to be growing lovers of God and others. God's name and character were at stake.

The Lord has loved, and He continues to love; He expects a return on His investment. Those loved the most with a perfect love should love and OAN the most. OAN love is one of God's means for the believer to become more like Christ individually and as body of believers.

1 Thessalonians 4:9: *Now about brotherly love we do not need to write to you, for you yourselves have been taught by God to love each other.*

For the believer, love is learned, demonstrated, and taught. God expected a return on His investment—loving them—as shown in verse 10 and 3:12. In both places, Paul exhorted his people to super-abound as OAN lovers. They are to continue in loving all the brothers but even more. They were to super-abound, to love as God loved them. True knowledge of God and self leads to greater love and loving on the believer's part.

2 Thessalonians 1:3: *We ought always to thank God for you, brothers, and rightly so, because your faith is growing more and more and the love that every one of you has for each other is increasing.*

The peace and help of God (verse 2) is evidenced by how fellow believers treat one another. Paul considered himself under obligation to thank God for God's work in the Thessalonians.

God is at work in His family members. God's work in them was evidenced by a growing faith and robust OAN love. The two go hand in hand. Their love demonstrated God's grace and love in them. They were living out Matthew 5:14-16 and the church benefitted.

VI. OAN, the Law, and Lawkeeping

Romans 13:8: *Let no debt remain outstanding except the continuing debt to love one another, for he who loves his fellowman has fulfilled the law.*

OAN involves true lawkeeping but not for salvation. Rather it is a testimony of what the believer is in Christ. Christianity is a lawkeeping religion because the Triune God is the Lawmaker and Christ is the Lawkeeper.

The law is good and lawkeeping is good (footnote 20). The Christian is to understand God's initial message as recorded in Exodus 20:20. After giving the Ten Commandments to the people: *Moses said to the people, "Do not be afraid. God has come to test you, so that the fear of the Lord will be with you to keep you from sinning."*

The giving of the Ten Commandments was an act of love, an expression of God's love and justice. They highlighted the fullness of God in His redemptive glory. Salvation depends on Jesus and His perfect obedience—His perfect lawkeeping. He fulfilled the Law by His self-giving love and perfect obedience. In love, His perfect obedience is reckoned to the believer's account so that God declared the rebel not guilty and not condemned.

Love and loving as one loved fulfills every requirement of the law. Love and lawkeeping are what Jesus did. OAN love is following the example that Jesus gave in His short, earthly ministry. Jesus, Paul, and John were not against lawkeeping (Matthew 5:17; Romans 7:12; 13:8-10; 1 Timothy 1:8-11; 1 John 5:3).

I repeat: Christianity focuses on lawkeeping. But it is not personal lawkeeping! Rather, forcefully, and confidently, Christianity focuses on Christ and His perfect lawkeeping! The Law and Word of God are summarized by the word love (Matthew 22:37-40) and Jesus is the Lover par excellence!

Moreover, the essence of lawkeeping is love—either of self or of God. If it is of self, a person will be a law unto himself out of *love of self*; he does all he can to fulfill his law or a version of any law including that given in the Bible. He functions as if is the supreme standard of lawmaking and lawkeeping. He believes lawkeeping is in his reach to earn and gain.

Or if it is of God, he will acknowledge and rest on God as the One and Only Lawgiver and Jesus Christ as the One and Only True Lawkeeper. Lawkeeping then becomes a fruit of being saved not a means to and for salvation. The believer has a right view of the law, lawkeeping, the Lawmaker and the Lawkeeper.

It was Jesus Who removed the burden of personal lawkeeping as a means of salvation and holiness. Jesus through His perfect obedience and perfect death as the true Sacrifice set the believer free from the bondage of personal lawmaking and lawkeeping. Therefore, the believer is free to pursue OAN love (which is commanded) out of gratitude, even relief, for what Christ has done for him. He will love, honor, and obey as a testimony to God's love.[20]

Attempting to keep the law for the purpose of a right standing before God or looking good in His sight indicates a love of self that is based on ignorance and arrogance: self-righteousness, self-dependence, and self-sufficiency with a goal of self-justification. It says that "I am boss" and "I set the standard for what is good and bad."

---

[20] The Law is an expression of the essence of God. As such, it is God's revelation of Himself. Moses, in Exodus 20:20, told Israel that the Law was good, it was antidote for fear of man, the proper instrument for developing fear of the Lord, and was given so the people would not sin. Paul wrote that the law was good, spiritual, and holy (Romans 7:12; 1 Timothy 1:8-11). Thus, the Law is the way of life for the redeemed (Leviticus 18:5; Ezekiel 20:11, 13, 21); but it is the way of death for the unredeemed (Romans 10:5; Galatians 3:12). Jesus' lawkeeping is the end of the Law: it accomplished God's purpose. Jesus in keeping the Law perfectly fulfilled the Law's requirements—to the fullest (Matthew 5:17-20; Romans 10:4). Christ filled the "law full" of its true meaning which had been sucked dry by the false religions of personal lawkeeping then and now. Jesus fulfilled all of God's expectations and demands of the Law and achieved God's good purpose in giving the Law. The perfect law pointed to the Prefect Lawgiver and the perfect Lawkeeper. Jesus proved that God is a righteous and just Judge and that the law is an extension of the Triune God (Genesis 18:25). Moreover, He proved God's love by His perfect lawkeeping.

Rather, it is self-deception and rebellion against God, and a return to the serpent's counsel in the Garden (Luke 18:9-14). Conversely, lawkeeping out of gratitude for God's grace; it is an expression of a true sense of what it means to be loved by God (John 14:15, 21, 23). It is fruit-bearing par excellence!

VII. OAN and Christian Liberty

Galatians 5:13: *You, my brothers, were called to be free. But do not use your freedom to indulge the sinful nature; rather serve one another in love.*

Paul was concerned about an abuse of Christian liberty (also see Romans 14:1-15:7). The false teachers had inserted personal lawkeeping into the picture as the means of salvation. They taught that something more than Christ and what He secured in His perfect lawkeeping was needed for a person to be saved.

This false teaching misunderstood God's salvation for man. Salvation was not considered freedom from sin, self, and Satan. Rather, salvation was considered a place or position that could be self-gained. The temptation for a former self-pleaser to return to self-righteousness to serve self was great and appealing especially when there was pressure (see the book of Hebrews for a similar situation).

The person was taught to earn points with God and therefore self by personal lawkeeping often at the expense of using others. The lure of personal lawkeeping is quite strong for believers in any age. Previous membership in Satan's culture (kingdom and family) leads to self-sufficiency and self-righteousness. Jesus is at best an "add-on."

Paul says "whoa." His message is something like this: "You were saved from a "do-it-yourself" attitude and the action proceeding from it. Therefore, don't misuse your freedom (see Galatians 3:1-5). The term *flesh* refers to the old lifestyle of self-service and self-exaltation which is the only activity learned while in Satan's kingdom and family.

Instead, Paul calls his people to serve others by *OAN slavery* (Romans 6:16-19). We need to capture the Bible's teaching on this subject. The passage teaches that a person is a slave to self and unrighteousness or to God and righteousness including OAN. That understanding and actions that flow from it will simply life. Moreover, slaves are to work heartily unto the Lord (Ephesians 6:5; Colossians 3:22-25).

Since the believer has been rescued and transferred from the kingdom of darkness into the kingdom of light, he now serves God and others as a God-pleaser and freed person (Acts 26:15-18; Colossians 1:13; 1 Peter 2:9). OAN is part of his new life.

Yet the believer is not complete as a God-pleaser. God's work of salvation continues. There is life after salvation. Living as one saved is to be accomplished in love, by love, and through love. This includes OAN.

Eternity came down to the believer in Christ and the Holy Spirit. A piece of heaven became a reality in the present (John 17:3; Romans 6:9-11; 1 John 3:1-3). One day, every believer will be face to face with love, in love, and by love because Love is a Person (1 John 4:7-12)!

Liberty is often considered synonymous with freedom: "this is a free country and I can do this." That fact is changing especially if you are a Christian. But the statement indicates that freedom is carte blanche to do what I want when I want. Rather, biblically, freedom is being what God intended you to be. That freedom cost: the blood of the Godman. Guard your freedom in Christ and never abuse it. The believer is free to enjoy and please God. OAN is a means to do that thanking God for His love and your salvation.

CHAPTER 6

Romans 14:1-15:7: Welcoming, Accepting, and Bearing With

Romans 15:7: *Accept one another, then, just as Christ accepted you, in order to bring praise to God.*

PAUL'S INTENT IN WRITING THE book of Romans was to give a reasoned, logical summary of the Christian faith. Beginning with chapter 12, Paul began to give many exhortations for the ministry of OAN; they were of a general nature. We studied some of these in the sections entitled The Mind of Christ and Love.

However, beginning with chapter 14 (14:1 through 15:7), Paul was specific. He addressed perhaps the only known problem in the Roman church. He called for OAN based on a proper understanding of "welcoming" and "accepting" using Romans 14:1-15:7 as a handbook of OAN.

Every local congregation and regional church has its share of people with differences of opinion. The present pandemic is a prime example. Consider and answer these questions: Do we or don't we: wear masks, social distance, meet here or there or not at all, sing-not sing, etc. How does God direct His Church to address differences of opinions individually and corporately? What standard is to be used? What are to be the results?

Members of the Roman Church had differences of opinion at least regarding the eating of meat and the observance of days. In response, individuals chose sides resulting in factions and division (1 Corinthians 1:10-17; James 3:13-4:3). In contrast, Paul, as he did to the Corinthians, commanded the people to get along God's way by emphasizing many biblical principles that pertained to interpersonal relationships.

In this section, we study OAN as "welcoming," "accepting," and bearing with; we learn how Paul applied these teachings to the Roman congregation. First, consider the terms welcome and accepting. The word translated as "accept" or "welcome" means "to take to oneself," "to receive to oneself," "to admit to one's society and fellowship," and "to treat with kindness."[21] Both *biblical accepting* and *loving* are a result of first being accepted and loved by God (Romans 5:6-10; 1 John 4:19).

I repeat: Christians are the most accepted and loved people; therefore, they must accept and love others as they have been accepted and loved. It is their duty, privilege, and right! Therefore, one brother is not to look down on another who holds a differing viewpoint. What is he to do?

---

21 The word in the original language is *proslambano*: Romans 14:1, 3; 15:7, Philemon 1:12, 17, Psalm 65:4: this Psalm of David praised God: *Blessed are those you choose and bring near to live in your courts.*

OAN involves accepting and welcoming but not as the culture says: *accept me just as I am* (Ephesians 5:1-2). Contrary to popular opinion, God did not do that. He cannot do that. If He did, He would attack the integrity of the eternal plan of salvation and the cross. The decision would be an affront to the Triune God Who sent His Son to live and die for unlovely people—His enemies (Romans 3:21-26; 5:6-10).

Through the work of the Holy Spirit, He changed them from the inside out with the expectation of change. He set for them a new, radical, and supernatural agenda: for God, to God, and by God, and for others. They had been changed supernaturally (Romans 5:6-10; Ephesians 5:1-2). God expects and deserves thoughts, desires, and actions commiserate with that change. This includes OAN!

Acceptance and welcoming involves a commitment to love someone for God's sake, in spite of who he is. That was the believer status when he was saved. He was saved in spite of himself (Romans 5:6-10)! One accepts, welcomes, and loves others by serving other believers and extending kindness to them even when it may be hard. This is OAN love.

As we learned in our discussions of submission and love, acceptance and welcoming are not doormatism. God is not at the beck and call of people. He is not an errand boy. Neither is the believer.

However, the believer is to have a servant's heart that is fenced by God's truth and biblical principles as he interacts with others. It was for Jesus and believers are saved in order to imitate Christ. Saying *no* can be as much or even more loving than an *eternal yes*. Jesus answered demands by *yes, no,* and *wait*.

I. Romans 14:1-3

Paul, in 14:1-15:7, categorized two groups with differing viewpoints as the weaker brother and the stronger brother. Some people had difficulty with eating meat but not vegetables (14:1-4) and another group (maybe the same group?) had problems with keeping of days (14:5-6). Another group had problems eating meat that had been declared unclean by Hebrew laws (14:14-15:3). Paul summarized these problems in 14:7-13 and 15:4-7.

But Paul focused on the attitudes (thoughts and desires vertically toward God and horizontally toward each other) of each person and each group; he was much less focused on the correctness of the opposing views. He placed attention on how to get along with those who held differing viewpoints by encouraging OAN. Salvation is a prerequisite for giving and receiving OAN. Differences of opinion are a reality among believers. The issue: how do you respond to the people holding them?

Sometimes both groups may be wrong. Both may be the weaker brother! Therefore, Paul focused on attitudes of each group. He understood that differences of opinion are not the same thing as conflict and that differences do not need to lead to conflict and division in the body of Christ. In fact, they must not!

Paul knew each group could cause trouble in the church if they maintained that they had truth and the other did not. Congregations are undergoing the same scenario especially during these times of pandemic and cultural suicide. Perhaps this is God's wake-up call for the Church.

Interestingly, Paul began chapter 14 by addressing the strong (those who have no problem or scruples eating meat):

Romans 14:1: *Accept him whose faith is weak, without passing judgment on disputable matters.*

Paul draws a distinction among *matters*. In part, he is making a distinction between principle and preference and application. He defined the weaker brother as one with a strong opinion regarding certain foods and perhaps drink, and the keeping of certain days. They believed that people should not eat certain foods and should keep certain days in a special way—perhaps treat Saturday as the Jewish Sabbath rather than Sunday. The stronger brother had much less concern about food and days but held to them as strongly.

As I said, Paul's basic concern was the attitudes of each group toward one another and thus to God. He calls these matters strongly-held opinions. They were disputable, in part, because the people were hanging on to them and their "assumed right" to do so. They failed to hang on to Christ and to each other. Some dispute what a disputable matter is! Paul was saying that is not how God in Christ by the Spirit treated you!

Paul says whoa! He exhorts his readers not to criticize, judge, or bring under scrutiny the weaker brother's thoughts and beliefs in order to use them against him.[22] The strong, and the weak, must not look down upon, break fellowship with, or in any way disparage the weaker or stronger brother because of differences of opinion.

The principle set forth is that differences of opinion do exist among family members. But they are not to be used to produce division or to separate brothers. They are to be used by each person to grow into Christlikeness. Difference of opinion must be handled correctly. OAN is one of God's tools to accomplish this. The issue is the person's heart rather than the difference of opinion!

Differences of opinion that exist because of differing views of biblical principles are one thing. Those differences need to be discussed and resolved. The mind of Christ, not the thoughts of men, must prevail.

However, differences of opinion based simply on preference are never to be used as a lever to divide the body. When principles and their application are involved, the Church leaders must come alongside the congregation and steer them in God's direction. Brothers and sisters are to exist side by side in Christ's body growing and maturing individually and as a body (Philippians 1:27-2:5).

---

22 The word translated "criticize" is *diakrisis* which means judgment, distinguishing, discernment, or scrutiny. The word translated "views" is *dialogimos* which refers to an opinion, reason, or intention: Luke 2:35; 5:22; 6:8; 9:47.

The goal is not to judge or change the other person but to include those with a difference of opinion in the fellowship of the whole congregation. Opinions may need to change and that may come as a result of OAN.

Romans 14:2: *One man's faith allows him to eat everything, but another man, who faith is weak, eats only vegetables.*

Paul defined the two groups: the weak as one who thinks he is limited in what he can eat and the strong as one who believes he can eat anything.

Romans 14:3: *The man who eats everything must not look down on him who does not, and the man who does not eat everything must not condemn the one who eats, for God has accepted him.*

Paul addressed the heart—the attitude, thoughts, and desires—of individuals in each group giving specific directions for the strong (the one who eats) and the weak (the one who does not eat). The strong must not despise or look with contempt on the weaker brother and the weak must not judge the strong (Luke 18:9-14).

Either activity produces division and dishonors God. The word translated look down upon is a strong word and means "to look down upon with disdain and superiority."[23] Despising and judging are expressions of pharisaical, self-righteous thinking and wanting that says "I am better than another;" they have no place in Christ's Church. It is antithetical to and prevents OAN.

---

23 The word in the original is *exeoutheneo*. See Luke 18:9; 23:11; Romans 14:3, 10; 1 Corinthians 1:28. The word translated "judge" is a general word, *krino*, which means "to distinguish."

What was the basis for the command? It is the fact that God has accepted, welcomed, and received each believer into His family. Their status changed so that they are fellow heirs and fellow brothers and sisters (John 13:34-35; Ephesians 3:7; 1 Peter 2:9-10; 3:7).

The ones God has received, others have no right to exclude (1 Corinthians 11). This same call must be sounded in regard to marriage and sexuality. What God has declared, let no one tamper with and attempt to separate and destroy!

God has put His mark on His people including those weaker and stronger in the faith, those married, and men and women in general and in the context of marriage (2 Corinthians 1:22; 5:5; Ephesians 1:13-14). Believers are marked out by God for God! Differences exist but they are not to be misused and abused! Therefore, OAN is not excluded because of differences of opinion but rather it is encouraged and in fact mandatory as a means of building up the body.

In addition, when each person is in bondage to his opinion and belief, it leads to tyranny in the church. OAN becomes non-existent and any fellowship becomes self-serving as each group recruits more members (1 Corinthians 1:10-17).

Dangers exist on both sides. Often non-biblical opinions are used to bolster one group's view and preferences simply to win. The strong may misuse their freedom and promote lax living without concern for the weaker brother and practice verbal cannibalism (Galatians 5:13-15; 1 Peter 2:16; 2 Peter 2:19).

On the other hand, there is the danger of legalism and externalism with the weak. Rather the strong are to make a place for the weaker brother in their hearts (attitude and disposition) and in their actions. Similarly, but less recognized: the weaker brother, who probably does not agree that he is the weaker brother, must keep the stronger brother in a place of love and concern.

II. The Necessity of Self-Inventory

Romans 14:4: *Who are you to judge someone else's servant? To his own master he stands or falls. And he will stand for the Lord is able to make him stand.*

Paul asks a self-inventory question: "Just who do you think you are?" Then he answers it for each person. Each person was functioning as the other person's lord! No one is another person's master or lord. Paul has placed the matter of attitude toward others in the context of lordship and self-evaluation.

This truth takes us back to the Lord's Supper and Jesus' answer to the James and John's kingdom regarding their place in the kingdom: serve rather than be served or focusing on your place and your opinion (Matthew 20:20-28; Mark 10:35-45).

Treating another as unworthy and with disdain because he holds a different opinion is judging him, is lording over him, and is showing favoritism (Romans 2:11; James 2:1-7; 1 Peter 5:1-4). Paul says these actions are a result of bad theology and flow from a heart in competition with God.

Every believer is the Lord's servant and only the Master has a right to judge. Therefore no one, including elders, is to lord it over another (1 Peter 5:1-4). No one is another's Holy Spirit. No one is another's master. Yet OAN is mandatory; it is essential for the good of God's Church and individuals.

Paul referred to the judgment seat here and later (see verses 10 and 12). "Standing" (... *For we all stand before God's judgment seat*: v.10) referred to giving an account of one's actions and attitudes toward another as well as his response to those who hold differing views (*So then, each of us will give an account of himself to God:* v.12).

"Standing" is not simply judicial. The word implies an inner-man function. God through His Holy Spirit enables a believer to stand and function as a God-pleaser in any situation (Philippians 4:13). The person is responsible for standing or falling. He can't blame God or others. The person is responsible for making it easy for another person to sin; he is not responsible for the sin, but he will answer to God for making it easy to sin.

If someone cries "uncle" saying he can't take it anymore because too many of his fellow believers don't think the way he does, or crumbles under criticism and hard times he must take responsibility for that sin. It is his own fault—not the Church's or God's. Every person is responsible for his own sin but also for the ease by which he facilitates another to sin. Fellow believers are to make it easy for someone to do right and hard to sin.

III. Motivation

In this section, an important question is addressed based on 1 Corinthians 10:31 (*So whether you eat or drink or whatever you do, do it for the glory of God*): Whose eyes do you consider and fear? Is it your own? Is it the eyes of people? Is it the Lord's?

Romans 14:5-6: *One man considers one day more sacred than another; another man considers every day alike. Each one should be fully convinced in his own mind. He who regards one day as special, does so to the Lord. He who eats meat, eats to the Lord, for he gives thanks to God; and he who abstains, does so to the Lord and gives thanks to God.*

Paul sets forth a universal principle of motivation. Believers are to do what they do for the praise and glory of God: 1 Corinthians 10:31; Colossians 3:17. Paul is teaching the principle that Jesus taught in Matthew 15:1-20 and Mark 7:1-23.[24] The heart is the heart of the matter. Philippians 2:5 emphasizes that the mindset of believers must flow from having and correctly applying the mind of Christ.

In verse 5 and 6, Paul exhorts every believer to be convinced of the correctness of his view. Thinking and wanting are whole-person functions in the brain (body) and the heart. Correct thinking and wanting flow from a heart change and changed actions and often feelings.

---

24 The word translated *regard* is *krino*—see verse 3, and the word translated *observes* is *phroneo* which means "to have a mindset," or "to be minded resulting in action": see Philippians 1:7; 2:2, 5; 3:19; 4:2. Romans 12:3; 14:6; 1 Corinthians 4:6; 13:11; Galatians 5:10.

Since the stronger and weaker brothers have the mind of Christ, they have the capacity to think God's thoughts and desire what God desires. Christlikeness is developed by bringing one's beliefs and convictions in line with God's truth and applying them God's way as patterned living.

A believer must not reach a conclusion based on impulse or reaction to or against something or someone. Rather his conclusion should follow study and discussion about the matter (Acts 17:11). Once convinced (rightly or wrongly), he is to express that belief in thankfulness to God in order to honor Him. Prior to being convinced, the *holding* principle of verse 23 applies (see discussion of that verse).

As a corollary, Paul teaches that no one must do what is contrary to his own beliefs. If someone is thinking wrongly and yet believes it is true and goes against that "truth" (some may say his conscience), he is guilty. The solution is to correct both the standard by which he trained his conscience and the activity of opposing that which he thinks is correct. The ultimate solution is a heart and conscience trained and steeped in God's Word.

Romans 14:7-9: *For none of us lives to himself alone and none of us dies to himself alone. If we live, we live to the Lord; and if we die, we die to the Lord. So, whether we live or die, we belong to the Lord. For this very reason, Christ died and returned to life so that he might be the Lord of both dead and the living.*

Verses seven through nine apply only to believers because the unbeliever is a self-lover continuously (1 John 4:7-12). Paul is pointing to the vertical reference of life. Clearly self-worship, often called "love" by the culture is forbidden in Scripture. It is idolatry. It is contrary to God—His Being and work and to OAN. Jesus made the point that He died to self and lived to please His Father (John 4:31-34: this truth is repeated throughout John's gospel).

Paul pointed to his radical departure from being a self-pleaser to being a Christ-pleaser as given in 2 Corinthians 5:9-15 and Philippians 1:19-21; 3:3-11. No believer is free to live for self because the old person has been crucified with Christ (Romans 6:6; Galatians 2:20). He has been purchased at a great cost: Christ Himself. Therefore, how can the believer live for self? He is not his own. He has been bought with a price (1 Corinthians 6:19-20).

Rather, a believer is a steward who is to give back to God in return for what God has done for and to him (1 Corinthians 4:1-5; Matthew 25:14-30 and Luke 19:12-27; Ephesians 5:15-19). One way he does this is through OAN which includes fellowshipping with those of differing opinions.

Since having the mind of Christ is a result of God's redemption, a believer's viewpoint and how it is expressed is the Lord's. Self, which had center stage in Satan's family and kingdom, now takes backstage. Self no longer motivates or directs one's actions and thoughts. The weaker and stronger brother must regard their activities from the perspective of OAN love. Each must be OAN-er and OAN-ee.

IV. Judging and Judgment

Romans 14:10-12: *You, then, why do you judge your brother? Or why do you look down on your brother? For we all stand before God's judgment seat. "It is written: 'As surely as I live,' says the Lord, 'every knee will bow before me; every tongue will confess to God.' So, then, each of us will give an account of himself to God.*

Paul is adamant: no one is to judge his brother. God is Judge and if someone judges his brother, he is attempting to take God's place (see James 4:11-12). And to prove the point that each one has his own Lord (see verse 4), Paul reiterated that one who judges his brother must stand before the Judge for an accounting.

Romans 14:13: *Therefore let us stop passing judgment on one another. Instead, make up your mind not to put any stumbling block or obstacle in your brother's way.*

At the same time, Paul clarifies that OAN involves judging but it is to be judging God's way. God is not against judging but against wrong judging. In Matthew 7:1-6, Jesus taught that judgment is required of believers (Acts 17:11; 2 Corinthians 13:5; 1 Thessalonians 5:21; 1 John 4:1-6). They were not to throw their pearls to dogs or pigs (Matthew 7: 6)! But judgment begins with self-judgment.

Jesus in Matthew 7:1-6 gave guidelines on how to judge. Jesus taught that a believer must be as aggressive in judging himself, and by God's standard, as he is in judging others by his own standard. Jesus is condemning self-righteous and censorious judging which destroys OAN.

Paul also gave guidelines regarding judging in Romans 14. Paul had spelled out who the stronger and weaker brother were (verses 2, 5). He underscores the underlying principle of the motivation for all of life: a person is to live and die for Christ, not self (verses 7-8). In this way, problems will be solved but better: the Church will grow!

Each person—the weaker and stronger brother and the one judging—must stand before the judgment seat and the righteous Judge. Therefore, for the honor of God and the blessing of the body and the individual, wrong judgment must stop and right judgment must begin (verses 4, 10, 12). There are serious consequences for trying to do God's job.

Paul does not teach non-judgment which is a judgment itself! Rather he teaches that judgment begins with self. He followed Christ teaching as did James (James 4:1-4, 5-10). Paul taught the Corinthians that God's judgment came upon them because they had failed to practice self-discipline and self-judgment when celebrating the Lord's Supper (1 Corinthians 11:28-32).

Paul exhorted both groups to evaluate themselves. Both were to judge in the correct manner and for the right reasons. There must be judging, but it is to be prudent and discerning (being sensitive to and aware of) the other person and his reasoning.

Both must discover what the other person's hindrances and stumbling blocks are as well as his own.[25] This is an aspect of OAN.

A hindrance makes it hard for a person to do right, and a stumbling block makes it easy for him to sin. It is a temptation over which a person may fall. They are contrary to the rule that believers are to make it hard for another to sin and easy to do right.

In order to help with your self-inventory, here are some OAN questions for you to consider:

- What is the difference of opinion and what is the basis for it?
- Who is the weaker brother and give the reasons for your answer?
- Who is the stronger brother and give the reasons for your answer?
- What is your role, if any, in contributing to any division?
- How can you do to build the other person up and encourage him rather than make it easy for him to sin?
- What is God's solution in terms of principles and how should they be implemented?

---

25 The word translated hindrance is *proskomma*. It is spoken of Christ Who was a stone of stumbling (Romans 9:32-33; 1 Peter 2:8) and it is used of an occasion for sinning (Romans 14:13, 20; 1 Corinthians 8:9). The word translated stumbling block is *skandalon*. The idea is a trap on which bait is placed and when touched the animal or person is entrapped. The idea is one of enticement and entrapment (Matthew 18:7; Luke 17:1; Romans 9:33; 11:9; 14:13; 16:7; 1 Corinthians 1:23; Galatians 5:11; 1 Peter 2:8). The believer is to make hard for a fellow believer (and himself!) to sin and easy to do right!

As a corollary teaching, the believer will give a threefold accounting at judgment: one for his wrong judging of others; one for a failure to judge and discipline himself; and one for a failure to OAN (1 Corinthians 11:28-32; 2 Corinthians 13:5; James 1:22).

Self-discipline is a fruit of the Spirit; it is self-control which is control of self! Self-control is to replace self-righteous judgment of others. Therefore, God's people must stop judging one another wrongly. Rather, Paul exhorts them to make this judgment: Be a OAN-er and you won't put a hindrance or stumbling block in a brother's way!

V. Standard for and Purpose of Judgment

Romans 14:14: *As one who is in the Lord Jesus, I am fully convinced that no food is unclean in itself. But if anyone regards something unclean, then for him, it is unclean.*

Paul follows his own teaching. He is convinced, and it is by the Lord that he is convinced (verse 5, 13). He had this on the direct authority of Christ. In this case, Paul sides with the strong—nothing is unclean. And yet if one counts something unclean, it is unclean for him.

Romans 14:15-16: *If your brother is distressed because of what you eat, you are no longer acting in love. Do not by your eating destroy your brother for whom Christ died. Do not allow what you consider good to be spoken of as evil.*

Paul guarded his freedom so as not to give license for the believer or even the unbeliever to sin (1 Corinthians 8:9-12; 9:21-22). The believer is to make it hard for anyone to sin and easy to do right. Guarding the use of one's freedom in Christ is part of OAN and the opposite of selfishness. Every believer's freedom is in Christ not separated from it. Paul encountered division because of a lack of OAN in the Roman and Corinthian congregations.

Paul taught the Corinthians that food was not the issue (1 Corinthians 8). Rather, the problem was a wrong view of God (8:4-6). Since there is only one God, eating meat that was served to idols which are only physical objects was not wrong. Simple yet profound!

In the Roman church (and the Corinthian church!), the issue was the belief that "I can hold on to whatever I deem correct and once convinced of it, I have the right to flaunt it and make fun of those who don't hold to my view." Bad theology existed in the Roman Church as well!

Paul taught that OAN love is the key to unity and glorifying God. However, some in the Roman congregation were following the example of some in the Corinthian congregation. Possession of knowledge, even truth, can puff up leading to the destruction of the people (1 Corinthians 8:1: *Now about food sacrifice to idols: We know that all possess knowledge. Knowledge puffs up, but love builds up*; verse 11: *So this weak brother, for whom Christ died, is destroyed by your knowledge.*).

Paul did not want what had happened in Corinthian church to happen in Rome. The issue was not being right but concern for the body and individual believers. Paul encouraged OAN which, as we have seen repeatedly, is summarized by loving God and one's brother (Galatians 5:13). Loving neighbor begins with believers in the Church.

VI. The Kingdom of God, Differences of Opinion, and OAN

Romans 14:17-18: *For the kingdom of God is not a matter of eating and drinking, but of righteousness, peace and joy in the Holy Spirit, because anyone who serves Christ in this way is pleasing to God and approved by men.*

Here is one key to OAN. Correct theology influences living—thoughts, desires, and actions (Titus 1:1-2; 2 Peter 1:5-10). Both groups had failed to understand the essence of the kingdom of God. If they had correctly understood biblical truth, they would have given and received OAN; there would be less or no tension and strife (1 Corinthians 8:1-13).

The principle is twofold: first: right theology always trumps falsehood and results in godly living. A right view of God results in a right view of food and days and a right view of those who hold a differing view—one's neighbor.

And second: the weaker brother is the one who is to come first in the thinking and desires of the stronger brother. Christians do have rights, but their exercise is limited by the effect on others. How does deferring to the weaker look in Church life?

Paul made the monumental statement: the kingdom of God does not consist of the physical and material things such as food, drink, position, or preference. Jesus taught this same truth throughout His ministry (John 4:31-34). The physical is important, but it is as a means and a vehicle of viewing God who is the Creator and Controller. This is His world! Nature sings of His glory (Psalm 19).

God's kingdom is not about the physical but includes the physical. The physical must be considered in light of righteousness, peace, and joy. The kingdom of God is to be discerned spiritually, through the eyes of saving faith and true hope (2 Corinthians 5:7). The physical takes its rightful place only in the context of God's kingdom including family membership.

It is God's way to give attention to the needy, orphan, afflicted, humble, poor/powerless, oppressed, widow/weak, fatherless, broken hearted, and lonely (Psalms 9:18; 10:17-18; 34:18; 146:9). God's way does not preclude the rich! God blesses some people with varying amounts and types of wealth—both physical and spiritual (Abraham, David, Solomon, and Job for starters).

Paul is speaking of the physical AND the spiritual aspect of each person and the body. John does that as well (1 John 3:16-18). Following God's design, the stronger brother is to correctly relate to the weaker brother: God takes care of His people both weak and strong! How this looks is dependent on the persons and their relationship as well as the issue.

However, there is an issue: the weaker brother may not agree that he is in that category. Both parties must come to the table of biblical truth ready to be taught, grow, and honor God. OAN is desperately needed for victory.

Kingdom life does not consist in exercising liberty as a believer. It does not consist of "my way," "my rights," and "what I deserve." Rather, it consists of God's way and what He deserves. Therefore, it consists of righteousness—right living before God and others; peace; and joy in and by the Holy Spirit.

The focus of life in the kingdom is on what God wants for His glory and the good of His church and individual believers. The believer invests in God and what He wants. God wants heaven on earth, which I define as loving fellowship! OAN allows believers a foretaste of heaven—unity and fellowship!

Contending for "self" and "me" is based on a *now* theology. The *now* is the physical, created, material, temporal, personal, and visible. It is facts—people, events, circumstances— which are taken in by the senses and interpreted. These facts are interpreted by one of two grids: feelings, wants, circumstances, and reason that is either distorted or divorced from biblical truth; or by the true interpretative standard biblical truth. A sinful *now* approach to life focuses on what is in it for me to the exclusion of the eternal and spiritual.

The congregation in Rome interpreted facts but their interpretative standard was their view of themselves and their view; feelings; wants; experience; circumstances; and their understanding devoid of biblical truth. A person's interpretation of facts follows from and leads to a way of life that Joshua placed before Israel: who will you serve: self or God (Joshua 24:14-15)? Differences of opinion were the context of Joshua's call!

When self takes center stage, its pursuit produces chaos and strife, the very opposite of righteousness, peace, and joy. Emphasizing certain foods or days was an example of simply "majoring in the minors." Paul uses this same argument with the Corinthians (1 Corinthians 6:13; 8:8).

Rather, God's name and the peace of the Church were at stake. When there is disorder, there is no OAN and the church is hindered from its functions, one of which is to display God's wisdom to the unseen world and another which is to equip the saints for maturity (Ephesians 3:10; 4:11-14 and also Matthew 5:14-16 and 1 Peter 2:9-10).

Order produces a milieu for teaching which leads to truth and life which leads to ministry both inside and outside the church (discussed in chapter 2). OAN is conducive to bringing about and maintaining that order which is necessary for proper education (Ephesians 4:11-14: footnote 2).

Righteousness, peace, and joy are blessings and gifts from the Holy Spirit that are conducive to and developed in the process of OAN. These are in opposition to focusing on the physical aspects of eating, drinking, and winning. However, eating and drinking is part of kingdom life, but they must be done to the glory of God (1 Corinthians 10:31). Moreover, eating and drinking falls under OAN and is to be part of good stewardship of the physical body! God blesses biblical stewardship.

The Holy Spirit brings the trio of knowledge, righteousness, and joy through His Word for believers to use to solve problems and to OAN. Jesus summarized the believer's activity in His kingdom in Matthew 6:33: *But first seek his kingdom and his righteousness, and all these things will be given to you as well.*

The believer's peace and joy is not dependent on people and their treatment of him. Rather, they produce and are by-products of righteous living for God's glory and the good of the Church. If OAN is ongoing, there will righteousness, joy, and peace which cannot be taken away from the church and the believer because they are from God.

How do we apply Paul's teaching to the Church today especially in light of the pandemic? My answer is not exhaustive, and I add thoughts later in the section. Hopefully all would agree that this God's world and the pandemic *and* differences of opinion are part of God's sovereign control.

Moreover, all circumstances including a person's own sin and sinning and being sinned against fall under God's providence. God has designed all things for good—God's glory and the growth of the believer in Christlikeness. God is the Designer and Organizer par excellence!

How can sin be good? Sin is not good. It is the absence of good, light, and life and it is the presence of evil, darkness, and death. But what God accomplishes in it is good (Genesis 50:15-21; Romans 8:28-29). God is not the author of sin, but nothing happens in His world without His sovereign control. If there was a maverick molecule or a random event, God would not be sovereign and God would not be God!

These truths are vividly expressed in Genesis 50:15-21 and Romans 8:28-29. The pandemic is a full-blown opportunity and mandate to learn God's principles and experience His grace in applying them. We must OAN. The question is how. Churches must come together committed to honoring the Lord.

How then do believers arrive at an answer to differences of opinion? Consider this scenario. A couple is planning a trip. One person wants to be safe and another frugal. How would you know what the person is thinking? You ask and learn! Wanting to stop and rest is one's person answer to being safe. The other person does not want to stop thereby saving money.

The same scenario may be seen in a pandemic. One person wants to distance self from others by staying home and another person wants to be in God's house for worship. What do you do with this difference of opinion and the people holding them?

It is a good start that the reasons of each party are made known. Another aspect of the proposed action is motivation. In the above example, was the desire to be safe and to be frugal motivated by a love of the Lord and a desire to please Him?

In the same way, are believers today sinfully fearfully by isolating themselves or foolishly arrogant by acting as if *business as usual*? These times are certainly unprecedented, especially for America. Moreover, America may be in the throes of increasing hard times including persecution. People don't like Jesus and His people (John 15:18-21; 2 Timothy 3:12; 1 Peter 1:6-7; 2:13-25; 4:12-13, 19). Christians must decide how they and the Church will respond locally and nationally. God knows what He is doing!

Whatever the final conclusion, it must be God-honoring. To that end, it must not be a *me* or *you* solution but *me-you* decision. It is not a compromise. Jesus never did. Rather, the parties must take the concerns and the motivation of each party; discover God-honoring solutions; and enjoy the unity of the body. Verse 19 addresses this with of the use of a powerful word.

VII. OAN: *Make Every Effort*

Romans 14:19: *Let us therefor make every effort to do what leads to peace and to mutual edification.*

This is the summary verse for OAN. It encourages, demands, and makes possible for believers to live and grow together in a milieu of differences of opinions (Ephesians 4:1-3). Each member must be OAN-er and OAN-ee. Both require pursuing peace and edifying others.

The word translated *make an effort* is an energetic word meaning "to pursue, to hunt down, to follow hard after, to prosecute, and to go after with a desire of obtaining." The idea is a bloodhound on the scent of the fox. The idea is a concerted effort: long obedience in the same direction. Here are several questions to answer to help you pursue peace God's way for His glory:

1. Do my attitudes and actions bring peace? Am I a peace lover or a peacemaker? James 3:13-4:3; Matthew 5:9. There is a difference between the two. Jesus did not come to bring peace but division (Matthew 10:32-38). And yet He gave peace not as the world gives it but divinely (John 14:27; 16:33).
2. Do my actions and attitudes build up or tear down? 1 Thessalonians 5:11.
3. How have I responded to situations in which people hold differing views to mine?
4. What is my way of persuasion, and does it foster peace or strife?
5. Why would God place me in a body of believers (or any relationship) that holds differing views than mine? See Romans 8:28-29.

VII. The Holding Principle

Romans 14:20-23: *Do not destroy the work of God for the sake of food. All food is clean, but it is wrong for a man to eat anything that causes someone else to stumble. It is better to not to eat meat or drink wine or do anything else that will cause your brother to fall. So whatever you believe about these things keep between yourself and God. Blessed is the man who does not condemn himself by what he approves. But the man who has doubts is condemned if he eats, because his eating is not from faith; and everything that does not come from faith is sin.*

In these verses, Paul repeats the same principle he taught in 1 Corinthians 6:12-13 and 10:23-24. Paraphrased, these passages teach that many things may be lawful for him—liberty—but he will not be ruled by self-pleasing, self-fulfillment, and self-indulgence simply to display his rights. God and His Church are bigger than any one or two individuals.

What is God's work that may be *undone—hindered*—by putting self-first? Paul addressed this activity when he spoke of *putting out the Spirit's fire*—quenching or offending the Holy Spirit (Ephesians 4:30; 1 Thessalonians 5:19). The Holy Spirit applied Christ's reconciling work secured at the cross to the believer and the body of Christ. He expects and will get a return on His investment in His Church and individual believers.

When peace and unity of the body are interrupted, the work of the Spirit is being undermined! He is grieved, offended, and the Triune God is dishonored. God's work of reconciliation is the model for His Church, and it is attacked when believers fail to OAN resulting in strife and contention (2 Corinthians 5:18-21; Ephesians 2:11-15; James 3:13-4:3).

To say again, freedom in Christ must always be restrained by its effect on others (Galatians 5:13-18; 1 Peter 2:16; 2 Peter 2:18-19). Rather than press one's beliefs on others (by compelling them to follow in one's footsteps) or simply to follow another thoughtlessly, the believer is to train his heart and his conscience by God's standard and then hold to it (verse 5, 14).

In verse 23, Paul sets forth the *holding* principle. It calls for sober reflection on both one's attitude and action using the Bible as one's standard (verses 5, 14). If one is in doubt regarding a certain thought, desire, and or action and does the doubtful thing, he violates God's word and sins. His conscience if it is trained by God's word will serve as a warning. He must be vigilant. Conscience may need to be retrained but it should not be ignored.

Therefore, Paul's exhortation is that one must not take an action against another or hold an attitude toward him unless he thinks his action and attitude is right before God. The *holding* principle is invaluable in OAN and applies to both the strong and the weak brother.

VIII. The Bearing-With Principle

Romans 15:1: *We who are strong ought to bear with the failings of the weak of those and not to please ourselves.*

This verse sets forth the *bearing-with* principle of OAN. The *holding* principle, discussed above, emphasized that maintaining and developing interpersonal relationships involves one's attitude—thinking and wanting. Being convinced in one's thinking regarding the correctness of his view must be motivated and applied by Truth and for God's glory and the benefit of His people (14:5, 14).

Next, Paul follows with the *bearing-with* principle. To understand this particular teaching, we must have some idea of what he means by "weaknesses" and "to bear." First consider the word translated "weaknesses" (*asthenia*). It refers to both physical and moral weakness.

In Hebrews 4:15-16, the author wrote that Jesus is our great High Priest who sympathizes with our weakness (see 10:34 for a similar use). The word *sympathizes* in the original language indicates more that simply "feeling what the believer feels." The author did not mean that Jesus simply "feels."

More completely, the word emphasizes experience. Jesus experienced the full weight of the human condition yet without sin. He did not simply experience what you or I experience. Rather, He knew what it was to be tempted to please self; to blame God, others, or God's providence; and to *punch* out of life because of feelings and circumstances—to live the lie! He knew those facts to the depth of His soul. In a word, He knew what it was like to be tempted to follow satanic logic and prove untrustworthy by pleasing self.

Experience and not feelings is part of the key to properly understanding the Holy Spirit. Even more, it is Jesus' response in the circumstances that is the key. Jesus identified with the full misery and effects of the curse of sin. That is something the believer cannot do. The believer may never fully comprehend the fullness of the holiness of God, His love and mercy of God, and his own sinfulness. Jesus saw all that as if He was a sinner, but He was not.

The Winner was considered the loser. Jesus had to know misery in a way that no believer will. And He did as the Victor and perfect High Priest Who had the solution for the human condition. He did not live the lie! He lived by truth which set Him free. He lived out of his relationship with the Father.

In our verse, Paul used the term weakness to refer to the spiritual immaturity of the weak brother. Spiritual immaturity occurs because of the acceptance of false teaching or being poorly informed and trusting in it. However, the stronger brother was in danger of living the lie as well. Knowledge is never to puff up (1 Corinthians 8:1-3).

Next consider the word translated "to bear." It means "to take up and hold; to support, to raise up; or to carry."[26] In Matthew 8:17, Matthew, quoting Isaiah 53:4 wrote that Jesus bore—took hold of—our diseases. The passage occurs in the context of

---

26 *Bastazo* occurs more than 25 times in the New Testament: John 10:31 ("in the hands"); John 19:17 (the cross); and John 20:15 (Jesus' body); Luke 11:27 (womb); Luke 14:27 (one's own cross), Luke 22:10 (water); Galatians 6:2 and 5 (burden: sin and its consequence, and load: responsibility and service).

Jesus' signs, miracles, and wonders which demonstrated Jesus' power and authority over nature, demons, diseases, and death. Moreover, Jesus ushered in a new age and a new existence.

Jesus took the position of a sinner though sinless (2 Corinthians 5:21)! He understood what it meant to be sinner. But there is more! He bore or experienced the human condition as and so He could be the perfect High Priest and Sacrifice.

At its core, the human condition post-fall is summarized as one of self-pleasing. God-pleasing was non-existent until salvation. Jesus faced the human condition: the choice between pleasing Himself or God 24/7. He gained the victory by taking every thought and desire captive; godly action followed 24/7! Jesus had no *time-outs* or reprieves. He was not able to change the rules nor did he so desire!

In Matthew 20:12, the workers bore (experienced) the burden of a day's work. In Galatians 6, Paul called for those who are spiritual to bear one's another's burden so that person would be able to bear his own load and return to function (6:2, 5).

What is the import of these passages in terms of bearing with? What is it that is to be borne by the strong and the biblically-based spiritual-minded? The concept is expressed perfectly by Christ. He knew Himself and others. He knew truth.

OAN-bearing with helps the person focus on, and flows from, a proper understanding of fallen man and the believer; it focuses on what the other person is experiencing then; and it focuses on how he is responding and for what reasons. The goal is not simply gathering information; the goal is to help him respond in a God-honoring way.

Jesus, the Godman, experienced the fullness of the human condition yet without sin (2 Corinthians 5:18-21). He looked sin, misery, condemnation, and Hell square in the face—head on! He came as the second Adam and new Israel. He did not fail as the first Adam had done! He is the great OAN-er. Therefore, OAN is alive and well! Jesus understood what it meant to be under God's wrath and His enemy. In every situation, He understood God's call for godly living for Him and His people. He identified with the human condition; yet, He was without sin. He experienced the human condition and the temptation of covenantal unfaithfulness (Hebrew 4:14-16). Moreover, He understood the provisions that He had in the Holy Spirit and that He would secure as the perfect Messiah for His people. He understood that He and the Father would send another Counselor just like Him (John 14:16-17; 15:26-27; 16:13-15)!

Jesus was OAN-ed by the Holy Spirit securing OAN for the Church (Isaiah 11:1-5; Matthew 4:1; Luke 4:1)! His experience was magnified and counted as the believer's because the believer was His and He was the believer's. He was and is God, the sinless, perfect Lamb of God Sin-bearing Substitute (John 1:29, 36; Hebrews 4:15; 7:26; 9:24-29; 1 Peter 1:19; 1 John 3:5).

We return to Matthew 8:17. Matthew referred to Jesus as the One Who was healing people physically, but He was also the fulfillment of Isaiah 53:4. Isaiah pictured the cross with Jesus as the perfect, Substitute Sacrifice for sinners.

Matthew (8:17) understood that the miraculous was but temporary physical healings by Jesus which pointed to His deity; they had a sign and authenticating function. They pictured and pointed to His work of spiritual healing both temporally on earth and eternally. Isaiah understood them as pointing to an eternal and spiritual *healing* secured by Jesus' death. This *healing* would start on earth and be completed in heaven.

Jesus did not take on the physical disease of the ones He died for, nor did He always reverse the consequences in this life. Rather He was the compassionate One Who daily experienced the full misery of the curse of sin in the place of sinners. Again, He was faced with the choice of thinking, wanting, and acting as the true Messiah or a counterfeit one.

He understood the burden and weight of perfectly functioning as the covenantal faithful One. He had no leeway, no margin of error. It was all or none before the cross and on the cross! Perfection was the only standard that Jesus lived by and was measured by.

In this way, He was preparing the sheep for the eternal presence of God. Eternal life begins on this earth at salvation. Jesus looked inward at the heart of man and offered Himself as God's solution.

He stayed the course being OAN by the Holy Spirit and OAN others. The results were and are electrifying and supernatural.

Taken together, Matthew and Isaiah pictured God's perfect eternal reconciliation of Himself and with man that was developed by Christ before the Cross, secured on the Cross, and applied by the Holy Spirit. "Bearing-with" is solution-oriented. Jesus walked through life perfectly so that on the cross the Father considered Him the sinner. Likewise, the bearer aids his brother; the OAN-er helps a fellow believer in the process of reconciliation and restoration beginning with each other and moving to fellow believers.

Paul makes a similar point in Galatians 6:1-5. Paul pictures a fellow believer who is so caught up in sin—entangled in it and its consequences; he is unable to extricate himself for whatever reasons (and there may be several).

Paul calls for the use of the *bearing* principle as part of OAN (verse 2: *Carry each other's burdens, and in this way you will fulfill the law of Christ,*) refers to the individual's problems including consequences, and his response imitating Christ who is the Chief Bearer; and in verse 5 (. . . *for each one should carry his own load*), the reference is to the "entangled" brother who will stand before God and to the brother who will OAN him to restore him to functionality.

Bearing or carrying the burden of another is giving biblical aid; the purpose: in order for him to be restored to a functional position; the motive: for his sake and the sake of the body. It is a type of reconciliation. The brother is estranged at least from God and other believers because of his sinful activity. He is not functioning in the body as he should.

The meaning of the word "to restore" in verse 1 (*Brothers, if someone is caught in a sin, you who are spiritual should restore him gently . . .*) is to so mend the fishing net so that the person can be useful again. By a return of function, he will be able to fulfill his own responsibilities at home and at church including OAN. The teaching fits nicely with 1 John 4:7-12. The one loved by God loves so that love and glory returns back to God! This is the true circle of life!

We return to Romans 15:1. There Paul wrote that *bearing-with* is an obligation for the stronger brother to the weaker and in Galatians 6 it is the obligation of the spiritual-minded to act as God's instrument of change. This follows Christ's pattern! In each case *bearing* is part of OAN.

In all cases of *bearing-with*, the opposite is pleasing self. Claiming one's own rights and having *I deserve* mindset is self-service rather than concern for God's character, His name, and one's neighbor.

If the weaker brother is involved in a sin from which he cannot or does not know how to extract himself, then Galatians 6:1-5 applies. Otherwise, Romans 14:23 and 15:1 apply. These verses strike at the heart of self-centeredness which is an enemy of God's Church and eliminates all OAN.

IX. Pleasing God and Others

Romans 15:2-3: *Each of us should please his neighbor for his good, to build him up. For even Christ did not please himself, but as it is written: "The insults of those who insult you have fallen on me."*

In verses 1-3, Paul returned to his teaching found in 14:7-9. These verses set forth a choice between self-pleasing and pleasing God and they answer the question: Who do you want to please? Pleasing God promotes a biblical concern for neighbor by imitating Christ (John 4:31-34; 5:19-20, 30; 15:12). These verses call for the practical application of the second great commandment of Matthew 22:37-40.

Weaker brothers and sisters can be aggravating. So can strong ones! It is easy to criticize (14:1) and make fun of—deride—them (14:3). Yet Jesus welcomed, accepted, and loved every believer even when each one opposed Him (Romans 5:6-10). Paul motivated his readers by calling them to bear with others because Christ did the same to them. The action that flows from the truth depends on what the person thinks about Christ work for him.

X. OAN: Hope and Unity

Romans 15:4-6: *For everything that was written in the past was written to teach us, so that through endurance and the encouragement of the Scriptures, we might have hope. May the God who gives endurance and encouragement give you a spirit of unity among yourselves as you follow Christ Jesus, so that with one heart and mouth, you may glorify the God and Father of our Lord Jesus Christ.*

Paul closed the section on OAN by giving additional reasons for encouragement and the motivation to get along. In verse 4, he set forth a core and ultimate purpose of Scripture which is to give hope in all ages. Biblical truth is buttressed by saving faith and true hope and is applicable for all ages!

Biblical hope is the confident anticipation that what God has promised is an unfolding reality (Romans 8:24-25: see my Book: *Out of the Maze: A Covenantal View of Hope*). Salvation is a foretaste of heaven. Scripture points believers heavenward to the God of hope while keeping their feet firmly planted on earth. He gave hope by sending His Son, by pouring out the Holy Spirit into the hearts of His people, and by preserving His Word (1 John 3:1-3).

In verse 5, Paul wrote that God is the source of encouragement and endurance, both of which are needed for growth in Christlikeness and the practice of OAN. Hope, encouragement, and endurance are gifts and graces that result from and in the peace of God which transcends all human comprehension—it is *mind-boggling* (Philippians 4:7).

Jesus gives peace because He is our peace (John 16:33; Ephesians 2:14-15). Peace means that relational coolness and hostility are much less or non-existent. Relationships are restored. God is honored. Life is simplified. It is this peace that produces unity of thinking and oneness of the body in part because contending for self is not a primary goal.

Having the mind of Christ fosters OAN and unity. In verse 6, he restates one purpose of OAN: to glorify God by bringing order and unity among believers. Is that your desire? Or is your desire to be right defined your way? It is time for you to reflect on God's truth! There is no time like a pandemic and a nation and Church in disarray!

CHAPTER 7
Family Affection

THERE ARE SEVERAL PASSAGES THAT focus on the principle of *intimate family life* within Christ's Church. They share a common word in the original from which the English word "Philadelphia" comes. These passages include Romans 12:10; 1 Thessalonians 4:9; Hebrews 13:1; 1 Peter 1:22; 3:8; 2 Peter 1:7.

The word means "one who loves his brother," or "brotherly love," or "family affection." Within God's family, God expects warmth, closeness, and affection, all characteristics of God's love of His children and OAN love. This concept is countercultural and even counterintuitive. Consider the following passages:

I. Romans 12:10: *Be devoted to one another in brotherly love. Honor one another above yourselves* (also addressed in the section: The Mind of Christ)

Life in the Father's house is not without trouble. Sinners and sin abounds! Some of the trouble comes from without while others are homegrown. Paul realizes that people can become cold in their relationships with others.

Believers may relate to each other with coolness and even coldness. They may relate to all in the body or only part of the body as strangers. For whatever reason, they have broken off relationships or they take part in relationships only casually. The silent or avoidance method of "getting along" may be the order of the day.

Paul calls for warmth and closeness between family members. This is a command, as is all OAN-activity; it is not a suggestion. OAN love searches out others and helps light the fire of affectionate thoughts, desires, and actions toward others. One specific application of this principle is laboring together. Believers who do mutual work with a common goal of pleasing God often discover wonderful God-honoring results.

Devoted to and *preferring another* means deferring from self that which may be due another or can be given to him. Holding up another by giving credit where credit is due fosters OAN and is a product of OAN.

II. 1 Thessalonians 4:9-10: *Now about brotherly love we do not need to write to you, for you yourselves have been taught by God to love each other. And in fact, you do love all the brothers throughout Macedonia. Yet we urge you, brothers, to do so more and more.*

Love is taught and learned in order to be demonstrated (Matthew 7:21-27; James 1:22, 27). Love without loving would be a misnomer! Apparently, this fledgling congregation was engaged in OAN. However, in verse 10, Paul teaches that OAN must be developed more and more (1 Thessalonians 4:1 teaches the same truth in terms of progressive sanctification). All congregations, especially new ones, need to be steeped in OAN.

Believers are to be growing in Christlikeness! This is partially accomplished by loving and being loved! No congregation can get enough OAN! Moreover, since there is only one true teacher—the Triune God—a believer's love must imitate God's love. In that way, an atmosphere of care and concern soon develops and grows.

III. Hebrews 13:1: *Keep on loving each other as brothers* (Also addressed in Chapter 4: Submission).

The author opens the final chapter with a call for OAN. There was confusion and division within the church. Persecution was there or soon to be. Interpersonal relationships had turned inward, and people were moving away from Christianity and previous brothers and sisters in Christ. Since OAN is affection and concern in action, it is one of God's antidotes for chaos, confusion, and strife. Therefore, the pastor sent out the call to the congregation to be lovingly concerned and affectionate toward one another. Brotherly love must be maintained and matured!

IV. 1 Peter 1:22: *Now that you have purified yourselves by obeying the truth so that you have sincere love for your brothers, love one another deeply from the heart.*

Peter is speaking in family terms. Times were tough for his congregation. Nero was on the warpath, and it was not safe to be a Christian. But Peter envisions a loving brotherhood not based on externals. Believers were loved into the Kingdom and in the Kingdom they were changed into lovers of God and others.

The relationship between brothers and sisters is to be as deep and wide as is God's love (Ephesians 3:17-21). Therefore, Peter changed the word translated love from *philadalphia* to *agapao*. This change may indicate that OAN love is a deepening, loving concern for each other. The emphasis of Peter's statement falls on the verb: *love one another deeply, from the heart.*

Peter did not want his congregation simply to tolerate one another but to love frequently, fervently, and intensely—wholeheartedly. This type of affection for fellow Christians extends itself and reaches out. Believers can be loved and must be loved by other Christians even when it seems impossible. That action is not hypocrisy. It anticipates heaven as life is visualized through the grid of Christ's love for each believer!

Peter called for increasing intimacy within God's family. This intimacy is demonstrated by OAN love. It is a genuine love from the heart. How is this possible and what would it look like? Saved people have been changed by God's grace so they are no longer at their core self-pleasers but God-pleasers. Pleasing God is accomplished by OAN love.[27] A proper motivation for OAN

---

27 The phrase obedience to the truth was also used by Paul to mean the obedience which results from following the command to believe and acting on it (Acts 17:30). Peter spoke of purifying or cleansing one's heart by faith (Acts 15:9). He used the term cleansing to indicate that one's salvation is a result of the Spirit's inside radical work. In the passage before us, Peter likewise refers to regeneration by the term cleansing and then focuses on life after salvation—he is speaking of responding to the gospel. There is the daily living of becoming more like Christ that follows because of the believer's inward change.

flows from the truth that Christ died for His enemies. I have made this point several times. It is so easy to ignore.

Peter had rejoiced over the cleansing of the heart and saving faith that occurred in the lives of some of the Gentiles (Acts 15:9: footnote 27). In his letter, he may have remembered this fact. Now, he says to his predominately Jewish congregation that it is possible to love one another more genuinely and sincerely than they were doing.

He encourages them to think differently about the usual motive of loving—to get what I can get. This motivation is not God-honoring and is not biblical love. Rather, he calls his people to a genuine wholehearted and intensive love—from the heart, because "I have been loved by God."

He knew that OAN would sustain his congregation during tough times. Imagine what it will do in a pandemic! Imagine what it will do in easier times! He gives general principles in his letter. I am sure he was there to give concrete examples of OAN. His letter is one example!

V. 1 Peter 3:8: *Finally, all of you, live in harmony with one another; be sympathetic, love as brothers, be compassionate and humble.*

This verse, as did Paul in Ephesians 4:31-32 and Colossians 3:12, sets out a general principle of conduct for believers interacting with other believers. In addition, Paul wrote a similar prescription in Romans 12:14-21 that directed believers toward unbelievers, but the principles are applicable to believers. In its context, this verse was especially important because of the constant threat of persecution.

Peter indicates it is not always easy sailing within the household of God. People sin and are being sinned against, in a myriad of commissions against God's Word and omissions of failing to apply and obey God's Word. Peter wanted his people to be on guard and hold firm to each other by holding firm to the Word of truth.

Specifically, this verse (and the others mentioned) sets forth the principle that OAN involves blessing (*eulogeo*) one another. God's people were called to bless one another; it was beneficial not only for the whole body but each one individually. Blessing another literally means "to speak well of." To bless another is to say good to them and about them. This contrasts the behavior described in James 4:11-12; Galatians 5:15; Romans 14:13; and Titus 3:3.

Peter calls the people to live in harmony with one another; one way to do this is by speaking well of them thereby doing good to one another (1 Thessalonians 5:11, 15). Peter is not teaching manipulation, lying or flattery but harmonious family living. Blessing is not agreeing to disagree nor is it making up empty words to make one "feel" good.

Rather, it is resting on the fact that the mind of Christ is a gift from God by which the believer has changed thinking and wanting. Therefore, seeking to speak well of another will be on one's agenda to promote changing and growing in himself, the other person, and the body of Christ. Communication is a gift from God who communicates with His people. Words are to be used for edifying and building up (Proverbs 12:18; 15:4; Ephesians 4:15-16, 25, 31; Colossians 3:8; 4:6; 1 Thessalonians 5:11).

An antonym for *eulogeo* is cursing another. If one is not blessing, he is cursing—speaking ill of someone even if the person speaks only to himself! If a person is not returning good he is returning evil (Romans 12:17-21; 1 John 3:16-18). Cursing may only involve *self-talk* so that no one hears except God. No matter because the heart activity is an expression of a bitter spirit which tears down (Romans 12:17-21; Hebrews 12:14; 1 John 3:13-16). God is not honored, and the body—both the physical body and the Church is damaged

Rather God spoke well of His Son—"this is My beloved Son Who I am well pleased." So, too, are believers to follow God's example and conduct family life by using words that build up each other. Blessing another is true OAN especially when the other person makes it hard to do so.

VI. 2 Peter 1:7: *and to godliness, brotherly kindness, and to brotherly kindness, love.*

False teachers were coming, and Peter was preparing his congregation. In verse 5, Peter calls his people to *add* to their faith (*For this very reason, make every effort to add to your faith goodness; and to goodness, knowledge;*). The word translated *add* is compound word and is used only here in the New Testament. It carries the idea of bringing in.

In this way, the people would contribute to the growth of their faith by adding fruits including fruits of the Spirit (Galatians 5:22-23). He continues his exhortation through a series of appeals (verses 6-8: *. . . .and to knowledge, self-control; and to self-control, perseverance; and to perseverance, godliness; and to godliness, brotherly kindness; and to brotherly kindness, love. For if you possess these qualities in increasing measure, they will keep you from being ineffective and unproductive in your knowledge of our Lord Jesus Christ.*).

Peter knew firsthand saving faith and true hope are foundational pillars for individual growth in Christ. Both are necessary for strengthening of the body. Peter knew *godliness through addition* prevents ineffectiveness, unfruitfulness, and unfaithfulness and is synonymous with growth in Christ. In verse 9, he characterized the person who does not have them as *nearsighted and blind and has forgotten that he has been cleansed from his past sins.*

In verse 5, Peter begins to catalogue a string of virtues which were designed for growth in Christ. This addition begins with goodness and knowledge and ends with love. In between, Peter stresses family living, commitment, and affection.

Peter is calling for what Paul called for in Galatians 5:6: *. . . faith working through love.* Saving faith is exercised and expressed or it is not saving faith. It is the root and OAN love is its fruit. Salvation and life after salvation are linked. When this occurs, it is a testimony of the Holy Spirit's work and leads to assurance of one's salvation.

CHAPTER 8

Encouragement, Comfort, and OAN

ENCOURAGEMENT AND COMFORT ARE BIBLICAL terms that are misused by the culture. The cultural mindset envisions encouragement as helping a person feel better about himself irrespective of circumstances and the person's role in problems. You see this emphasis in times such as a pandemic. God is not in the picture or if He is, He is only a babysitter or He is someone only to make you feel better.

I. Cultural Encouragement: A Misnomer

The culture reasons that since a person "is his feelings," circumstances and other people determine how he feels. In essence, the person is considered a victim to chance or things or the *stars*. Actually, the world and culture are speaking of God's providence—His control. But since to the world, God is non-existent, not in the picture, or impotent, it really does not matter!

Moreover, the culture thinks feelings are the "inner-self" and "getting in touch with them" and changing them is the key to a victorious life. Therefore, every person is a product, even a victim, of what is going on around him; but he is told to get in touch with his feelings, something inside of him, or something outside. *Just do it*. When the person—the victim—is down and feels bad, the answer is to help him feel better about himself.

The culture, and unfortunately the Church is following in its footsteps, has attempted to produce good feelings in any number of ways. Sometimes it is by using God through going to church, changing church, giving, reading the Bible, and or praying; sometimes it is through the use drugs and or medications even championed by church leaders. At other times, there is an attempt to make a person think differently about himself (mindfulness therapy, cognitive behavioral behavior to mention a few).

The Bible emphasizes changed thinking and wanting about self, others, and God. But the culture ignores, rejects, or denies biblical truth by using self-help books and groups, or a one-on-one meeting with a friend or a professional counselor. The Church can fall prey and misuse biblical principles. Living the lie is rampant and will be until Christ returns.

These approaches appeal to people because relief in some form is a major goal in our society. Victimhood and non-responsibility are touted as major culprits. The *greater good* is relief. It is the goal, and the person is directed outside of himself for "inside relief." Pleasing God is not considered or God is used for relief.

These approaches are superficial and lead only to temporary relief at best, because man is more than feelings. Feelings, thoughts, and desires are linked. Rather, man lives out of his heart and godly change requires God's grace.[28]

By God's design, changed thinking and wanting lead to changed feelings. So-called mindfulness therapies can change the way a person thinks which often leads to better feelings. God's design of man is ignored and or denied. Relief is not the issue. The issue is living out one's relationship with Christ. A change in thinking and wanting begins with the person's view of and response to God and then of the other person. The two are linked. This requires the supernatural work of the Holy Spirit. Relationships matter.

According to Webster's dictionary, to encourage means "to hearten," and "to give courage, spirit, and hope" thereby

---

28 The heart is that part of the inner man known only to God perfectly, to oneself imperfectly, and little or not at all by others. A person thinks, doubts, fears, hopes, expects, plans, and trusts in the heart. He acts in his heart—inner man. That action would be known only to him and God. Man is a duplex being: a spiritual and physical or material being. He has an inner man, and he has a body and acts in both. But he is whole person, body and soul or heart. Moreover, everyone lives out of their heart. As such, everyone lives out of an identity (who he thinks he is) and sets an agenda for himself based on his identity. A person will pursue what he thinks he needs and wants. It is in the heart that his functional motivational or want system and his functional belief system are located. Somehow the heart and the brain (there is no word for brain in the Bible—it is part of the body) are connected; but there is no neural or neurochemical connection. What a person wants and thinks affects his actions and his feelings in both the inner and outer man. Encouragement and discouragement are heart matters appealing to truth or untruth and one's desire to be a God-pleaser or self-pleaser. They are displayed in the inner and in the outer man in varying degrees.

strengthening by giving help or aid. Comfort is usually considered as encouragement given during trouble; it means "to give hope and strength," "to cheer up," and "to ease the grief of the person." Webster's definitions imply giving a person something that he lacks by targeting his inner self which the Bible calls this the heart. Webster is trying to capture a biblical truth.

II. The Biblical View of Encouragement

The Bible translates encouragement and to encourage generally using *paraklesis/parakaleo* which mean "to call alongside of." The biblical concept of "coming alongside of" runs counter to the culture's view of encouragement.

The words (*paraklesis/parakaleo*) are translated in a variety of ways: "to strengthen and establish, to assist, to aid, to help, to comfort, to encourage." The words can also indicate an exhortation which is translated as "to beseech, call on, summons, exhort, or invite." The ideas expressed in these words are alluded to in Webster's definition.

In contrast to the culture, the goal of biblical encouragement is to help the person become more like Christ within the context of God's providence—the circumstances and people around him. The encourager has both a short-term and long-term perspective of life. Therefore, he helps the person live now by persevering and enduring to the end using trouble to do so. That is Christ's and the Holy Spirit's way (Hebrews 12:1-3; see my book, *Endurance: What It is and How It Looks in a Believer's Life*)!

In addition, OAN encouragement builds on the fact of a changed family membership. The believer has God as his Father, Christ as his Brother, and fellow Christians as his brothers and sisters. OAN encouragement is simply one family member helping the other. One's view of this family membership influences his giving and receiving encouragement.

An encourager is a brother or sister who ministers biblical truth in an appropriate manner with the proper motivation and goal. His purpose is assisting in whatever way needed in order to establish a person firm and strong so that he doesn't give up or give in to feelings. Christlikeness is a key for both giving and receiving encouragement.

In Romans 15:4-5, 13-14, contrary to the culture's emphasis, Paul makes clear the source and purpose of encouragement: *For everything that was written in the past was written to teach us, so that through endurance and the encouragement of the Scriptures we might have hope.* And: *May the God of hope fill you with all joy and peace as you trust in him, so that you may overflow with hope by the power of the Holy Spirit. I myself am convinced, my brothers, that you yourselves are full of goodness, complete with knowledge, and competent to instruct one another.*

God is the God of encouragement and the basis for the believer's encouragement is his relationship with God in Christ.[29] Since God the Holy Spirit is the Bible's author and the Triune God is the God of hope, all of Scripture was written to give hope.

True hope is intended to encourage and to comfort for the purpose of strengthening and firmly establishing God's children in His ways in order that they may endure to the end (2 Corinthians 1:3-4). It does so by instructing God's people in who God is and in what His will is (verse 4; 1 Thessalonians 4:18). The believer is encouraged and comforted as he receives and applies biblical truth through OAN.

---

29 Believers are united to and are in relationship with Christ and He with them. Once saved, the relationship can never be broken; it will impact and influence the believer's thinking, wanting, and doing daily. Moreover, God relates differently to the believer and the believer differently to God. God is now his Father and Jesus his brother. The Christian has a new family and receives manifold blessings all of which are encouragements. Consider:
1. Romans 3:24: The believer is justified (declared not guilty) but only in Christ. God reckons/counts him as having lived a sinless, righteous life only because of Christ did and counted it as the believer's.
2. Romans 8:1: There is no condemnation or guilt in Christ. God holds nothing against the believer.
3. Ephesians 1:3-6: In Him, believers have been blessed with every spiritual blessing, chosen in eternity past, adopted, and gifted.
4. Romans 8:2: In Him, the Christian is made free from personal lawkeeping for salvation.
5. Colossians 1:2: In Him, believers are saints and faithful brothers.
6. 2 Corinthians 2:14: In Him, the Christian has triumphed (Romans 8:35-37; 1 Corinthians 1:1 John 5:4).
7. 1 Timothy 3:13; 2 Corinthians 3:12; Philemon 8: Believers have hope and boldness only in Him.
8. Jude 1: Believers are preserved in Christ.
9. Ephesians 1:12-14: The Christian possesses the Holy Spirit and is sealed with hope and promise.

As a result, the believer can change his view of himself and what he should do to provide for others. He recognizes his own insufficiency and lack of resources, and he relies on grace to understand and apply biblical principles in the sufficient Word of God for his own growth and the growth of others.

In place of helplessness and hopelessness, the believer brings hope and encouragement and the promise of endurance so that he and fellow Christians will respond to God's providence God's way. Webster's definition of encouragement, which places an emphasis on giving something that a person lacks, more closely comports with the Bible's definition of encouragement than the culture will admit.

Deepening and necessary knowledge of God's trustworthiness and covenantal faithfulness are facilitated by the biblical encouragement of fellow Christians. They bring God's truth to bear on the problem and all persons involved. As a result of OAN encouragement, God's children learn to place their trust in and act on God's presence, promises, power, purpose, plan, and provisions especially in hard times.

In this way, the inner man is strengthened in thoughts and desires (feelings are not strengthened; they are linked to thoughts and desires). This produces encouragement and endurance both of which lead to true hope (verse 4). Hope, encouragement, and endurance are linked and are out workings of the mind of Christ. The trio promote and maintains the unity of the body (verse 5 and Romans 5:1-5).

III. Encouragement: A Necessary Ingredient for Victory

Four ingredients—hope, encouragement, endurance, and oneness of mind—are foundational and essential for church life and foster all types of OAN including counseling (Romans 15:13-14; see footnote 41). At the same time, encouragement is part of OAN which holds together true hope, sound oneness of mind, and the unity of the body.

At some point, every believer experiences conflict in terms of his thinking, wanting, and motivation for acting. Pleasing God or self is a constant choice until Christ returns. It was for Christ, and it is for the believer. The war within the heart of man can be described as a moral drama in which a person decides for self or for God daily, even 24/7. Often there is angst and turmoil within (John 14:1-3; Romans 8:14; Galatians 5:16-18). Unlike the culture's teaching, the core issue of life is not one's feelings. It is a worship and service issue.

Fundamentally, the issue is the issue of the heart from which flows thoughts, desires, and actions. The Bible tells believers to guard their heart, it is the well-spring of life (Proverbs 4:23). The core question for every person is this: despite your feelings, who will you serve: self or God (Joshua 24:14-15)? Jesus faced this question every moment of every day while on earth. He proved covenantally faithful. That fact is and should be an encouragement for every believer and the Church.

And as previous members of Satan's family and his disciples, believers developed habits of self-worship which are manifested as self-reliance, self-sufficiency, and self-righteousness. The Bible speaks of this foolishness as "wise in one's own eyes" and "trusting in self."[30] It is idolatry. It is living the lie and losing but usually denying it!

Saved people retain the inclination and orientation of and for "self-reliance for my benefit and glory." Therefore, the desire to feel good and have life *easy* (uncomplicated) can become seemingly overpowering motivations of even those saved.

The *pleasure principle* was established in the Garden: obey God and live; disobey and die (Genesis 2:15-17). Jesus had the perfect view of the pleasure principle: please the Father. After the fall, the *pleasure principle* was still operative in mankind (see page 243). However, it was and is distorted. The pleasure was for self, by self, to self, which resulted in a false and complicated life. It came by pleasing self, using others and even God for that purpose. There was no desire or effort to honor God (Proverbs 5:21-22; 13:15b; 26:11).

Old habits of thinking and wanting persist. When times are tough and no change in circumstances or in people is in sight, the

---

30 See Proverbs 3:5-8; 26:5, 12, 16; 28:11, 26; 29:25.

believer's tendency is to view his resources as insufficient, people "too big," and God "too small." The believer is living the lie!

Rather we have a BIG God. By *big* I am not referring to size or quantity. The idea of God's *bigness* rests in His essential Being—His necessity, His aseity—His self-existence and self-dependence, and His incomprehensibleness (1 Kings 8:27; Psalm 94:8-11; 139:7-12; 145:3; 147:4-6; Isaiah 40:15ff; 55:8-9)! He made the heavens and the earth, and He fills them with His presence. He is everywhere and everywhere He is all of God is there! He is not like silly putty stretched thin! He is Lord of lords and King of kings.

Even among believers, problems, circumstances, and people are viewed as larger than God even though believers know or at least say this is God's world. God does control and sustain all His creatures in His world, but people—even believers—expect to be treated better than the Father treated the Son (Matthew 14:22-36; Acts 17:24-28; 1 Samuel 17; Deuteronomy 1:26-46; 31:8; Joshua 1:6-9).

Make no mistake: the issue is not bad feelings, people, or circumstances. These may well be realities—facts. But these facts must be rightly interpreted. Moreover, God and man must be rightly interpreted. The issue is one's interpretive grid and standard through which the person filters and views life's circumstances and draws conclusions.

Moreover, life has no life of its own! Mother Nature, evolution, and chance are offered as explanations for happenings. How absurd and illogical! Life is God's providence—His control—

being played out. Man's battle is predominantly a moral one and is summarized as a worship-allegiance-service heart issue: who will you serve and worship (Joshua 24:14-15; 1 John 5:21).

In response to God and His hard providence, various feelings occur. These include being down, losing heart, being fainthearted, being terrified and fearful, and being skeptical, confused, or doubtful. Bad feelings as are certain thoughts and certain desires are part of the curse of sin and God's curse on mankind.

However, feelings don't just appear. Neither do thoughts and desires. Responses don't just appear. All have an origin. As I have said, feelings flow from thoughts and desires that a person brings to every circumstance. Those thoughts and desires were initially for self and against God until the person was saved. Now he can think and desire God's way for His glory!

But patterned satanic thinking, wanting, and doing still reside in the believer. That pattern changes as he recognizes and acknowledges that feelings are linked to thoughts and desires that reside in both the heart and the body-brain. Change thoughts and desires lead to change actions. Love of self is replaced by love of God and others.

IV. Hope or its Lack: Encouragement and Discouragement

While encouragement means "to hearten" someone for the purpose of their endurance and perseverance—growth in Christ, its antonym is discouragement which means "to dishearten." Discouragement carries the idea of little or no true hope, sinful fear, and even cowardice and may result in self-pity, fretting, and eventually giving in and giving up as presented in Psalm 37 and 73.

Asaph, the author of Psalm 73, acknowledged that he lived the lie until verses 16-17. He was living the lie (verses 3-11) which he thought he would never do (verses 12-15). Asaph rightly pictured the arrogant and wicked (verses 2-3, 5-9, 11). Yet he envied them thinking they had the *good* life (verses 4-5). He wondered if he had made a mistake being a believer (verse 14). He was living the lie.

But God brought him to his senses, and he came to his senses (verses 16-17). He began to perceive himself, the circumstances and others through God's eyes. God's Word and power became a reality, and he began to couple them with God's presence among His people—Immanuel. Inner-man turmoil and bad feelings were the result of wrong thinking and wanting. He made a radical change as explained in verses 21-22). He had been animal-like! He voiced the presence of God and His eternal security (verses 24-25).

David the author of Psalm 37 gives a formula for encouragement. In verse 1, he writes not to fret or be discouraged because of evil men—it is part of God's providence. His antidote which is applicable to times of pandemics and cultural disarray: *trust in the Lord and do good* (verse 3). And in verse 7: *Be still before the Lord and wait patiently for him; do not fret* ... (Psalm 46:10: *Be still and know that I am God; I will be exalted among the nations; I will be exalted in the earth*). David encouraged himself with truth about God and self. This led to proper conclusions about the circumstances and his presence in them.

Several other Old Testaments passages highlight the facts that encouragement recognizes that a person fails to demonstrate or lacks something and seeks to rectify the lack; the term discouragement acknowledges the lack.

For instance, as the children of Israel were about to enter the Promise Land, God gave them the specific command not to be discouraged which was their pattern when faced with uncertainty (Deuteronomy 1:21-32; 31:6-8).

God gave the same command to Joshua, David, Solomon, and Jehoshaphat (Joshua 1:6-9; 8:1; 10:25; 1 Chronicles 22:13; 28:30; 2 Chronicles 20:15, 17). The Hebrew word translated as discouraged is *hatat* which means "to be broken." If someone is broken, he lacks something. The word also carries the idea of lack of courage (the opposite of strong-hearted) often linked to ungodly fear.

When God commanded the people not to be discouraged, He was using His presence and His words to strengthen the inner man. The people were to take heart in God Himself—His goodness and power. Being satisfied that God was God, they were to enjoy and trust their God. They were to make a willful, active, and cognitive choice to trust God rather than themselves. Too often, people blame feelings, and live the lie.

Next consider what David thought, desired, and did as recorded in 1 Samuel 30:6 (*David was greatly distressed because the men were talking of stoning him; each one was bitter in spirit because of his sons and daughters. But David found strength in the Lord his God.*). In the face of the Amalekites' revenge, David returned to find the camp had been destroyed by fire and families had been captured (verse 3).

David's men threatened to murder David. In response, David's expressed godly grief by focusing on God's faithfulness and his relationship with Him. He sought the Lord's will and he acted in saving faith and true hope. God granted him victory. He did not live the lie although it would have been easy to give in to feelings.

Similarly, Numbers 32:7-9 emphasize the fact that the word *encourage* means to give a person what is lacking and *discourage* means to lack inner strength. Moses is speaking to the Transjordan Tribes in Numbers 32. In verse 7, he asked the Gadites and Reubenites why they would discourage the Israelites by not going to war with the rest of Israel since God had given the Promised Land to all of Israel.

In verse 9, he reiterated how, on their return, ten of the spies discouraged the Israelites from entering the Promise Land; they failed to acknowledge God the Giver, His gift, and evidence of His covenantal faithfulness (Genesis 12:3-7).

Make no mistake. The words of the spies did not discourage the people. The people's interpretative standard was self, feelings, and selective vision and hearing—what they saw and heard with their physical eyes and ears. They responded to the words of the spies as they done throughout the wilderness journey: patterned disbelief and distrust thinking the worst of God. They were habitual grumblers.

In each case God's honor was at stake. The word for discouraged in those two verses is a phrase that includes *leb*, meaning heart, and *nu*, that is used only nine times, and means "to forbid or disallow." Moses was concerned that the two tribes were basing their actions on the report of the spies. Literally, he asked the two tribes why they would "forbid Israel's heart" from trusting God. In the end, the two tribes assured Moses that they were not shirking their responsibility of conquering the land (32:17).

Why did the report of the spies produce a lack in Israel's heart (Numbers 13:27-29; 14:1-4)? The words of the spies were only the context and not the cause of Israel's response. The Israelites had a divided heart; when listening to the spies' report, they expressed their distrust of God. Self took center stage, and God and His agents were easy to blame. So, it is in every age. When we will ever learn!

These Old Testament passages help us to understand the importance of encouragement and OAN as one of God's means to strengthen the inner man by supplying that which is lacking in the believer. God does not desire His people to live the discouraged life.

To that end, God has supplied the believer with everything he needs for life and godliness—Himself (1 Corinthians 10:13; 2 Peter 1:3-4). In addition, He has provided for His Church and individual believers. Encouragement of one believer by another believer enables the proper use and appreciation of God's provisions.

Further the above passages help to emphasize that people and circumstances can be burdensome which is true. Yet it is not the circumstance that is the key. It is the believer's response to it and to God. Tough situations are times in which believers are tempted to live the lie. Even with believers, it easy to become discouraged which is evidence of "weak heart."

However, many people will point out that discouragement is not necessarily sinful. But we must be careful. We can get caught up in definitions in an effort to avoid facing our own sinfulness. Discouragement is more than a feeling. It originates in thoughts and desires in the context of the person's interpretation of his situation and his God.

The feeling that people label discouragement is most often evidence of a "weak" heart and faith. But it does not need to lead to grumbling and complaining, thanklessness, joylessness, helplessness, hopelessness, immobility, and depression.

Again, we must be very careful of the *slippery slope* mentality, which asks, "How much discouragement can I have before I am sinning?" Depression and other members of a list of terms (disappointment, discouragement, discontentment, despair, and depression) are the result of wrong thinking and wanting that leads to the use of—and reliance upon—bad feelings as the reason for immobility and the lack of fulfilling of personal responsibility.

All of these terms indicate dissatisfaction with God and His providence. This is a manifestation of living the lie. They all must be repented of and replaced by changed thinking and wanting. Depression is best defined as giving up on God and responsibilities because one gives in and follows his feelings. Even a believer can get down, but he is never out (see Paul in 2 Corinthians 1:8-10; 4:8-10).

"To encourage" means to strengthen the inner man (one's heart). Since the inner man is the domain of the Holy Spirit's indwelling and activity, strengthening of the heart can be done only as the believer uses His sword—God's Word—which is applied by His grace.[31] Proper knowledge and proper use of the knowledge is a must for biblical OAN.

Return to David in 1 Samuel 30:6 for a description of *coming to your senses* the correct way (also see Luke 15:17-18). After receiving devastating news, David shed tears, heard criticism, and received abuse from his men; but then he strengthened or encouraged himself in the Lord and set out to obey.[32] David

---

[31] The Old Testament words *chazaq*, *ames*, and *azaz* further capture the emphasis of strengthening and the source of that strength (1 Samuel 23:16; 30:6; Deuteronomy 3:28).

[32] The words in question may be translated as "encouragement" or "to encourage," "strong, strength, strengthen, and prevail," and even "hard" or "obstinate" such as used in the book of *Exodus* for the hardening of Pharaoh's heart and in Deuteronomy 2:30 for the king of Sihon.

could have *buried* himself in discouragement and wallowed in self-pity. He could have lived the lie.

He did not! His thoughts and desires were in sync with biblical truth and actions followed. He looked to his God who is the God of circumstances. He encouraged himself in the Lord by seeking His will. And he was blessed in the doing (John 13:17; James 1:25; Luke 11:28).

V. The New Testament passages, Encouragement, and Comfort

In the New Testament, encouragement is often associated with strengthening as in 1 Thessalonians 3:2 and 2 Thessalonians 2:16-17 and Acts 14:22; 15:23.[33] The biblical concept of encouragement is to bring strength and support to a brother or sister for the purpose of enduring God's way. Comfort is that specific encouragement that is given when there is present or potential danger and trouble.

In Philippians 4:13, Paul wrote that he could do all things because it is Christ Who gives him inner strength through the indwelling Spirit by the application of biblical truth.[34] By *all things* Paul meant honoring and pleasing God when it seemed—*felt*—impossible. Paul would not live the lie. He had done that!

---

33 The word translated as support or strength is *sterizo*. In Acts 14:22; 15:23, the word translated as strengthening is *episterizo* which means "to place firmly on or support."

34 The word translated "strengthens" is *endunamoo* which means to make strong. Its root is *dunamis* which means power. The English words dynamite, and dynamo are derived from it.

He knew who he was and who His God was! One means of God's inner strengthening is a brother-to-brother ministry of encouragement through OAN.

Everyone needs encouragement. But only believers have it, and only they can give and receive God's encouragement from others. You may ask, "On what basis is this true?". All believers in varying degrees and at different times are tempted to function as they did when they were unbelievers. The temptation is most noticeable during tough times or what I call *I don't like* situations. Again, we have to be careful with definitions.

Joseph and Paul help us with our definitions and making sense of them God's way: Genesis 50:19-21 and Romans 8:28-29. Often godly gain only comes with and in pain. Perhaps a more accurate term is affliction or trouble in lieu of suffering. Such was the case with Job (see Job 40:2-5; 42:5-6). Such is the case with Jesus and the cross. But there is no comparison between what Jesus experienced and what the believer or unbeliever experience.

Some situations are simply hard. You could list a myriad of ones. Yet biblical truth applies in any and every situation. The cross proves it, the resurrection affirms, and the Holy Spirit seals it (Romans 5:5; Ephesians 1:14; 2 Corinthians 1:20-22).

Sometimes a person can think all of life is hard! He may be correct but help him determine his standard for arriving at such a conclusion. In any circumstance, the believer can doubt and practice functional unbelief.

As a result, or even preceding the situation, he will, or has denied, deny the presence, power, promises, purpose, plan, and provisions of God in thought and action. He lives the lie and denies that he is! Such is the remaining habituation and sinfulness for the believer's life when an unbeliever.

Most believers will acknowledge God's presence in tough times—although there is a tendency to consider God far away and distant. It feels that way but for the believer the feeling focuses on the lie. Sometimes God's presence is a burden (Genesis 4:7; Psalms 32 and 38; Proverbs 28:1; Job 23:2, 8-9; 33:7). It is easier to acknowledge His power by using the term *allowing* the problem rather than ordaining it. Either way, the person does not appreciate God's purpose, intent, and motive.

When it comes to God's goodness which includes His intent and motive in ordaining (*allowing* it is too weak!) the situation, the believer often resists acting on the fact that God is a good God and Father, and that His goodness is being demonstrated in and through the present situation. He is in danger of living the lie.

Moreover, the one in trouble often has greater difficulty in acknowledging God's faithfulness (*Is God really for me? Can God be trusted to help me now?*). God's goodness focuses on His provisions for the believer to respond as a victor rather than a victim. When a person is engulfed in a tsunami of feelings, the person must *whoa* himself. He asks: what is true, right, and good? He brings himself back to truth: God is!

God's faithfulness focuses on His trustworthiness as a covenant-making and covenant-keeping God for His glory and the benefit of His child. True OAN brings these facts home to the believer so that he rides on eagle's wings (Isaiah 40:29-31).

The believer who functions as an unbeliever will not compete and complete the race, enter the winner's circle, or gain the prize as Jesus did Who joyfully endured all the way to the cross and beyond. Jesus is now seated at His Father's right hand interceding for His people (Hebrews 12:1-3; see Hebrews 7:25 and Romans 8:34).

Considers these truths:
- The Scripture encourages the believer by presenting truth in a three-fold fashion.
- Truth about God—who He is and what He has done and promised to do;
- Truth about the person himself—he lives out of functional motivational-want system and functional belief system—often for his own glory (see footnote 25);
- Truth about the situation—this is God's world and there is no chance or random events, wandering atoms, or maverick molecules. If there were, God would not be God.

VI. More Reasons Why All Believers need Encouragement

What other reasons do we have to support the statement that all believers need encouragement? First, Scripture tells us so. Even unbelievers encourage one another but in evil which is an expression of self-confidence and a disdain for God's omnipresence (Psalm 64:5-6; Proverbs 1:10-14, 22). Scripture commands mutual encouragement through OAN (Romans 1:12; 15:14; 1 Thessalonians 3:2; 4:18; 5:11-15; 2 Thessalonians 2:16-17). That fact attests to God's seriousness for believers helping believers.

Everyone is to be an encourager for the purpose of edifying and building up. God knows that believers who live in a fallen world with its pressures will only be victors, super-conquerors, if His encouragement and comfort are presented and made alive along their way (Romans 8:35-39).

God has provided not only His command and instruction regarding encouragement but also faithful OAN encouragers. Barnabas, the son of encouragement, was vital not only to Paul personally but to the early church and the spread of the gospel (Acts 4:36; 9:27; 11:22-26; 13:1-3; 15:35-41; 2 Timothy 4:11). Paul sent Tychius to encourage the churches by giving vital information regarding the ministry of the spreading of the gospel (Ephesians 6:22-23; Colossians 4:8-11).

A second reason for saying that every believer needs encouragement requires a simple look around. We live in a fallen world because of the effects of God's judgment on Adam and his first sin (John 16:33; Romans 5:12-14). Because of the curse of sin, there is much that is bad in the world that people face regularly—sin, misery, and death.

The believer is a redeemed sinner but an imperfect one. He sins, and he is surrounded by both redeemed and unredeemed sinners who can make life miserable sometimes without trying. There may not be any specific problem a person is facing.

Rather, the ebb and flow of life in a sin-cursed world amid sinners carries its own problems. In the world, diametrically opposed ways of life clash, pandemics come, tires go flat, toilets run over, people do not act "right," and things do not work the way we would like. These are some of the general hardships of living in fallen world. Yet, *life* and the world do not have a life of its own. These are the stage of God's providence.

In addition, the believer may be facing more specific pressures including bodily problems, decision-making, poverty, riches, being sinned against, receiving conflicting voices of advice, or his own sinfulness. However, no matter the circumstances, the situations are first and foremost the context in which a person plays out his inner-man conflict between self-pleasing and God-pleasing.

It is in God's providence whether hard or easy that the believer demonstrates his allegiance to the Lord or to self and his former father and master, Satan. Since no one is complete in terms of conformity to Christ, it is easy to lose one's moorings and focus. The person focuses on something else other than biblical truth. When that happens, he has been living the lie and continues in it.

As we noted earlier, everyone lives out of his heart using functional want and belief systems. At times a believer functions as an unbeliever. In God's providence, there are times when it is easier to sin than at other times. OAN is the ministry that helps make it easier for the person to please God and hard to please self.

Therefore, instead of viewing all of life from the perspective that God is in charge of His world and therefore all is right, a person is likely to view circumstances from his own experience, via his feelings, through his own reasoning, and with his own resources.

It is "natural" to place self above God and others. It is what sinners do, even saved ones (Psalm 51:1-6). The believer does this often in ways that he doesn't recognize or acknowledge. If that happens, a person will be overwhelmed by his lack of resources and his own insufficiency. It is easy to move away from God functionally, if not professedly, especially in hard times. Living the lie is a constant temptation and motivation.

A third reason to emphasize the need for encouragement centers on progressive sanctification or growth in Christ. Believers are changed and called to be changing and growing individually; they are to be an instrument of growth for fellow believers. Both are done through OAN. As a corollary, not only is every believer an encourager and edifier, he is also a receiver of encouragement.

The ministry of encouragement flows both ways: every believer is to be an encourager and an "encouragee." The latter may be even more difficult than the former. Often, the believer circumscribes his world, and he does not want any one in. I call that approach the *fig leaf* function of life.

In Genesis 3, after sinning, Adam and Eve put on fig leaves seemingly to protect themselves because of their shame and guilt (Genesis 2:25-3:9; Proverbs 28:1). They attempted to hide from each other fearing what the other would do, and they attempted to hide from God. Such is the futility that has resulted from Adam's sin and God's judgment of it.

Therefore, every believer needs to be strengthened in the inner man—encouraged. Otherwise, he may choose to follow old habits of inordinately and singularly pursuing "feeling good" and ease which will not endure to the end. When that happens the individual gives in, gives out, and eventually gives up. The culture calls this depression. The Bible calls it living the lie.

He may leave the church, family, or job. He "punches out of life" in some form or fashion. Either way, OAN is hindered as the person is too busy focusing on himself and what he can get so that he is neither a OAN-er nor a OAN-ee.

God's Church needs the ministry of encouragement for individuals to grow and change into Christlikeness thus completing its "equipping" function of maturing believers (Ephesians 4:11-14: footnote 2).

VII. Jesus' Comfort and Encouragement

Jesus began His Sermon on the Mount by giving certain characteristics of members in His kingdom. They are modeled after Him! He was poor in spirit, meek, mourned, merciful, a peacemaker, and was persecuted. When you see a believer, you are to see Christ—not completely or redemptively! But the believer is to be growing in Christlikeness and it is to be noted by others.

Jesus included those who mourn and His promise to them: *"because they will be comforted"* (Matthew 5:4). The ultimate comfort that the Messiah brings to His people is Himself and salvation through the redemption of sins (Luke 2:25-35, 36-38; 23:51; 24:21; Isaiah 40:1-3). Yet salvation is always linked to life after salvation on this earth! It is a package deal!

Sin and its consequences and the heart from which sin flows weigh heavy on a person. God's comfort in Christ is one answer to mankind and his sin problem. Part of a believer's inner-man war within may occur as he reflects on his sinfulness and the heart from which it flowed (Psalm 32, 38, 51). Salvation does not mean perfection. It does mean a personal and accurate assessment of himself before God.

A person may wonder how a just God can love such an unworthy creature like himself. It is a necessity that he does ponder this truth! He may think his sinfulness makes it impossible for God to love him, let alone save him. Like David in the Psalms mentioned above, the saved person eventually agrees that confession and repentance are his friend. They are God's means to restoring fellowship. OAN aids in arriving at that conclusion!

Ask yourself: how much sinfulness does one have to recognize in himself before he will turn to God and His grace? For the believer, he must be aware that focusing on one's own sinfulness without a proper view of God's work in him and His grace is an example of pride. Similarly, the same God who worked in him is also at work in the fellow believer! Sinful pride limits the believer to appreciate God's grace in himself and others.

Sin and sinfulness is no match for God's love and justice! In fact, they are to highlight grace! Confession is best served when the confessor has a proper view of himself as a sinner and of God as Savior and Comforter.

In every sin, self takes center stage and is a return to the serpent's satanic counsel in the Garden. Pleasing self will never sustain anyone and it creates its own problems: guilt, fractured relationships, power struggles, and fights and quarrels (James

4:1-3). Believers come to know this fact and begin to stop living the lie.

God's encouragement enables one to look away from self and to God. It is antithetical to sinful pride. When one searches for truth, he finds it; the Son, the Holy Spirit, and in Scripture (John 14:6; 16:13; 17:17). There he finds the truth about God, His answers about God and himself, and the peace than surpasses all human understanding. He becomes wise unto salvation and for life after salvation (2 Timothy 3:15-17). OAN facilitates a proper self-examination and confession of sin.

One encouragement that is critical for daily living is given in 2 Corinthians 5:18: *All this is from God who reconciled us to himself through Christ and gave us the ministry of reconciliation.* God reconciled Himself to each believer. The basis for this reconciliation is given in verse 21: *God made him who had no sin to be sin to be sin for us, so that in him, we might become the righteousness of Christ.*

A proper understanding of the doctrine of reconciliation is critical to growth in Christ and OAN. It is a relational word and flows from God to the sinner through Christ by the Holy Spirit (Ephesians 2:18; 3:12). Wrath, enmity, and the verdict of guilty and damnation were replaced with fellowship and intimacy with God.

The Triune God made peace with His enemies (Romans 5:10-11; 2 Corinthians 5:18-21; Ephesians 2:16; Colossians 1:21-22). He ceased

His hostility and estrangement. Therefore, the saved person is to function as OAN peace-maker rather than a peace lover which hinders maturing in the faith (2 Timothy 3:15-17: James 3:13-18).[35]

The comfort Jesus promised to mourners in Matthew 5:4 paralleled the woes promised to the rich in Luke 6:24. He, who is rich in self, including things, will not know God's comfort in this life nor in eternity (the rich young ruler: Matthew 19; the Rich Man and Lazarus: Luke 16; and perhaps Nebuchadnezzar: Daniel 4—we do not know if the ruler ever repented).

Self-renunciation rather than self-gratification and self-pleasure is the road to encouragement and comfort and one basis for it (Matthew 10:32-38; 16:24; Luke 9:23; 16:25; Romans 13:14). Self-renunciation is a blessing and a result of proper knowledge of self and of God. It proceeds as the person dies to self and is alive to and lives for God. Growth in Christlikeness is two-pronged: die to self and alive to God.

This truth is countercultural and counterintuitive and a theological mountain for some people to climb. Encouragement and comfort come from the Word of God through the Holy Spirit rightly applied. OAN is one vehicle for accomplishing this truth. These truths hinge on the fact that God is the trustworthy

---

[35] A peacemaker is one who seeks to bring shalom because God reconciled Himself to His people. Therefore, there should be no barriers to one-on-one fellowship between believers. In contrast, a peace-lover seeks ease and comfort of life at the expense of pleasing God in order to feel good. The peace-lover seeks "to smooth things over" or to minimize one's sinful thoughts or actions simply to avoid conflict and bad feelings.

Promise-keeper whose *yes* is *yes* in Christ (Psalm 119:49-56 especially verses 50 and 52; 2 Corinthians 1:20-22).

Hebrews 12:1-3 teaches that Jesus looked for (eagerly searched out) the joy set before Him; He endured (stayed the course —ran the race—continued heavenward) the hardships that was part of His Messiahship. He knew the Triune Gods plan and His role as Messiah. But He was not simply a player. He was the Player in a drama established in heaven. He was the Mourner: He grieved over unrepentant Israel (Luke 13:34-35, 19:41-44; 23:37-31).

He functioned as the God-pleaser par excellence in order to successfully complete His task as Messiah. Sometimes we speak of life as the *journey* and as a *race*. Jesus thought, desired, and acted in such a way that He completed—ran—the race God's way for His glory. Jesus encouraged Himself by focusing on the now—His task—which enabled him to focus on end and the winner's crown.

Jesus never doubted His own resources or considered people and problems larger than God. He joyfully endured even though He was left to "fend" for Himself as His disciples deserted Him. His encouragement sprang from His relationship with the Father and the indwelling Holy Spirit.

Moreover, God deserted His Son—the God-man, on the cross so that believers will never be forsaken (Matthew 27:46; Mark 15:34). God has provided something for His Church that His Son did not have at that one moment: encouraging OAN. Such is a loving God's provision for His people and His Church. The Church is to use it well!

VIII. Encouragement and the church at Philippi

Paul regarded the Philippians dear to him because of their growth, help, and encouragement in the gospel ministry (1:3-5; 2:19-21; 4:3, 15-19). His letter to them was a letter of joy. However, there were bigoted teachers, persecutions, and division in and facing the Church (1:15-17, 27-30; 4:1-2).

Paul wrote that he expected there to be encouragement (*paraklesis*) because of each one's relationship with Christ—they were a family (1:27-2:2). He knew the believer's relationship was not only the basis for encouragement; it was necessary and instrumental in having and fully developing the mind of Christ (2:1, 3-5).

Armed with the mind of Christ, changed thinking and wanting about God, self, and others would occur so that Christ's honor and God's glory, not self-interest, would motivate each person. In turn, the Philippians would close ranks, and unity of Christ's body would result.

He also knew that the preaching of the gospel was *paraklesis* and rejoiced that Christ was being preached no matter who preached it and for whatever motive (1:15-20; 1 Thessalonians 2:3-4; Acts 13:15ff). Paul gave at least two reasons for the saints at Philippi to be encouraged: God's relationship with them through Christ and the preaching of God's truth in which they were a partner. This encouragement was a blessing and would result in true OAN.

IX. Encouragement and the Church at Thessalonica

Turning to 1 Thessalonians let us see how Paul applied the ministry of encouragement to the church at Thessalonica.

1 Thessalonians 5:10-14: *He died for us so that whether we are awake or asleep we may live together with him. Therefore encourage one another and build each other up, just as in fact you are doing. Now we ask you, brothers, to respect those who work hard among you, who are over you in the Lord, and who admonish you. Hold them in the highest regard in love because of their work. Live in peace with each other. And we urge you brothers, warn those who are idle, encourage the timid, help the weak, be patient with everyone.*

The *therefore* in verse 11 connects Paul's exhortation with his teaching pertaining to the Lord's second coming recorded in 4:13-18. He was countering the false teaching that said no Christian would die before Christ's return. However, Christians were dying, and Christ had not returned. The congregation wanted answers as to what would happen to those who had died and if those alive at His coming had some advantage.

Truth which is a source of encouragement always trumps falsehood. He began chapter five by giving further teaching regarding the Lord's return (verses 1-8). As did Jesus, he taught that the Lord's return would come unexpectedly (Luke 21:34)—it would be a surprise to some (like a thief in the night: verse 2); that day would also be marked by destruction rather than peace and safety (verse 3).

In verses 4-8, Paul referred to 4:13 emphasizing the reality that the believer isn't to view life with despair as the unbeliever does who grieves without hope. There are some things true only of the believer. He is not in darkness, so the Lord's coming will not surprise him (verse 4). He is a son of light and of the day (verse 5; Ephesians 5:8-14). He has a destiny—eternal life—that began on earth at salvation (John 17:3; Romans 6:9-11).

Therefore, he is not ignorant (verse 6: *asleep*); he is alert and level-headed (verse 8: sober minded). He is not appointed to wrath but rather to a secure salvation through the Lord Jesus Christ (verse 9). These truths are edifying and encouraging.

In verse ten, Paul gave the encouraging bottom line answer to the Thessalonians: whether alive or dead, all believers live together with Christ. Why? Christ is for all believers (1 Corinthians 15:19-20, 44-58). The Christian's final destiny is a matter of individual and collective or corporate eternal security. The believer is to be in the presence of Christ forever not only individually but with his true brothers and sisters.

Paul is practicing the ministry of encouragement by exhorting his readers to watchfulness and wakefulness. Paul follows Christ's teaching and James' message (Matthew 24:42-44; 25:1-13; Luke 12:40; James 5:7-8). Paul's theme from chapter 4 until now (5:11) is "do better since you are doing well now" (4:1; 5:11).

In verse eleven, Paul encouraged the Thessalonians to be both an encourager and the "encouragee" by keeping alert and watchfully anticipating Christ's return. In this way they will be prepared for it.

Since salvation is summed up by the word "love," Paul was saying, "You were loved by God when you were unlovely and humanly speaking unlovable; you are to love each other in this life as you prepare for eternity; now you are to further abound in OAN love" (John 3:16-21; Romans 5:6-10). He then taught them how to do so through the ministry of OAN love.

In verses 12-13 of 1 Thessalonians 5, Paul discussed the Thessalonians response to their leaders. God intended the leaders' place of authority to be recognized. The leaders were to be appreciated and respected which would provide order and unity both of which are conducive to teaching truth and practicing OAN. He then added: *live in peace with one another*.

The truth taught to the Thessalonians in verses 12-13 fits nicely with the Holy Spirit's teaching spelled out in Hebrews 13:7, 17. Both leaders and the sheep have a responsibility to God and to each other. That is true OAN! Paul directed the congregation to think highly of their leaders (1 Thessalonians 5:13). Paul directs the leaders to care for the flock. Both of these activities require having the mind of Christ (Philippians 2:3-5).

Paul urged peace among the brethren in verse 13 and also in verse 15 (*Make sure that nobody pays back wrong for wrong but always try to be kind to each other and to everyone else*), Paul commands peacemaking within the body of Christ (see Romans 12:17-21 which applies more to the believer's relationship with an unbeliever). Peace is a gift and blessing that is given by God who is the God of peace (John 14:27; 16:33; Romans 5:1; 15:13, 33; 16:20).

X. Encouragement, Comfort, and OAN

1 Thessalonians 5:14: *And we urge you brothers, warn those who are idle, encourage the timid, help the weak, be patient with everyone*) expresses specific aspects of OAN. Paul's urging (*parakaleo*) is the essence of the ministry of encouragement. He calls both leaders and lay people to specific OAN activities: counseling, encouraging (a different word than *parakaleo*), boldly supporting and strengthening the weak, and being patient with everyone.

Verse 14 highlights at least four important points pertaining to OAN. First, OAN involves discernment and commitment. Paul lists three groups of people to help make his point. One approach does not fit all. Believers must be able to discern who is the idle (sometimes translated as unruly), the timid, and the weak and then determine the best way to present God's truth.

OAN requires discernment and commitment on both parties part: it requires a commitment to God's truth both in terms of knowledge and application of it for oneself and others; it requires a desire to please the Triune God; and it requires the desire to be a blessing to those in God's family. Without discernment and commitment there is no OAN.

Paul used specific adjectives for those in need of specific OAN activities. As noted, he pinpointed several groups. He begins with the idle. They need to be counseled. The word for idle (or unruly) is *ataktos* which is a military term meaning "to be out of step or out of rhythm."

The idle person uses the efforts of the group for his own gain. Apparently, some in the congregation had refused to work, borrowed from others, and were generally non-industrious based on Jesus' near-return.

The idle person needed to be lovingly confronted out of concern and care for him and the body. This is the import with which the word counsel (*noutheteo*) means. The word is used only by Paul; it carries the idea of concern expressed through care and confrontation to bring about change (see footnote 41). Change occurs as the person puts on or replaces self-serving thoughts, desires, and actions. God-pleasing thoughts, desires, and action flow as a patterned activity with the right motive in order to please God.

The second group he mentions is the timid or faint-hearted (*oligopsuchos* or small-souled: see James' use of the word in James 1:8; 4:8). These people could be discouraged—weak-hearted. They needed a courageous heart.

They have not been nourished by biblical truth for whatever reason and needed to be *fueled by truth*. That fueling may occur through any number of OAN activities such as one-on-one teaching or group Bible studies or simply encouraging him to give more attention to the substance of the sermon.

The third group Paul focuses is the weak (*asthenia*: this includes both physical and spiritual weakness). These people must be held up and supported. A *bearing up* ministry may be necessary as discussed (section entitled Welcoming, Accepting, and Bearing.

Paul makes a second major point: OAN involves a purpose: growing the body which includes:
- Respect for the leaders (see verses 12-13; Hebrews 13:7, 17);
- Peace-making activity by everyone in-lieu of peace-loving and trouble-making (verse 15); A ministry of peacemaking produces peace through patient endurance.
- Counseling (each member is both a counselor and counselee)—verse 14;

The word translated as encourage in verse 14 is a different word than *paraklesis*; it refers more to the manner of engaging another.[36] God calls for a ministry of encouragement and gives many options as to how to encourage and do OAN. Scripture does not specify the manner. The encourager is to be part of the solution rather than the problem. He must show meekness and discernment which are fruits of the Spirit.

The words for encouragement here and meekness in Galatians 5:22-23 carry the idea of humility and knowing how to pour soothing balm on troubled waters without ignoring the problem.

- Supporting, holding firm, or somehow being attached to the weak so he will not fail or fall. [37]
- This aspect of OAN is similar to Paul's *bearing* principle (Romans 15:1).
- Titus 1:9 teaches that true encouragement comes by healthy (hygienic or sound) preaching and teaching. Paul taught Titus as he did the Romans (15:4, 13): Scripture which is God's truth is the source of encouragement.

Paul's third major point: OAN is a means of fulfilling Ephesians 4:11-14 which describes one of the purposes of the Church: the equipping of the saint. All OAN activities called for in 1 Thessalonians were instrumental for doing that.

The equipping of the saints leads to the building up of Christ's body until all believers attain to the unity of the faith, full knowledge of Christ, and maturity which is Christlikeness (2 Peter 3:18).

---

[36] The word translated "comfort" is *paramutheomai* which means to speak kindly, soothingly, comfortingly: 1 Thessalonians 2:11; 5:14; John 11:19, 31.

[37] The word translated supporting is *antecho*: Matthew 6:24; Luke 16:13; Titus 1:9.

A fourth major teaching point: OAN not only involves the things done but also the way they are done. OAN can be done in a variety of ways using a variety of styles. The Bible gives general principles and may give leeway in their implementation. Teaching, counseling, and exhortation are part of a ministry of OAN encouragement.

XI. Peace, Peacemakers, and Peace-making

Believers are to be peacemakers because Christ is peace who has given peace. He has broken down the barrier between God and sinners (John 16:33; Matthew 5:10; Romans 5:10-11; 12:17-21; 2 Corinthians 5:18-21; Ephesians 2:11-16; Colossians 1:21-22; James 3:13-18).

Peace has effects within the person (Philippians 4:7) and within the body (Colossians 3:15-16; Ephesians 5:19). It is subjective, but it is more—it is objective. It is more than a feeling. It is relational resulting in knowledge of a change in God's enmity and wrath toward the believer. It is the confidence that the believer is no longer considered God's enemy. God has established the bond of peace and what God has established will not be broken. That is encouragement!

God placed the wrath and judgment on Christ that the believer deserved (Romans 3:21-26; 2 Corinthians 5:18-21). Relationships have changed! There is now peace; that fact should boggle a person's thinking and encourage OAN (Philippians 4:7)!

God's peace promotes a teaching milieu which is conducive to unity of and in the body. Peace among the brethren is a result of God's peacemaking which is fostered by OAN. This *vertical peace* is the reason why Paul commands peace *horizontally*—among the brethren via a ministry of OAN which facilitates reconciliation.

Peace within the body of Christ begins with the leaders—how they shepherd the flock (1 Peter 5:1-4). It then moves from the sheep to the leaders and respect for the leaders as well as to other sheep. The leaders are to facilitate OAN by giving it and even receiving it! Leaders must lead by example. Christ did! Peace is fostered by OAN and OAN develops, promotes, and maintains peace.

Believers are to live with an *already, not yet* mindset and perspective. The *already* is what the believer is in Christ by the Holy Spirit now—on this earth. It is resurrection life and eternal life that began at salvation (John 3:3-8; John 17:3; Romans 6:9-11; 1 John 3:1-3). The *already* includes a foretaste of and a piece of heaven now. The *not yet* awaits the second coming—the fullness of being in the presence of the Triune God.

God's glory has been revealed from heaven in His incarnate Son through the Holy Spirit. The believer has a down payment of that glory through the indwelling Holy Spirit (2 Corinthians 1:22; 5:5; Ephesians 1:14). Heaven came to the believer in Christ and the Holy Spirit!

As a result, the believer has a different focus for life—the *already*. Although the believer has not yet seen God with his physical eyes, he has seen Him with the eyes of saving faith and true hope (2 Corinthians 5:7, 9; Titus 2:11-14; 1 Peter 1:6-9). He looks forward to the *not yet*. In that way, he is of earthly good. In this way, he imitates Christ, the Victor, who always kept a proper eternal perspective and vertical focus (Hebrews 12:1-3).

The hope that he will "see Him as He is" should motivate the believer to grow in Christlikeness on this earth; growth includes OAN (1 John 3:1-3). The anticipation, certainty, and security of the *not yet* motivates the believer to run the race with endurance as Christ did perfectly and Paul did imperfectly (Hebrews 12:1-3; 2 Timothy 4:7-8). OAN helps bring the *already* and *not yet* in proper position holding them together.

CHAPTER 9

Encouragement through Exhortation

ENCOURAGEMENT MAY TAKE THE FORM of exhortation. Paul was an *"urger"* and "exhorter," but he gave exhortation a specific basis. Paul's ministry of exhortation must be seen through his mindset: *I am but an instrument in developing Christlikeness in you* (1 Thessalonians 2:7-12; see Galatians 4:19). Therefore, Paul always exhorted people in the Lord, in the name of Christ, or some other reference to God or Christ.

He did it under the influence of the Holy Spirit. Exhortation, as is all OAN, is an Intratrinitarian activity. Paul emphasized that his ministry of exhortation was not new or of his own invention. Rather, it was the Triune God's and Paul was but a vessel.

He never considered his exhortation simply a pep talk. He knew people did not change solely based on moral exhortation or simply telling. His ministry of exhortation was always predicated on what the believer already was in Christ. [38] This

---

[38] In other words, the imperative (his exhortation) assumed the indicative (what the believer was already in Christ).

truth sets the believer free! Paul did not want the people to live the lie!

Paul encouraged his readers by way of exhortation (he urged, he appealed, he insisted) in any number of circumstances as demonstrated in the following verses. Consider some of them.

Romans 12:1: *Therefore, I urge you, brothers, in view of God's mercy to offer your bodies as living sacrifices, holy, pleasing to God—this is your spiritual act of worship.*

1 Corinthians 1:10: *I appeal to you, brothers, in the name of the Lord Jesus Christ, that all of you agree with one another so that there may be no divisions among you and that you be perfectly united in mind and thought.*

1 Corinthians 4:16: *Therefore I urge you to become imitators of me.*

2 Corinthians 5:20: *We are therefore Christ's ambassadors, as though God were making his appeal through us. We implore you on Christ's behalf: Be reconciled to God.*

2 Corinthians 10:1: *By the meekness and gentleness of Christ, I appeal to you—I, Paul, who am "timid" when face to face with you, but "bold" when away!*

Ephesians 4:1: *As a prisoner for the Lord, then, I urge you to live a life worthy of the calling you have received.*

Philippians 4:2: *I plead with Euodia and I plead with Syntyche to agree with each other in the Lord.*

1 Thessalonians 2:11-12: *For you know that we dealt with each of you as a father deals with his own children, encouraging, comforting,*

and urging you to live lives worthy of God who calls you into his kingdom and glory.

1 Thessalonians 4:1: *Finally, brothers, we instructed you how to live in order to please God, as in fact you are living. Now we ask you and urge you in the Lord Jesus to do this more and more.*

The above passages focus on the believer's lifestyle: thoughts, desires, and actions, within the body. Paul understood that each believer was a new creature in the new creation and called his readers to think, desire, and act differently—as one supernaturally changed (2 Corinthians 5:17: the *kaine ktisis*: new creation or new creature or both).

A constant theme in the New Testament is: *be what you are in Christ*! It often follows Paul's *but now*: Romans 3:21, Ephesians 2:4, Titus 3:4. The believer has been changed! The work was one hundred percent the work of the Holy Spirit. The believer contributed zero percent. As a saint, the Holy Spirit still contributes one hundred percent but the believer also gives one hundred percent. His one hundred percent is evidence of the Holy Spirit's one hundred percent. The Holy Spirit works in and with the believer but never for him or against him.

Paul and John did not consider this new way of thinking, wanting, and acting as a burden (1 John 5:3). Rather, a ministry of exhortation was a blessing and acknowledgment of what God in Christ and His Holy Spirit had done and were doing in the life of the believer and the Church. Paul knew that now was the time for growing and changing and fruit bearing because there was a God to be praised and worshipped.

And yet there is a "dark" side of encouragement—*paraklesis*—which is found in Hebrews 3:13; 13:18-19. The book of Hebrews is the book of exhortation based on the fact that Christ is better than: the angels, Moses, Joshua, and the Old Testament rituals and high priests. It was written at a time when Jewish Christians were tempted to forsake Christianity and return to Judaism. Fellow believers were to come along side of each other as a blessing.

However, the author warned: sin desires its way! Rather the sinner desires his way! The phrase: *sin is crouching at your door* is often understood as sinfulness is ever present even in the believer (Genesis 4:7: *If you do what is right, will you not be accepted. But if you do not do what is right, sin is crouching at your door. It desires to have you but you must master it*).

Cain brought his sacrifice *and* himself to God. Self was at the center of his worship. God rejected him and his offering. Hebrews 11:3 tells us why: He was unfaithful to God—he was an unbeliever—and faithful to himself. In response, he was angry at God. Believers and unbelievers get angry at God!

Another view of the passage focuses on the sin offering—not sin itself—that is available to him. The sin offering was himself in full dependence on God. God said living as a true worshipper was available to Cain (John 4:24). But so was self-pleasing. The pull to please self and false worship was crouching at the door of Cain's heart; this is it is true of everyone (Genesis 4:6-7; Hebrews 3:13; 11:3-4).

Only the believer can and will choose to please God, His way for His glory. It was relatively easy to convince oneself that life was better back home in Judaism given the hard times. Such was the serpent's counsel in the Garden. God's message to Cain highlighted this point but Cain failed to think right to desire right, and to do right. He lived the lie!

The author of the book of Hebrews knew that many in the congregation would interpret the circumstances as an indication that a change was needed. It was time to return to Judaism. Christians were shunned by families and friends. Persecution in some form was ongoing. In this setting, OAN encouraging was an attention-getter. It was a warning that forced the person to consider the all-sufficient Christ as better than anything Judaism or the culture had to offer.

The issue then and now is fundamental to Christian growth. All of life is in relation to the Triune God. Everyone is a theologian and worshipper. Therefore, living is a theological activity. Proper OAN helps the person acknowledge and act upon those facts.

CHAPTER 10

Encouragement through Comfort

THE MINISTRY OF COMFORT IS a specific part of the broader ministry of encouragement. The sense of the word comfort speaks of consolation over and against trouble, problems, burdens, misery, and even death. The OAN-comforter provides that which is lacking in the person enabling him to endure God's way for God's glory. The Triune God is honored as believers grow in Christlikeness.

Giving true hope and strength in trouble or easy times is the Bible's definition of comfort. The author of the book of Proverbs asked God for neither riches nor poverty (Proverbs 30:7-9). Each has its own problems!

The believer lives the lie when he views himself as in a *black hole* with little or no hope of remedying his situation or getting victory in it. The tunnel seems so long and dark, the mountain too high, and the hole too deep. His focus is on himself in the circumstances without adequate resources.

However, the circumstances may be *bigger* than him but not his God. In fact, they came from God's hand. But the person down and out does not recognize or denies that he has a Person to trust and depend on. That Person has not let him go! The believer is in a theological battle. A small view of small God leads to living the lie and misery.

A person is in need of godly comfort all the time but especially when he is grieving (especially if that grief has originated from ungodly grieving—without true hope—or godly grieving has been complicated by wrong thinking and wanting); when he is fearful or doubtful or confused or perplexed, and or seemingly at the end of his rope. Such was the case as described in 1 Thessalonians 4:13. These are times in which it is easy to sin by living the lie and following the world's philosophy of life.

Some, if not most, in the young Thessalonian congregation grieved without hope—as do unbelievers—because they embraced wrong teaching regarding Christ's return (see my book: *Joy in Grief: God's Answer for Hard Times*). They were living the lie. Acceptance of false teaching leads to sinful thinking and wanting and subsequent actions.

Giving comfort is an aspect of the *cheering up* function of encouragement. Believers are called to comfort one another as they have been (Acts 20:12; 1 Corinthians 14:3; 2 Corinthians 1:4-6; 2:7; 7:6-7).

Yet the Bible's view of comfort is not the culture's "cheer up—things could be worse" or "cheer up—everything will work out for the best." Jesus discussed what true comfort and true cheering-up is and in John 16:33 (*I have told you these things, so that in me you may have peace. In this world you will have trouble. But take heart! I have overcome the world*) and John 14:16-18, 27 (*And I will ask the Father, and he will give you another Counselor to be with you forever—the Spirit of truth. The world cannot accept him, because it neither sees nor knows him. But you know him for he lives with you and will be in you. I will not leave you as orphans; I will come to you . . . Peace I leave with you; my peace I give to you. I do not give to you as the world gives. Do not let your hearts be troubled and do not be afraid*).

Jesus contrasted two types of peace in verse twenty-seven. Both types related to trouble and affliction in the world. One was centered on self and changed circumstances through the person's own resources. The other centered on a Person—Christ—and a personal relationship with Him and hope and contentment (John 1:9; 3:17-21).

In his gospel, John teaches among other truths that peace and light, life and truth are linked. Deny light and there is no peace. Deny truth (Truth and truth), and there is only falsehood and chaos. When you deny truth, you deny life and vice versa (John 14:6; 17:17). You are denying God who is life, light, and truth.

As I have written previously, the Triune God is peace and the peace-Giver (Romans 15:13, 33; 16:20; Ephesians 2:11-15; John 14:16-18). In Christ, the disciples had peace; in the world, they had pressure and trouble, but Christ had them. They were in the world but also in Christ by the Holy Spirit. Therefore, they were in the world but not of the world. God's world of peace comes alive through the ministry of OAN. Believers are victors not victims.

The believer has a double existence: he is in the world AND he is in Christ. Believers do not exist alone but in the family of God. Therefore, world events—God's providence and control—are the stage to demonstrate one of the blessings of being in Christ: God's peace-giving and the believer's peace (Philippians 4:7). This results in growth in Christlikeness, intimacy with the Triune God, and the joy of one's salvation.

Joyful believers are contagious and a blessing. Moreover, Jesus desired that His joy would be in the apostles and that it would be complete (John 15:11—also see 16:20-22, 24; 17:13). Jesus had revealed truths regarding fruit bearing (15:1-8: I am the Vine, my Father is the Gardener, and you are the branches).

Jesus emphasized that the person must stay connected with the true vine, which is Jesus, if he is to bear good fruit! He will bear fruit if unconnected or disconnected but it is God-dishonoring! Separation from Jesus in any form has tragic results for the person and the Church. The person's fruit is satanic in nature which often masquerades as wisdom (Genesis 3).

Jesus then followed with a love *story,* or at the least a statement about love. He highlighted the fact of the Father's love of Him and His love of the apostles (John 15:9: *As the Father has loved me, so I have loved you. Now remain in my love.*). These statements were designed to engender a deeper understanding of the deep, deep love of God (Ephesians 3:17-21). The apostles were facing Jesus' death but without the confidence and peace that Jesus had and was theirs. Love was His answer.

Moreover, Jesus linked joy and love. Love is eternal because God is, and He is love. Joy begins in heaven and extends to earth. Jesus loved the apostles to Himself: out of hell and out of the hopeless misery of this life. He brought them to Himself. He taught these truths the night before He died. Love is joyful and joy is linked to love. These were words of encouragement to the apostles who faced unprecedented times. However, they did not get it right away.

Joy differs from happiness. Happiness focuses on happenings which are God's providence. Joy is deeper. It looks to the God of happenings. Joy comes from a personal relationship with Christ by the Holy Spirit. Joy, love, and obedience are linked (John 15:10). True OAN helps bring this triad to the person in his or her situation. In that way God is glorified and the believer grows which is joyful in itself!

True comfort begins with salvation and a personal relationship with Christ by and through the Holy Spirit (Romans 8:1—*there is no condemnation for those in Christ*). God delivers His people from sin, the kingdom of darkness, and the family of Satan due to His relationship with them.[39]

---

[39] Colossians 1:13. Ultimately and preeminently, Jesus is the consolation of Israel, the new Israel, the redemption of the new Jerusalem, and the fulfillment of the Messianic hope that all believers, Jew and Gentile, long to know and be a part of (Luke 2:25-35, 36-38). Because of Christ's life, death, and resurrection, salvation is a reality for the believer—from every tribe, tongue, and kindred (Revelation 5:9)—which affects his daily life in terms of thoughts, desires, and actions.

He delivered them from His wrath and gave them peace by giving Himself to them (Ephesians 2:11-15). The apostles were in the world but more so, they were in Christ. Their relationship with the world had changed due to their relationship in Christ by the Holy Spirit.

The believer is bathed in love, truth, light, and life all from the Triune God's loving hand. Salvation and true comfort are realities because Christ is the Victor over the world and believers are in Him (Romans 8:35-39).

People deny these truths—they live the lie—most often expressed when hard times come. However, God has not changed! OAN helps brings these truths front and center. When that happens, the Church and individual believers grow in Christlikeness and there is victory. By virtue of one's personal relationship with Christ, the believer is in the presence of God and that relationship will never be broken. The Christian will never be excluded from God's family. God is his eternal Father and Jesus is his eternal Brother.

Therefore, as Paul says in Romans 8:35-37, in (not out of!) all kinds of situations, trouble, and affliction, Christian are more than conquerors; they will never be separated from God's love, provisions, and protection. The believer may run and even try to separate himself from God (see Psalms 32 and 38). But God will not lose any of His (John 6:37-43). If He did, He would not be God!

As good as the above are, the Triune God made it even better if that is possible! Jesus and the Father sent another Comforter, one of the same kind—the Holy Spirit—Who guides in all truth (John 16:13). Consider the concept of truth! It is Intratrinitarian in its origin, nature, and effects. Truth sets the believer free. That freedom is a growing one and will never be exhausted.

By the down payment of the Spirit, God makes good on His promises of salvation and growing believers into the image of His Son (2 Corinthians 1:22; 5:5; Ephesians 1:13-14; Romans 8:28-29; 2 Corinthians 3:18). He does this by providing His Word to equip the child of God (2 Timothy 3:15-17). These truths are encouraging! God is taking care of His people.

Therefore, the believer is never alone, is never without resources, is never outside of the Light, and is never without the ability and capacity to respond to all things in a God honoring way for God's glory and his good (Romans 8:28-29; 1 Corinthians 10:13; 1 Thessalonians 5:18). That is true comfort and hope!

I. Encouragement, Comfort, and 2 Corinthians

In 2 Corinthians, which is arguably Paul's most personal letter, he taught the beauty and the necessity of comfort by focusing on the God of comfort. Consider several such passages. First, 2 Corinthians 1:3-4: *Praise be to the God and Father of our Lord Jesus Christ, the Father of compassion and the God of all comfort, who comforts us in all our troubles, so that we can comfort those in any trouble with the comfort we ourselves received from God.*

Paul began the letter by introducing himself and Timothy as God's servants (verse 1). He quickly moved to God, naming Him the Father of Jesus and of compassion, and the God of all comfort (Isaiah 66:13).

Both Paul and John, echoing James 1:17 taught that God was the Fountainhead of all good things: comfort as here (Paul) and love (1 John 4:7-12). Therefore, God's comfort is trustworthy, useful, and unique—one of a kind. God is committed to comforting His people as the Good Shepherd (Psalm 23; 121; John 10, 15).

Paul taught that believers were comforted by God for two purposes: to experience something of what God's comfort is like (the believer as a "comfortee") and to imitate God as a "comforter." Both purposes move to the heart of OAN.

The believer is both one who has been loved and comforted (a 'lovee' and 'comfortee'), and he is a lover and comforter. The source of the model for and the method of OAN love and OAN comforting is God:

	Source	Obligation	Lesson
Love (1 John 4:7-12)	God	to love	God is love
Comfort (2 Corinthians 1:3-11)	God	to comfort	God is the God of comfort

It is well to remember our definition of comfort. Comfort is godly encouragement—heart strengthening—especially when there is trouble and hard times. It is cheering up the inner man.

Trouble is part of living in a fallen world; it is unavoidable. Paul taught that the God of comfort provides His comfort because He is not far from His people—He is the ever-present God who provides a relationship through Christ, by the Holy Spirit and energized by the Bible for daily living (Jeremiah 23:23-24). Therefore, not everyone can comfort. Only the believer who has received God's comfort can be OAN-comforter.

One truth of Scripture that is often misunderstood concerns God and trouble. The word for trouble is a common one and includes affliction of any kind. The ultimate source of trouble is God. Many deny this fact. However, if any event, person, or activity is outside the will of God He is not God. He is not the sovereign God of the universe that He claims to be.

In a general sense, God brings trouble to His servants, but we don't know the specific reason for any one person at any one time. And He is not the Author of sin. The Bible does give general reasons for trouble. One is God's zeal for Himself and judgment. God has zeal for Himself. He will not share His glory with competitors (Exodus 20:4-7; Isaiah 42:8; 48:8-11). Therefore, He judges and He disciplines.

Another reason is for the testing and refining (Genesis 22:1; Exodus 15:25; 16:4; Deuteronomy 8:1-4; Judges 2:22-3:1; Romans

5:1-5; James 1:2-4; 1 Peter 1:6-7). It is not as if God does not know the believer. But the believer must be refined so that his purity is as pure gold. God deserves holiness and purity. See the Levitical System and God's call to be holy as I am holy (Leviticus 10:1-3; 16; 11:44-45; 1 Peter 1:16)!

An important reason for bringing trouble is to train His people to seek Him and His of comfort. A piece of heaven—union with Christ and the indwelling Holy Spirit—is here but not heaven itself. God desires believers to develop a pattern of seeking Him in everything continually (Matthew 6:33). In that way, believers imitate Christ.

Moreover, believers will be prepared to comfort others (2 Corinthians 1:4, 6). Paul expressed this thought from his own life in several places: 2 Corinthians 4:1; 16-18, 12:7-10; Philippians 3:7-11. Jesus, the True Comforter, knew people were in bondage and heavy burdened with the false teaching and the wrong use of the law. He urged them to seek Him and taste and see that He was good—experience Him and get close to Him (Matthew 11:28-30; Psalm 34:8).

Paul, who had been heavy burdened with his self-righteousness and self-sufficiency, learned this lesson as recorded in Philippians 3:1-11. He experienced no joy, peace, or comfort as he lived for self: a Jew of Jews, proud of his ethnicity, and a zealot for personal lawkeeping (verse 3-6).

Rather, and radically, comfort came in a growing, personal relationship with Christ (verses 7-11). Paul sought God and found

Him because God found and saved him. He was saved by the Triune God, and he knew it. In his salvation Paul was comforted. Receiving comfort and help motivated Paul, and should believers, to live as one comforted. Life after salvation includes functioning as a "comfortee." .

Paul then lived as a OAN comforter because that is what believers do (Galatians 4:8-9)! Depending on God and acting on that dependence is the key to being comforted; serving others via OAN is a key expression of being comforted and made a comforter.

God's comfort, and the receiving of it, is so profoundly wonderful that it cannot be hidden under a basket; further, the person who has experienced it will not be tearless (Matthew 5:14-16; Luke 7:36-50). These will be tears of joy (John 16:20-22)! To have received God's comfort means to have been OAN-ed and loved by Him and others and to appreciate those facts. Believers should have their appetites focused on OAN.

In 2 Corinthians 1: 8-11, Paul gave specific reasons for his afflictions. First, in verse 9 (*Indeed, in our hearts we felt the sentence of death. But this happened so that we might not rely on ourselves but on God, who raises the dead*), Paul gave one of God's purposes in ordaining trouble: to motivate him and believers away from self-dependence and toward dependence on Him—the exercise of saving faith and true hope.

Reliance on self is so ingrained in the believer that it must be rooted out. Knowledge of that fact helps explain why God uses affliction to draw His people closer to Him. These truths are vital aspects of divine comfort (Genesis 50:15-21; Romans 8:28-29: see John 14:1-3.)

This fact is an aspect and one lesson of the cross (1 Corinthians 1:18ff). A truly comforted person looks to God's presence, power, provisions, promises, plan, and purpose rather than to self and his own resources. One result is involvement in OAN—both receiving it and giving it.

Second, in verse 10 (*He has delivered us from such a deadly peril, and he will deliver us. On him we have set out hope that he will continue to deliver us*), Paul taught that deliverance both in and from daily affliction was a taste of salvation, a foretaste of, and continuing reminder of God's promise of eternal redemption.[40]

Paul was reminded that God is the only true Promise-keeper and is the only true object of hope. Therefore, Paul changed his thoughts and desires about himself, others including his enemies, and life. He lived well so he could die well and move to heaven. Pleasing God was becoming more and more his motto for life.

True hope is the confident expectation of and eager anticipation to receive that which already is but is not yet fully realized but which is perceived through saving faith (see my book: *Hope: Out of the Maze: A Covenantal View of Hope*).

---

[40] The word translated "delivered" is *ruomai* which means "to draw or snatch from danger": Matthew 6:13; Luke 11:4; Romans 7:24; Colossians 1:13; 2 Corinthians 1:10; 1 Thessalonians 1:10. See Psalm 13.

Paul's earthly deliverances whetted his appetite for his final deliverance when he would be in the presence of God forever. He stayed the course and cared for the flock.

Third, also in verse 10, comfort results in and helps sets the believer's hope on God and not on a change in circumstances or people. Everyone has hopes and expectations and an agenda to pursue them. God created man a hope-seeking being. True hope and comfort guards the believer from living the lie.

Hoping for change in people, things, and circumstances is tenuous at best. That change may never come or may come in a way that one does not want or expect. Rather, God's promises, provisions, and purposes are based on His faithfulness and trustworthiness which never change. God gives His people what they need when they needed in ample supply. We must remember "life" is God's providence.

Fourth, consider verse 11 (. . . *as you help us in your prayers. Then many will give thanks on our behalf for the gracious favor granted us in answer to the prayers of many*). The proper response of the comforted will be joyful and humble thankfulness no matter the outcome. Foundationally, Paul's gratitude was based on his salvation and the ministry with which he was entrusted (2 Corinthians 4:1; 1 Timothy 1:12-16).

However, he knew that salvation and life after salvation were linked. As he worked out his salvation daily, he was grateful for his own growth in Christlikeness (Philippians 2:12-13).

By God's grace, he was focusing not on the affliction and pain but on the God of the trouble and the gain which was for him to become more like Christ. Gain through loss and pain is a major lesson of the cross. Paul was learning that lesson (Paul explains God's truth and his response in 2 Corinthians 12:7-10: *What to Do With a Failing Body* at www.jimhalla.com).

His gratefulness also stemmed from the fact that he knew that God had provided the Corinthians for him, and God was answering their prayers. Paul knew that God and the Corinthians were a source of comfort, and he was for the Corinthians. Those discontented, especially during trouble, must ask if they have experienced God's comfort. If not, they must ask why not and then humbly and hungrily seek it.

In the next chapter (2 Corinthians 2:7: *Now instead, you ought to forgive and comfort him, so that he will not be overwhelmed by excessive sorrow*), Paul presented a different setting for the giving and receiving of comfort. Paul urged the Corinthians to comfort the forgiven brother so that he would not be overcome by excessive sorrow and grief.

As forgiven people, the congregation was called to be comforters. The forgiven brother was to be a comforted brother—a "comfortee." Judicial forgiveness (that which comes from God once-for-all as the Just Judge of the world), is a down payment on comfort. Forgiveness of sin with the removal of guilt, condemnation, and separation from God is true comfort.

For every believer, there is no condemnation for those in Christ Jesus (Romans 8:1). Christians must grasp this fact, or they may function like the servant and the Pharisee in Matthew 18:21-35 and Luke 7:36-50. In the situation described in 2 Corinthians 2, Paul called for OAN forgiveness. Judicial forgiveness had set the whole church at Corinth on the road to peace and comfort. Personal forgiveness and reconciliation must follow.

As comforted people, Christians are capable to love and to forgive because they have been loved and forgiven. Paul called the congregation to be comforters and the returned brother was to receive the gift of comfort in the same manner as Mary responded in Luke 7:36-50.

Further in the letter (2 Corinthians 7:6: *But God who comforts the downcast comforted us, by the coming of Titus*), God gave comfort and help by using people—in this case Titus—to comfort. God uses secondary means to secure His end of comforting (Colossians 4:8-12).

II. Encouragement, Comfort and 1 Thessalonians

In his first letter to the Thessalonians, Paul addressed an important issue that had produced confusion: false teachers taught that no Christian would die before Christ's return and yet people were dying. What now? Paul stated emphatically that those still alive at the coming of Christ did not enjoy an advantage over those who had already died.

He began to offer comfort early in the letter found in 1 Thessalonians 2:11-12: *For you know that we dealt with each of you as a father deals with his children, encouraging, comforting, and urging you to live in a manner worthy of God, who calls you into his kingdom and glory.*

Paul imitated giving comfort and help modeled after God's giving of it (2:7-12). He did so as part of OAN encouragement. In verse 11, Paul characterized his ministry: he was like a father taking care of his children. He encouraged them; he comforted and soothed them; and he urged, exhorted, and challenged them.

For what purpose did he do so? Paul ministered as a true OAN-er in order that the Thessalonians would walk in a manner worthy of God. Comfort is purposeful. As a proper response, the "comfortee" should demonstrate a patterned lifestyle that displays Christlikeness and the fruit of the Spirit because he had tasted the goodness of God and is forever changed (Ephesians 4:1; Philippians 1:27; Colossians 1:10).

Paul continues his ministry of comfort in 1 Thessalonians 3:7: *Therefore, in all of our distresses and persecutions, we were encouraged about you because of your faith.* Faithful people model their faith in all circumstances and thereby are a means of encouragement to others (Romans 4:18-25; Hebrews 11; James 2:14-26).

And in 1 Thessalonians 4:18 (*Therefore, encourage each other with these words*), Paul concluded his teaching on Christ's return by exhorting his readers to be encouraged by his teaching. These were not any old words—they were words of truth. Functionally, Paul taught that truth encourages.

"What is truth?" asked Pilate (John 18:38). He did not know the Triune God. If he did he would have known that God is truth (Psalm 31:5; Isaiah 45:19; 65:16); Jesus is truth (John 14:6), the Holy Spirit is truth (John 14:16-17; 15:26; 16:13), and so is God's Word (John 17:17). Paul presented truth as inherent in and from the Triune God. Therefore, truth is personal and a source of comfort and encouragement. OAN encouragement and comfort requires speaking God's truth in love (Ephesians 4:15, 25).

And in Paul's second letter (2 Thessalonians 2:16-17), Paul closes the chapter with a benediction suitable for all ages: *May our Lord Jesus Christ himself and God our Father, who loved us and by his grace gave us eternal encouragement and good hope, encourage your hearts and strengthen you in every good deed and word.*

Paul was comforting and encouraging much like Peter in 1 Peter 5:10. His readers were facing false teaching and confusion. Paul and Peter encouraged the people by getting to the heart of the matter—informed and courageous hearts.

OAN encouragement and comfort is from the heart: Holy Spirit-given, energized, motivated, and directed for the purpose of strengthening the inner man. Paul and Peter pointed the people to the only source of all and true comfort (2 Corinthians 1:3-4); to the good and true hope of eternal life that begins in this life at salvation (Romans 6:9-11); and the secure inheritance of heaven that never spoils, fades, or corrupts (1 Peter 1:3-5).

The anticipation of being in the presence of God lacking nothing was and is a wonderful thing (Revelation 21:4). And yet Paul points his people to the present life. Paul looked to the heavens but as a means by which to live his present life as he recorded in Philippians 1:19-21; 3:12-15.

Comfort has an eternal perspective, but it is also a present reality. A truly comforted person is of earthly good (1 John 3:1-3). He is a comforting, loving, and encouraging OAN-er thereby imitating Christ and honoring the Triune God. He benefits and the body of Christ benefits!

CHAPTER 11
OAN, Encouragement, and Stirring-up

"STIRRING UP" IS AN ASPECT of encouragement, exhortation, and OAN. By "stirring up" the Bible is referring to someone who is a stimulator and an enticer. A OAN-er is a person who is be a proper stimulator—a proper *burr under another's saddle*. Consider Hebrews 10:22-25: *let us draw near to God with a sincere heart in full assurance of faith, having our hearts sprinkled to cleanse from a guilty conscience and having our bodies washed with pure water. Let us hold unswervingly to the hope that we profess for he who promises is faithful. And let us consider how we may spur one another on toward love and good deeds. Let us not give up meeting together, as some are in the habit of doing, but let us encourage one another—and all the more as you see the Day approaching.*

There are several words in the original language that are written in a "stirring up" motif. These words include our word in verse 24 and in Acts 15:39, and two different words in Romans 10:19, and Ephesians 4:26 and 6:4. OAN involves being a "stirrer-upper" and there will always be fruit of that endeavor either good or bad.

Which kind of stirrer-upper are you? Biblical OAN involves being *a burr under another's saddle* as a fruit of the Spirit and as a help to others in their development of the fruit of the Spirit. The irritation is a reminder to keep focused on being God's kind of person. No one really likes irritations, but God says we are to His kind of irritation!

The author gives a three-fold exhortation to the people as a way of encouraging potential defectors to remain true to Christ. That exhortation began in verse 22: *come close* or *draw near* is related to faithfulness—living out of saving faith.

The second component noted in verse 23 is *holding firmly* which is related to the object of saving faith and true hope; and the third is given in verse 24 and is related to *love*: giving thought to ways to stimulate others in the congregation to love on another.

The author of Hebrews understood that his people were facing decisions; some were withdrawing from the fellowship of the body in order to go back to Judaism. In verse 24-25, the author–pastor taught his congregation that OAN is God's answer for strengthening the bonds of unity, peace, and fellowship within the body (Ephesians 4:1-3). It involves faith, hope, and love.

Self-service and self-pleasing were due to a lack of love. This lack expressed itself as concern for self and unconcern for the body which would lead only to isolationism and division. There would be no OAN. In the case of the congregation and God's name, "stirring up" one another was critical for the well-being of the Church and its members; it was one of God's antidotes for apostasy.

Selfish individualism is opposed to OAN. It results in a distancing of oneself from another and from God. It is entirely different than the social distancing being urged in the pandemic. Isolationism can be generated by and lead to the thinking that there is no compelling need for an association with God's people. The downward spiral of thinking in that manner leads to action: forsaking and abandoning Sabbath Day keeping and meeting together as a body.

Wisdom based on God's truth not sinful fear must prevail. Mutual edification and encouragement through OAN are concerns for Christ and for His people. The pandemic has brought the Church to reconsider how to implement this teaching. How have you and your church worked out OAN principles in the context of being set apart?

The author wrote that the motive for OAN-stirring up rests upon the truth that the Day is drawing near (approaching). To what day does he refer? Many think it likely refers to the fall of Jerusalem in 70 AD. The author knew his people were considering returning to their former life of Judaism and would be objects of slaughter by the Romans. The physical reality of death pointed to the spiritual reality of eternal damnation (Hebrews 6:4-6; 10:26-31).

However, some think that this is a reference to Jesus' return. It is not an either or. Either way or both ways (which I prefer:

an immediate fulfillment and a later fulfillment), believers have a responsibility to be a "good" burr under another's saddle because this life is finite and dangerous and eternal existence follows—in heaven or hell.

Peter gives an insight into "stirring up" in 2 Peter 1:13: *I think it is right to refresh your memory as long as I live in the tent of this body*. Peter uses the term translated as *to refresh* as a reminder or as a call to stir up the people. Peter wrote his second letter to warn his congregation about impending false teachers.

He began chapter 1 by turning them to the all-sufficient God and His Promises and Power (verses 3-4). Through the ministry of exhortation, he stirred them up. He urged them to add to their faith—*godliness and faithfulness through addition* (verses 5-11).

He then continues to stir them up by reminding them of *these things* even though they were established in the truth (verse 12-15). *These things* are the basic truths of the Christian faith some of which Peter had outlined in previous verses. Truth is a vital necessity for life and godliness (Titus 1:1-2).

The book of Deuteronomy is another book of repetition, remembrance, and not forgetting. God's people, too often, have selective memory or boredom or dullness of hearing (*nothros* according to Hebrews 5:11).

These latter terms may be expressed as "I have heard this before" or "This is the same old thing—nothing new, so why should I listen." God knew it was important to remind His people of truth. It was one of His antidotes for spiritual decline. OAN-stirring up is God's way of shaking His people from the inside-out!

The stirring up aspect of OAN is desperately needed today. God's people must gather around the Lord, each other, and truth. God's Word calls for it! It is one of the ways His Church will prevail.

CHAPTER 12

OAN, Encouragement, and Counseling

Romans 15:14: I myself am convinced my brothers that you yourselves are full of goodness, complete in knowledge, and competent to instruct one another.

OAN CONSISTS OF CHANGED PEOPLE helping others change and grow. It involves knowledge and wisdom (which is applied knowledge). Here Paul says that wisdom is goodness in action and includes being able to counsel. This is true, not simply of the leaders of the Church (in an official capacity), but of all Christians (in an unofficial capacity). In a real sense, the Church is a counseling center (Ephesians 411-14; footnote 2).

Counseling is a ministry of discipleship and OAN. It is one-on-one discipleship. It is ministering truth not from the pulpit but person-to-person. It can be classified as remedial discipleship and preventive discipleship. It can be an official ministry of the Church done by the leaders and those trained or simply believers helping believers.

In the first instance (remedial discipleship), there is concerted and specific help given to a believer officially or unofficially in a specific area of life in order to help move him from where he is into Christlikeness.[41] In the second instance (preventive discipleship), believers come alongside of each other in order to keep other on the path to greater Christlikeness.

Colossians 1:28: *We proclaim him, admonishing and teaching everyone with all wisdom, so that we may present everyone perfect in Christ.*

Colossians 3:16: *Let the word of Christ dwell in you richly as you teach and admonish one another with all wisdom, and as you sing psalms, hymns, and spiritual songs with gratitude in your hearts to God.*

The leaders of the Church have the primary and official role in the counseling ministry. But fellow members are to practice one-on-one discipleship was as well (Romans 15:1-3; Galatians 6:1-5). This individual ministry best functions under the guidance of the leaders of the Church. A singular philosophy of ministry —truth and change—must come from the pulpit, from an official counseling ministry in the Church, and from individuals simply coming alongside of a brother or sister.

Moreover, OAN includes counseling yourself and others. The word for counseling—*noutheteo*—literally means "to place

---

41 The verb *noutheteo* is used eight times: Acts 20:31; Romans 15:14; 1 Corinthians 4:14; Colossians 1:28; 3:16; 1 Thessalonians 5:12, 14; 2 Thessalonians 3:15 and the noun *nouthesia* is used three times: 1 Corinthians 10:11; Ephesians 6:4; Titus 3:9.

or put in the mind" in order to reset it (see footnote 41). The believer has the mind of Christ. Counseling facilitates the proper use of it.

Biblical counseling as the words imply has the following truths: change is needed in a person's thinking, wanting, and actions; the process of change takes place out of loving concern and care for the person; change is facilitated through a loving encounter with the person; by using God's truth as the standard for the how and *what* of change, believers grow.

The word in the original implies that wrong thinking, wanting, and motivation is present with wrong actions and secondly, that biblical truth, correctly ministered and applied sets the person free.

"Placing in the mind" can be done only by confronting oneself or another person with God's truth. Sadly, often the word *confront* carries the idea of hostility or harshness. The word does not refer to manner. Since God is man's environment, there is no escaping God (Psalm 139). We are confronted by and with God constantly! He is the ultimate Confronter! We are to confront God's way!

People may assume the word confront indicates harshness and brashness. Those who counsel from the Bible may be accused of being confrontational. However, the word indicates a face-to-face ministry with biblical truth on the table as a guide, lamp, and mirror (Psalm 119:99-105). The manner of the person coming alongside of another should be conducive to bringing about change in the attempt to honor God.

Sometimes, "leaning" on another is considered harsh—confrontational. It may be the style and manner that is the issue. But God is the great Leaner. Believers are to imitate Him. Hebrews 4:12 teaches that every believer is confronted by Him in His Word which penetrates to the core of the person's being. Sadly, most believers don't want to be exposed by the Word of God no matter how it is presented.

The result of "placing in the mind" will be changed thinking and wanting; changed action will follow at varying speeds. The whole person is changed. God' truth replaces unbiblical thinking such that the believer begins to develop more and more the mind of Christ.

CHAPTER 13
OAN: Kindness, Compassion-Tenderhearted, and Forgiveness

> Ephesians 4:31-32: *Get rid of all bitterness, rage and anger, brawling and slander, along with every form of malice. Be kind and compassionate to one another, forgiving each other just as in Christ God forgave you.*

IN THESE VERSES, PAUL CONTINUED his teaching (begun in 4:1) regarding body life, including the importance of OAN. The Christian walk—a patterned way of life in terms of thoughts, desires, and actions—is never solitary.

Because of the supernatural change of salvation, walking and talking together as members of God's family should be completely and radically different than it was in Satan's family (Ephesians 4:15,17-24; 25-32; 5:8-14; also see Romans 12:1-2; 13:12-14; Colossians 3:8-10).

Because the believer is changed and is changing, Paul called for a patterned, major replacement or *put off*) of those responses learned when in Satan's family and kingdom. These habit patterns include thinking, desiring, and acting and some are listed in verse 31; they stem from a satanic-derived *me-first* approach to life and they harm the body, both the individual's physical body and the body of Christ.

The whole person—the person's heart and body especially the brain—is affected by the fall. These changes are ingrained so that self-pleasing as a motive competes with pleasing God, God's original design for man. Those responses include but are not limited to bitterness, anger, wrath, slander, and every sort of evil.[42]

At salvation, the believer begins to replace old habits. He begins to display habits of thinking, wanting, motivation, and acting (the *put on*) that are patterned after Christ's active obedience some of which are listed in verse 32.[43] Notice the use of the terms habits and patterns. The believer puts off his old wardrobe that indicated membership in and allegiance to Satan and self. He puts on the wardrobe—the fruit of the Spirit—that characterizes him as a child of God. He does because he is in new family with a new wardrobe.

---

42 *Putting off* and *putting on* are biblical terms and include the idea of undressing and unclothing yourself from old, dirty clothing and putting on a new wardrobe. Effectively, old habit patterns of thinking, wanting, and acting that please self are replaced by habit patterns of thoughts, desires, and actions that please God.

43 While on earth, the sinless Godman lived a perfect righteous life. He had no unbiblical habit patterns to *put off*, because He had no innate, inherent sinfulness. He had no Adamic legacy, and He had no prior membership in Satan's family and kingdom. He did not need to change clothes! His thoughts, desires, actions were perfected. His perfection must be demonstrated daily in every thought, desire, and action.

New habits of patterned wanting, thinking, and acting will occur one thought and desire at a time. The trio of thoughts, desires, and actions occur in both the inner man (heart) and the body including the brain. Life after salvation is a whole-person change as the believer moves toward heaven (1 John 3:1-3).

Paul knew that unreconciled relationships fostered disunity, chaos, and confusion in the body of Christ. They dishonored God and they did not benefit the body of Christ and the individual. Paul's aim was to promote each member's relationship to each other. In that way the Church would fulfill the functions described in Ephesians 3:10 and 4:11-14 and Jesus' teaching in John 13:34-35. God would be honored, and the Church blessed.

When kindness, tenderheartedness, and forgiveness (Ephesians 4:32) are practiced, it is a testimony to the fact that the mindset and patterned lifestyle described in verse 31 is being replaced. When that happens, the Holy Spirit is not grieved, or better He is not offended (verse 30) and the individual Christian and the whole body benefits.

Further, Paul clarifies the *how* of OAN in verse 32. The *how* involves at least three characteristics and activities: kindness, tenderhearted/compassion, and forgiveness.

I. OAN and Kindness

A major *how* of OAN is kindness (*chrestos*); the term indicates a supplying of what is suited, fit, needed, or profitable to and for another. It may involve supplying things including oneself, words, and actions so that life is simplified for the person (Matthew 11:30; Luke 5:39; 1 Corinthians 13:4; 15:33; 1 John 3:16-18). Or it may involve people and their disposition in terms of being good-natured, gentle, willing to help, and be useful toward others (Luke 6:35; Romans 2:4; 1 Peter 2:3).

A believer's kindness should and will imitate God's kind actions as seen in Luke 6:35 (*But love your enemies, do good to them, and lend to them without expecting to get anything back. Then your reward will be great, and you will be sons of the Most High, because he is kind to the ungrateful and wicked*) and in Romans 2:4 (*Or do you show contempt for the riches of his kindness, tolerance, and patience not realizing that God's kindness leads you toward repentance*)?

Kindness is always purposeful (Romans 2:4). Loving an enemy requires God's grace and an inward change of the heart in the lover. While the term enemy may refer to one who is a non-believer, too often there is enmity between believers (James 4:1-3). Paul calls for all bitterness, however small or large, to be put away and replaced by a specific aspect of love, that being kindness.

Unresolved issues and problems lead to unreconciled people and God-dishonoring relationships and vice versa. That is not God's way for His Church. The lingering effects of unsolved problems can be complicated by anger, bitterness, and resentment leading to division between individuals and the whole body of Christ. Believers are to search for ways to be useful and profitable to one another through OAN.

II. OAN and Compassion-Tenderhearted

A second aspect of the *how* of OAN is compassion (tenderhearted). A true OAN-er is compassionate. In Greek thought, the intestines were considered the seat of feelings and emotions. The word translated compassion or tenderhearted is *eusplagchnos* which is used here and in 1 Peter 3:8 (*Finally, all of you, live in harmony with one another; be sympathetic; love as brothers, be compassionate and humble*).

Paul is speaking of strong feelings toward another—"to feel deeply or to pity"—at the gut level—not the heart. Paul and Peter are not teaching that the believer is his feelings or is to be led by them. Both of them taught and practiced the truth that feelings including compassion flow from changed thoughts and desires about God, self, and others including enemies. Actions follow.

In the verb form, the root word is used only in the gospels and most often described Jesus' attitude toward the multitudes and individuals. [44] Compassion imitates Christ as He related to

---

44 *splagchnos*: The word refers to the gut—the GI tract—and is derived from the Greek interpretation of man: Matthew 9:36; 14:14; 18:27; 20:34; Mark 1:41; 8:2; 9:22; Luke 10:33; 15:20. The noun form is used less often: Luke 1:78; 2 Corinthians 6:12; 7:15; Colossians 3:12; Philemon 1:8, 12. Emotion in the Bible is related to the viscera—internal organs of the gut—rather than the heart.

people. Compassionate also describes the heart of the believer. The believer's heart has been *tenderized* so that he functions like Christ.

Being a compassionate OAN-er takes several forms including being a good listener especially when moved by true concern for the person. Compassion is expressed by words and deeds such as the example of the Good Samaritan (Luke 10:25-37) and the other servants in Jesus' parable describing the unmerciful servant (Matthew 18:21-35). Compassion includes anticipating the needs of another and providing for them (1 John 3:16-18).

III. OAN and Forgiveness

A third aspect of the *how* of OAN is forgiveness. There are two words found in the New Testament translated as forgiveness: *aphiemi* and *charizomai*. Our word is the latter, and its most common meaning is "to show or bestow a favor or kindness to," "to pardon and graciously remit a person's sin" (Colossians 2:13; 3:13; Luke 7:42-43; Romans 8:32; 2 Corinthians 2:7, 10; 12:13).

In other words, forgiveness does not keep track! Its root is *charis* which is translated as *help* and *grace*. The believer is the most graced, helped, and forgiven person; therefore, he is to be the most forgiving person!

What is forgiveness? (For more on the subject see: *Forgiveness* at www.jimhalla.com). Theologians use the term judicial forgiveness to indicate God's gracious removal of the believer's sin debt. The removal is based on the righteous life and death of Christ that is counted by God as the believer's and the righteousness of Christ is placed on his ledger sheet! Judicial forgiveness is a one-time act on God's part as the just Judge.

God counted (or reckoned or placed on the ledger sheet) what Christ had perfectly accomplished in His life and at the cross as the sinner's. On earth, Christ, the perfect Lamb of God, after perfect obedience and covenant-keeping, took the place of hell-deserving sinners. He went to hell on the cross. He experienced the fullness of God's perfect and complete wrath because:

One: He fulfilled the law's demands by His complete and perfect life of trust and obedience while on earth. He thereby qualified Himself as the perfect Priest and Sacrifice. Some speak of this as Christ's active obedience.

Two: then as the perfect Substitute, He bore sinners' guilt, shame, condemnation, and punishment nailing them to the cross as He died the perfect Sacrifice (John 1:29, 36; Colossians 2:15; Hebrews 9:11-14; 10:1-4; 1 Peter 1:18-19). Some theologians speak of this aspect of the cross as Jesus' passive obedience.

The believer's record was wiped clean by God the just judge based solely on the work of Christ's perfect lawkeeping and sacrificial death. In the place of unrighteousness, God "saw" only Christ's perfect lawkeeping! God declared the person not guilty! God counted to the believer's record the perfect life of Christ and its merit. What Christ did and accomplished, God counted as the believer's!

What Christ did was impossible for fallen man to do or even desire to do (Romans 8:5-8)! Such is one aspect of the gospel. It is even better, if that is possible! Every believer must remember that Christ is a resurrected Savior not simply a crucified One (1 Corinthians 15:1-3).

As I have said, resurrection life begins now and is to be enjoyed now as we wait for eternity (Romans 6:9-11; 1 John 3:1-3). Excitement about the whole spectrum of resurrection life leads to OAN. God considers or reckons every believer as having committed no sin and having a not-guilty record. The believer is justified—he is declared right and righteous before God. His legal standing is perfect. He is accepted, but only in Christ.

One simple definition of justification is given in the Westminster Shorter Confession #33: it is the act of God's free grace wherein He pardons all our sins and accepts us as righteous in His sight only for the righteousness of Christ imputed to us and received by faith alone. The sinner is forgiven! As such he is a different person. Bondage to his mown lawkeeping to remove guilt and the stench of what he was in himself is no more!

Once God justifies an individual (God declares him not guilty: Romans 8:1), God keeps His promise not to hold that person accountable, liable, or guilty: *I will remember your sins no more* (Isaiah 38:17; 43:25; 44:22; Jeremiah 31:34; Micah 7:19-20; Psalm 51:1, 9; 103:8-14). These passages refer to judicial forgiveness and God's activity as the Just Judge.

I repeat: God's judicial action was a one-time action never to be repeated. Christ will not re-crucify Himself! Heaven forbid! God never goes back on His word. As the just Judge, the Triune God will never use Adam's first sin or the sins of the believer to harm the believer in any way. He has promised not to bring them up for the believer's hurt. God does not break promises (Romans 8:32-34; Hebrews 7:25; 1 John 2:1).

However, there are still temporal consequences for sins. Poor stewardship of the body must be confessed but God's judicial forgiveness does not necessarily remove its results. Moreover, as the good Father, God disciplines—the word carries the idea of training to change—and forgives His children (Hebrews 12:5-11).

Thus, it is proper to speak of a second type of forgiveness. There is Fatherly forgiveness which is ongoing; it must be distinguished from judicial forgiveness which is a one-time-forgiveness as Judge.

God as Judge forgives the now-believer into His family and kingdom! Again, judicial forgiveness is a one-time forgiveness never to be repeated. The believer's record is clean because God has cleaned it with the blood of Christ. On it, God counts the perfect record of Christ on it. What Christ did as the believer's substitute, God counted it as the believer's—a perfect record. This is simply an amazing fact! So often it is misunderstood or worse, denied. How can God be that good or powerful!

However, as a loving Father, He brings up to the believer his sin. He disciplines him. This word implies educative instruction and correction. This activity on God's part is a means of bringing about change in the person and is an act of love. One purpose of discipline is developing conformity to truth—God's Word and Christ. Discipline enables believers to mature in Christlikeness.

In response to God's forgiveness of him (His promise *to remember your sins no more for the person's hurt*), the Christian will forgive others out of gratitude for what God in Christ has done for him and for others. We don't have time to discuss forgiveness at length, but it is mandatory to remember: 1. You can't forgive an unbeliever, and he can't forgive you; 2. You must be ready to forgive and make it easy for him to do so (see Forgiveness at www.jimhalla.com).

The believer's forgiveness of another is patterned after God's forgiveness of him meaning that the person promises not to bring up the specific offense done against him to God, others, self, or the other person to gain some advantage. That is a promise every Christian can and must keep because "like Father like son" (Matthew 5:48; 1 Peter 1:16; Matthew 21:21-35; Luke 7:36-50).

I encourage people to confess the specific sin and specific biblical principle(s) violated. I also ask them to confess and repent of the pattern of the sin, the excuses for that sin, and the hardness of heart from which it flowed. In that way, relationships can and are to be restored.

The granting of forgiveness (it involves a promise) results in people being restored to each other. It breaks the bar of separation between parties. OAN helps to remove the bar and facilitate a growing relationship. Relationships are reestablished in the rubble of hurts, bitterness, distrust, and resentment (verse 31). OAN facilitates forgiveness and forgiveness facilitates OAN!

The two believers are to grow their relationship with each other and with God. God is honored, the body of Christ is protected, and individual believers are benefitted. OAN requires forgiveness and forgiveness requires OAN. Colossians 3:12-13 *Therefore, as God's chosen people, holy and dearly loved, clothe yourself with compassion, kindness, humility, gentleness, and patience. Bear with each other, and forgive whatever grievances you may have against one another. Forgive as the Lord forgave you.*

Paul gives his readers an identity reminding them who and what they are in Christ (Romans 6:9-11). They are chosen, holy, and dear to God (1 Peter 2:9-10). God is the great Chooser. He handpicked His people from eternity past and then consecrated them to Himself in the present (Ephesians 1:4; 1 Peter 1:3-5).

He has snatched them from the kingdom of darkness, from the present evil age, from Satan's family, and has made them His dear children (Romans 7:24-25; Galatians 1:4; Colossians 1:13; 1 John 3:1-3).

Because they know who they are, believers are called to think, desire, and do certain things as they relate to fellow believers. In that way, they are relating to God. A proper horizontal focus requires a proper vertical focus!

As I have noted previously, Paul calls this change in thinking, wanting, and doing *putting off* and *putting on*. Putting on one garment requires the person to take off one garment and replace or change it with one that is entirely different. The chart will help in following Paul's admonition.

	Put On	**Put Off**
1	Compassion/tender heartedness	Little regard for, hardness to, hard heartedness.
2	Kindness	Evil, malice, hindrance, hardness, callous, insensitive.
3	Humility	Esteeming oneself high, high minded, arrogant
4	Meekness	Ungrateful, grumble/complain, un-accepting of God's providence
5	Patience	Impatient, short fused, irritated, frustrated
6	Putting up with	Intolerant, judging others stricter than self; others change not me
7	Forgiving	Holding grudge, bitter, resentment, hostile

One principle that stands out in Paul's teaching is man's internal motivation. Every person, saved and unsaved, conducts himself and lives out of his heart according to an identity. A person's functional belief system and functional want system are inner-man (heart) activities. Each person has an agenda for self.

As an unbeliever, he was trained and trained himself to please and worship self—he was a previous member in Satan's family (Romans 6:11-14; 8:5-8; Ephesians 2:1-3). As a believer he is perfect in standing and position but not in the practice of godliness.

I repeat a vital point: believers have remaining sinfulness and remaining habituation. Habit patterns of self-service, self-trust, and self-exaltation linger and die hard! Change requires a great, divinely-motivated and energized effort to change that occurs through the indwelling Holy Spirit (Romans 8:9-11; Philippians 2:12-13).

He does not do the work for the believer but the changed thinking, wanting, and doing that occurs in the believer is evidence of His presence. The controlling power or operative principle of the law of self-pleasing has been broken (Romans 8:2). Paul goes on to write that believers are no longer controlled by self but Christ-in-him through the Holy Spirit (Romans 8:9; Galatians 2:20).

Paul continues and writes that if Christ is raised via the Spirit (*and He is!*), then, so, too, is the believer because he is in Christ (Romans 8:11). The believer has no justifiable reason why he does not grow in Christlikeness. This includes being involved in OAN!

Therefore, Paul, joyfully and vigorously calls fellow believers to put off Satan's prior influence and put on Christ because Christ has put on them! There in Christ because He is the true Vine (John 15:1-8). He is united to them and them to Him (Romans 13:14; Galatians 2:20; 3:27-29; 5:24; Ephesians 4;22-24; Colossians 3:8-10). The believer has been radically and supernaturally changed.

One way the Christian demonstrates the Holy Spirit's indwelling is by *putting on* the practice of kindness, tenderheartedness, and forgiveness of and for each other. Further, he grasps that God has been kind, compassionate, and forgiving to and of him. He is able to understand that OAN is a ministry in which family members treat others in God's house the same way God has treated them (again see Matthew 18:21-35; Luke 7:36-50).

James offers a similar insight into the issue of OAN (James 5:14-16). He asks: *Is anyone among you sick?* The word translated sick is *asthenia* which can refer to both physical and moral weakness (sin). If a person was sick, James wrote that two things should be done: the one who is sick should call the elders, and sins should be repented of and forgiven.

As a result, any God's dishonoring relationships can be restored. In addition, the elders are to pray with and over that person and provide appropriate care for the physical body. The elders may need to facilitate relationship-building between believers and between the believer and God. The elders are call to minister to both the body and the inner man—the whole person.

Some physical illnesses can be a direct result of sin especially if it is unconfessed, or a physical illness can be aggravated by sinful responses to God's providence, by guilt and by unconfessed sin (see Psalms 32, 38, 51). As a result, there is bitterness, resentment, and even hostility. As a result, broken relationships and disunity develop.

The confessing of one's sin to another and the forgiveness that follows is the soothing balm that brings relief and joy to the heart of believers and peace to the body of Christ. It is not to be taken lightly or misused. The context of forgiveness may be OAN, and OAN helps to smooth the road so that repentance can be sought, and forgiveness granted.

CHAPTER 14
OAN Hospitality

THERE IS A GROUP OF passages that contain the words *philoxenia* or *philoxenos* which mean "kindness to, sharing with, and befriending others" and are translated as hospitality. These words are compound words meaning "lover of strangers." However, OAN hospitality is directed toward believers.

The love of the Lord draws people into Christian fellowship. As a result, relationships are strengthened and flourish—both vertically (to God) and horizontally (person to person).

In one sense there should be no strangers within God's family. OAN hospitality is a type of litmus test for OAN love. OAN hospitality is an activity that must be cultivated. Practice makes perfect. The Christian must look for opportunities.

Israel was a redeemed stranger bought and brought out of Egypt (Deuteronomy 5:15; 10:18; 26:12; Leviticus 19:34; Exodus 22:21; 23:9; Ezekiel 47:22-23). OAN was alive and well in the Old Testament. This past history is one motivating factor for the Church today to OAN.

God's covenant community in the Old Testament pointed to the Church which is the New Israel (Galatians 6:16; 1 Peter

2:4-10). Therefore, hospitality is to be wisely and consistently directed toward all Christians.

Another motivation for practicing hospitality is God's overwhelming concern for those in need (the defenseless, alien, foreigner, and stranger (see Psalm 9:9-12; 10:14-18; 34:18). These people were in the nation of Israel. OAN begins in the household of God (John 13:34-35). In the same way, the believer is to show the same concern through OAN hospitality.

Passages include:

Romans 12:13: *Share with God's people who are in need. Practice hospitality.*

1 Timothy 3:2: *Now the overseer must be above reproach, the husband of but one wife, temperate, self-controlled, respectable, hospitable, able to teach.*

Titus 1:8: *Rather, he must be hospitable, one who loves what is good, who is self-controlled, upright, holy, and disciplined.*

Hebrews 13:2: *Do not forget to entertain strangers for by doing so some have entertained angels without knowing it.*

1 Peter 4:9-10: *Offer hospitality to one another without grumbling. Each one should use whatever gift he has received to serve others faithfully administering God's grace in its various forms.*

Two verses (1 Timothy 3:2; Titus 1:8) indicate that an elder, among other characteristics, must be hospitable which is part of a full OAN ministry. The elder's ministry is in an official capacity but since all believers are called to be hospitable, it is exemplary as well.

In 1 Peter, Peter exhorts his congregation to provide physically, socially, and spiritually to members of God's family as part of OAN. It cost believers in Peter's time. But Peter, a wise pastor, knew that OAN would help maintain the unity and bond of peace in these tough times. The members of God's family are to be there physically to meet all types of needs including material ones (1 John 3:16-18).

Hospitality involves service to others as a good steward of God's grace. Stewardship and hospitality are linked together. Helping others is OAN. The focus is on God, off self, on others, and on serving God; therefore, there should be no grumbling or complaining.

There is a corporate responsibility for hospitality. All believers are to return interest on God's investment of His grace in His Church and its members. Scripture leaves open the *how to* of hospitality.

What are some hindrances to hospitality? One is a failure to understand hospitality as part of OAN. Another is an unwillingness and fearfulness to spend time and energy in developing a relationship with someone.

This latter factor can be summarized in what I call the *fig-leaf* function of life. As a result of Adam's sin, all of his posterity is exposed: naked, ashamed, and guilty. In his own strength, a person attempts to clothe himself in what he considers is a *protective shell* (Philippians 3:3-6). He fails in this life and certainly in the next (Proverbs 13:15b; 28:1; Matthew 12:36-37).

As a result, he avoids relationships and getting to know people in more than a superficial way. Or he uses people for his gain. He thinks he is keeping others out, but he is only exposing his ignorance and arrogance because God created man as a social being for the good of one another (Genesis 2:18-23). Animals, also God's creation, were not the answer! They can serve a purpose but are not a replacement for biblical OAN.

In 2 John and 3 John (2 John 8-11; 3 John 5-8), John gave direction regarding the *when* hospitality. Believers are to be at peace with all men but as John's two letters taught, OAN is a discipleship ministry by believers, for believers, and of believers.

In his second letter (verses 8-11) he addressed the problem of being hospitable when one should not be. John gave a strong warning: Watch out because false teachers abound and are dangerous. Do not take them into your home! You may become like them. Such was one of God's injunctions to the Israelites as they prepared to enter the Promise Land (Deuteronomy 7:1-6).

As a result of showing hospitality to such as these, a member of the Church can become entangled in false teaching and produce division in the body of Christ. John wrote that these false teachers must be shunned. Shunning as a protective measure is to be included as part of OAN ministry.

In his third letter John (verses 5-8) also addressed the *"when"* of hospitality. It should be offered to those interested in the truth of Scripture where there will be intimacy around the Word in sharing time, energy, and even money.

John commends Gaius for his efforts in ministering to traveling missionaries. He calls him "faithful" and "loving." Gaius was contributing to the spread of the gospel message and growth of the Church and individual believers. OAN was another fruit of the Spirit. It taught relationships matter—both good and bad ones! John urged Gaius to continue (verse 8).

CHAPTER 15
OAN and Intimacy

Romans 16:16: *Greet one another with a holy kiss. All the churches of Christ send greetings to you.*

1 Corinthians 16:20 and 2 Corinthians 13:12: *Greet one another with a holy kiss.*

1 Thessalonians 5:26: *Greet all the brothers with a holy kiss.*

1 Peter 5:14: *Greet one another with a kiss of love. Peace to all who are in Christ.*

OAN INVOLVES CLOSENESS AND KNOWING others in an intimate way. Each of these passages urge greeting one another outwardly and visibly (kiss). What does *greet each* other mean especially in a time of protective "social-distancing?" Do we jettison God's command because of a pandemic? What is the Church to do?

First and foremost, the Church cannot let the issue separate Christians (Romans 14:1-15:7). The Church must be on God's side. OAN must be done. The issue: how do we OAN in this day and age? Individual churches must side with God. How can we be wise and good stewards? The world is watching how the Church is going to handle this situation.

A Christian greeting may resemble the culture's greeting but the two are not the same. It is more than having the capacity to *engage people* or being a *people person* or having the gift of gab or simply being friendly and nice or even giving a "high-five."

Rather, OAN greeting is not based on distance. It is to be outward and visible; holy, and chaste; warm and affectionate; praise-worthy, sincere, and non-discriminatory. It is to be effectual—it should lead to harmony and peace. In that way it models the Trinity.

Why? OAN is based on truth: every believer is a fellow heir. OAN when demonstrated outwardly and physically, it builds up the body and points to the truth given in 1 Peter 1:3-5. God is the Giver of hope and the Bequeather; He has heirs and safely and eternally holds an inheritance for them waiting for them to arrive. Peter intended that promise to build up the body when a pandemic of persecution and murder was picking up steam!

How OAN will look in times of lock-downs and pandemics is left to the local churches. Hospitality is to continue in some way and in some form. Pandemics did not catch God by surprise!

In contrast, the culture in the past (before pandemics) greets and praises someone without a godly reference. Society encourages the greeting of another for several reasons including:

he is present (there), he is popular, or he is preeminent (Matthew 23:5-7; Luke 11:43; 20:46; James 2:1-9).

Today, unbelievers still want to *hang out together*—socialize although Covid concerns have dampened down some enthusiasm for it. This is true because man was created a social being. OAN is inbred in people by God's creational design, but sin distorted the world's understanding of it—its meaning and its expression (Genesis 2:18-20).

Job's three friends, while armed with bad theology, wrong ideas, false assumptions, and misconceptions, were physically present with Job. They had the gift of silence initially. The three sat silently with Job for one week (Job 2:11-13). They were practicing OAN! The ministry of silence can be a godly ministry!

Mere physical presence can be an encouragement. However, in Job's case, *being there* did not solve Job's problems. The three friends were a burden to him when they spoke. They began to apply their wrong ideas and thoughts to Job's situation. Wrong theology acted upon led to a greater burden for Job.

Ephesians 5:19: *Speak to one another with psalms, hymns, and spiritual songs. Sing and make music in your heart to the Lord,*

Colossians 3:15: *Let the peace of God rule in your hearts, since as members of one body you were called to peace. And be thankful.*

The passage in the letter to the Ephesians occurs in the midst of Paul's admonition regarding a wise Christian walk—a patterned lifestyle of pleasing God. Ephesians 5:13-18: *But everything exposed by the light becomes visible, for it is light that makes everything visible. This is why it is said: "Wake up, O sleeper, rise from the dead, and Christ will shine on you. Be careful, then, how you live—not as unwise but as wise, making the most of every opportunity because the days are evil. Therefore, do not be foolish, but understand what the Lord's will is. Do not get drunk on wine, which leads to debaucher. Instead be filled with the Holy Spirit.*

In verse 15, Paul gave a warning: *Be very careful, then how you live.* Paul uses the term *how you live* to refer to the believer's walk or patterned life of thoughts, desires, and actions.

The believer has a different motivation: to live and walk and to grow as a God-pleaser. The walk includes OAN in the form of worship, mutual fellowship, talking with one another, and discipleship. The believer is to be careful how he conducts himself and his life. He is to do so as a wise person (verse 15)

Paul described a wise person in terms of a lifestyle of good stewardship and discerning God's will. A wise person is one who determines from the Word what God's will is and his responsibility in accomplishing it (Romans 12:1-2). The believer will find general principles and specific application of them. He is to be a good steward of his time and opportunities and work hard at understanding God's truth (verses 16-17).

He is motivated by the influence of the indwelling Holy Spirit rather than self-interest (verse 18). The picture Paul paints is vivid. Instead of the influence of wine or alcohol (or any other substitute) the believer is to be permeated and controlled by the Holy Spirit (verse 18). The believer is to be interested in pleasing God and not offending or grieving the Holy Spirit.

The believer, full of the Holy Spirit, has the mindset and motivation of Christ in all areas of life. He is not perfect, but he is growing. Wisdom is to be demonstrated—seen (James 1:22-25; 3:13-18). Therefore, believers will interact with each other in a characteristic manner as described in verse 19 and Colossians 3:15-16.

They will speak fruitfully to each other and enjoy praising and worshipping God together. Fellowship and OAN are part of discipleship, none of which are to be burdens. Paul's emphasis is not only on outer-man activities (singing) but thinking, wanting, and action that flow from both the inner and outer man. Paul speaks of a whole person.

Paul's picture is one of a melodious choir making music in their hearts: a joyful heart is good medicine for the physical body, for the heart, and the corporate body (Proverbs 12:25; 14:30; 15:13, 30; 16:24; 17:22).

Sweet sounds (even without words, a person's presence have *sounds* and influence!) flow from one believer to another because they flowed from the Triune God to the individual believer and the Church. OAN is a biblical mandate, pandemic or not. How do you implement the command and privilege to OAN?

The believer and the Church are called to grow. A pandemic and election results are God's milieu for growth and OAN. OAN addresses both the inner and outer man—the whole person individually and the church body—corporately.

CHAPTER 16
Passages addressing a negative aspect of One Anothering

ONE: TITUS 3:1-3: *REMIND THE people to be subject to rulers and authorities, to be obedient, to be ready to do whatever is good, to slander no one, to be peaceable and considerate, and to show true humility toward all men. At one time we too were foolish, disobedient, deceived, and enslaved by all kinds of passions and pleasures. We lived in malice and envy, being hated and hating one another.*

Paul's letter to Titus is a "how to" letter for organizing recent converts into well-functioning and orderly congregations. Problems abounded in these groups including how to live as new creatures in Christ and how to bring order out of disorder. Paul knew that OAN was essential for unifying them and preventing division and strife in these fledging congregations.

He began chapter 3 by reminding Titus to call his people to submit—be subject to all ordained authority (verse 1). As we have learned (see section on submission), submission is OAN submission which is Christ-like submission. It is for the good function of God's people (Romans 13:1-7; 1 Peter 2:13-3:6).

In verse 2, Paul calls for general OAN activities designed to bring God's people together individually and as a body. Paul made the same point in Philippians 2:3-4 and Romans 12:9-13; 13:8-10.

Further, Paul emphasized the fact that OAN required a radical change in the OAN-er. The phrase *at one time* in verse 3 refers to the believer's former family and lifestyle (walk and live as discussed elsewhere including mention of Ephesians 5:15-18). The natural consequence of that membership is a desire-feeling oriented, "me-first" style of living that Paul succinctly summarized in Galatians 5:13-18: *You, my brothers, were called to be free. But do not use your freedom to indulge the sinful nature; rather, serve one another in love. The entire law is summed up in a single statement: "Love your neighbor as yourself." If you keep on biting and devouring each other, watch out or you will be destroyed by each other. So I say, live by the Spirit and you will not gratify the desires of the sinful nature. For the sinful nature desires what is contrary to the Spirit, and the Spirit what is contrary to the sinful nature. They are in conflict with each other, so that you do not do what you want. But if you are led by the Spirit, you are not under law.*

Paul is referring to the moral drama played out in the heart with resultant inner and outer man thoughts, desires, and actions. Theologians call the former state and mode of existence a reflection of total depravity and total inability (see Romans 3:9-19; 8:5-8; Ephesians 2:1-3). It is the legacy of being "in Adam"[45]

---

45 *In a person* is a relational term. When Scripture uses the phrase *in a person*, it means a person is related to or united to another representatively. "In

Unsaved, fallen man has no desire and capacity to please God. Rather, he is at war with God attempting to dethrone Him. Such is sin and more accurately sinfulness. These truths are denied even by believers.

When the first Adam first sinned, he, and all posterity, forfeited the position of coregent and vicar of God's earth; he was exiled out of the Garden and expelled from personal intimacy with God; he and mankind became a son (some deny this fact but see John 8:44) and a servant in the kingdom and family of Satan.

As I have written previously but is worth repeating: the orientation and mantra of *me-first* characterizes the kingdom of darkness and deadness—the old man, the old nature, life apart from and opposed to the Spirit. Sadly, but gladly, it is present in believers (the sad!) until Christ returns (the glad!).

The serpent proposed false counsel—satanic counsel—that stood in contradistinction to God's truth which is now expressed in and by Jesus and Scripture. Truth trumps falsehood and Satan. Because Jesus is the Way, the Truth and the Life, Satan represents himself as a counterfeit second Adam and second Jesus (2 Corinthians 4:4-6 and Galatians 4:4-6 and John 14:6)!

The effect of being in Satan's kingdom and family is comprehensive and pervasive—it involves the whole person in terms of thoughts; of motivation, affections, and desires;

Adam" refers to every man's relationship to Adam who was the representative head of all mankind. As Adam was in the Garden, so was each person representatively. What Adam did, everyone who followed him did. Christ was born of a virgin and is sinless and is His own representative.

and of willful actions. It is characterized by a lifestyle flowing from thoughts and desires.

This pattern still lingers in the believer despite the fact that the believer is indwelt by the Spirit and not Satan. The believer has what is termed remaining or indwelling sin. Every believer has remaining sinfulness and the habituation to please self. The desire to please self dies slowly and never completely in this life.

The tendency to live according to Satan's counsel and under his influence is expressed in different ways in the Bible. Proverbs 22:15 says it is foolishness and it is bound up in the heart of a child. Proverbs uses the phrases "wise in one's own eyes" and "trusting in self" to express the principle of man's prideful, false autonomy (Proverbs 3:5-8; 26:5,12, 16; 28:11, 26; 29:25). In 2 Timothy 3:1-5 and Titus 3:3, Paul termed the patterned lifestyle as a form of godlessness manifested as foolishness and disobedience under the umbrella of enslavement to self via self-pleasing.

People are born sinners, sinning from the "get go"—from the womb (Psalm 51:5). No one needs to teach another to sin. Each one learns to become a more efficient and astute sinner until the "But now." That is Paul's term for a radical transformation produced by divine activity termed regeneration (Romans 3:21; Ephesians 2:4-6; Titus 3:4).

One of fruit and privilege of salvation is OAN described in verse 8: doing good, fine deeds by looking toward the interests of others rather than one's own (Titus 3:8: *This is a trustworthy saying. And I want to stress these things, so that those who have trusted in God may be careful to devote themselves to doing what is good. These things are excellent and profitable for everyone).*

Two: John 5:44: *How can you believe if you accept praise from one another yet make no effort to obtain the praise that comes from the only God?*

Jesus is referring to the mindset that assumes living under God's eyes is unimportant. Rather, what is important to the person is the gaze of self and others. According to this mindset, another person's opinion counts more than God's scrutiny (Proverbs 5:21-22; John 9:22; 12:43; Galatians 1:10; Hebrews 4:12-13). The person wants something!

John is speaking of sinful fear—fear of man—in contrast to godly fear—fear, awe, and reverence of God because of a true understanding of who He is and who man is. John knew men were worshippers by nature both in giving worship and in receiving it. After the fall, man worshiped himself denying that he is an idolater by nature (Romans 1:18-23)

Sin distorted this God-given fact; post-fall and even with salvation, both the believer and unbeliever, seek to be praised and worshipped. The unbeliever regularly and the believer too often desire to be God and receive only what He deserves.

Praise-seeking can take several forms. One may desire simply to be noticed, to be thanked, and even paid. Those desires in themselves may not be wrong. However, OAN activity that is for me, by me, and to me is part of *me-first* lifestyle learned and practiced in Satan's family. Further, it is anti-Matthew 5:3 and anti-Philippians 2:3-4 and fosters division within the body (James 3:13-4:3).[46]

Three: Romans 1:27: *In the same way, the men also abandoned natural relations with women and were inflamed with lust for one another. Men committed indecent acts with other men and received in themselves the due penalty for their perversions.*

In Romans 1:18-25 Paul wrote that fallen man suppresses or tries to deny and hold down or hold back truth about God and himself. Truth includes facts about God and man: God is the Creator and Controller, and man is a dependent creature.

Unregenerate mankind is a truth-suppressor and consequently he functions as a truth-exchanger (he accepts lies rather than truth); therefore, he is an idolater inverting the Creator-creature distinction.

In verse 27, Paul is speaking of relationships and a specific perversion of the heart manifested as homosexuality. He speaks of dishonorable passions-desires and the result of the pursuit to fulfill them. These desires are dishonorable and the person seeking after their fulfillment is dishonorable. Self is serving self. These people serve self at the expense of serving the Creator and caring for others.

---

46 See the following verses which address the topic of fear of man: John 9:22; 12:42-43; Galatians 1:10; Ephesians 6:5-9; Colossians 3:22-25.

They serve and worship the creature—self. Idolaters distort their God-designed worshipping capacity that is reserved solely for God. Their fulfillment involves using another person for one's own interest and gain. Others are sacrificed at the altar of *self-love*.

Sodom and Gomorrah and David's desire of using Bathsheba are prime examples of the sinful use and expression of God-ordained sexuality and intimacy (Genesis 18-19; 2 Samuel 11:2). It is the wrong kind of OAN! They lived by the *pleasure principle* that was distorted at and by the fall. Pleasure is for me *now*; *it* is not from or for pleasing God. The person is after good feelings: for me, to me, and by me at the expense of God and others (an inversion of Romans 11:36).

The term *self-love* and its expression are often spoken of as a "sexual attraction" in the culture. Not so. Initially, David did not know Bathsheba as a person but as an object to be had to satisfy himself. He used her to fulfill his desire of self-pleasure. Such was the culture of Sodom which is fast becoming the culture of America.

Four: James 4:11-12: *Brothers, do not slander one another. Anyone who speaks against his brother or judges him speaks against the law and judges it. When you judge the law, you are not keeping it, but sitting in judgement on it. There is only one Lawgiver and Judge, the one who is able to save and destroy. But you—who are you to judge your neighbor?*

James used the word *katalaleo* to indicate speaking against another or speaking down. The word indicates the use of destructive speech to accomplish speaking down or about someone. The remedy or put on is to speak someone up—*eulogeo*: speak well of him; *Eulogeo: eu*—good, well; *logos*: word) is often translated as "to bless" or "to speak well of." This speaking well is to be guided by truth.

Speaking another down is judging not only the other person (see Romans 14-15) but also the Lawgiver—God. Truth telling must be in love, for God's good purpose, motivated by love of God and neighbor, and appropriate for the occasion (Ephesians 4:15, 25).

The Bible draws a line regarding the choice of words used by people. Words will be used either as a blessing and building up or for destruction and tearing down (Proverbs 10:19; 12:18; 16:21, 24; 17:27; 18:8; 22:21). Words convey thoughts and desires. Paul exhorted the Thessalonians to encourage one another and continue to build each other up (1 Thessalonians 5:11).

Five: Acts 7:26: *The next day Moses came up upon two Israelites who were fighting. He tried to reconcile them by saying, "Men, you are brothers; why do you want to hurt each other?"*

Within families, even God's family, there can be both verbal cannibalism (see Galatians 5:15) and physical cannibalism with physical injury (James 4:1-3). Paul describes this activity in general terms in Titus 3:3 and 2 Timothy 3:1-5. At its core is satanic reasoning and wanting. Moses intervened and perhaps properly. But he was rejected and fled to the wilderness for forty years!

CHAPTER 17
Summary and Questions

OAN MINISTRY IS A TESTIMONY of and grows out of the believer's relationship with Christ. Further, it is based on the guarantee and the down payment (*arabone*) of the Holy Spirit within the believer and the body of Christ and it is for all ages (Ephesians 1:14; 2 Corinthians 1:22; 5:5; 1 Corinthians 3:16; 6:19).

Since God is the Fountainhead of all love, OAN is an obligation of the one loved—the believer (1 John 4:7-12). It is also a privilege and blessing for the believer because it points to the Lover and membership in His family. Therefore, it is and should be considered an enjoyment for God's people.

The essence of OAN is love. God's people corporately and individually were OAN-ed by God resulting in a saving relationship between God and His people and between God and each Christian. Believers were loved by God into the kingdom when they were unlovely and unlovable by man's standard (Romans 5:6-10).

Humanly speaking, God had no business loving the unlovable. Too often for the believer, loving the unlovely makes little sense and is even harder to do. Yet recognizing the fact that the believer has been loved despite himself by Someone far greater than he, is a heart-opener!

The believer humbles himself and rejoices. He is grateful—which is an understatement—that God is a loving, trustworthy God. Now the believer takes on the obligation and privilege to act as OAN lover.

Consider these facts:

One: OAN is not natural because of the curse of sin. It takes God's radical change from the inside out. Post-fall, all men are self-pleasers and self-focused. This is the legacy of membership in Satan's family and kingdom and remaining sinfulness. God loved the believer out of his former family and kingdom into His kingdom and family. OAN is something the believer does out of gratitude for what God has done for him. He moves from self-pleasing to God-pleasing including OAN.

- Questions: Define OAN and answer: What is your understanding of OAN? How do the facts motivate you?

Two: OAN is commanded and is possible because of Christ's life, death, and resurrection, and the indwelling of the Holy Spirit in God's Church and the believer (Romans 5:5; 8:9, 11; 1 Corinthians 3:16; 6:19; 2 Corinthians 6:16-19; 2 Timothy 1:14). God does not give His people commands that they are unable to keep.

- Questions: How do the above facts fit the Immanuel principle (*God with us*: See Matthew 1:23 and wilderness wanderings in the book of Exodus: the pillar of fire and smoke: Exodus 13:21; 14:19-20; 33:9-10; Psalms 99:7; 105:39) and what is its significance?

Three: OAN involves service (*diakonia*) which is demonstrated OAN love: 1 John 4:7-12. Service is ministry.

- Question: How are you doing in the area of OAN? Give reasons. Then examine yourself and write out your plan to OAN. Be specific.

Four: OAN requires and thrives upon wisdom and discernment: James 3:13-18; 1 Thessalonians 5:14.

- Question: what is your understanding of the triad of truth, life, and ministry as it relates to OAN?

Five: OAN is heart-directed and purposeful: 1 Thessalonians 2:7-12; 2 Thessalonians 2:16-17.

- Question: Only the believer can love (1 John 4:7-12), comfort (2 Corinthians 1:3-4), forgive (1 John 1:7-9), and OAN. How do you respond?

Six: OAN involves activity in the whole person: thoughts, desires, and actions; Right Attitude; Thinking and Wanting.

1. Every member of the body belongs to the whole (Romans 12:5);
2. There is to be an equal concern for each member of the body (1 Corinthians 12:25);
3. There is to be patience—bearing with one another in love (Ephesians 4:2; Colossians 3:12);
4. OAN involves the development of the mind of Christ

within the body—proper thinking and wanting for self, others, and God (Philippians 2:5-11). This is one of the goals of sanctification and a specific function of the Church: Ephesians 4:11-13: *It was he who gave some to be apostles, some to be prophets, some to be evangelists, and some to be pastors and teachers, to prepare God's people for works of service so that the body of Christ may be built up until we all reach unity in the faith and in the knowledge of the Son of God and mature attaining to the whole measure of the fullness of Christ.*

5. It flows from the principles taught in Romans 12:10; Philippians 2:3-4; Colossians 4:6. Right speech which includes both words and the manner of speaking.
6. Luke 24:13ff: Post-resurrection, Jesus is on the road to Emmaus and appeared to two disciples. There was a "throwing back and forth of speech" (verse 14). The two were clueless to the reality of Jesus' resurrection. Yet Jesus unveiled Himself in words and fellowship until their hearts burned within (verse 32).

Seven: Within the body of Christ, there is to be an exchange of ideas for the purpose of burning hearts. There is to be an agreement and acknowledgment of a common purpose out of mutual interest of growing and changing into Christlikeness.

1. Proverbs 27:17: *As iron sharpens iron, so one man sharpens another.*

2. Romans 12:3-8: Believers are to think correctly about self and others with sober judgment.
3. Romans 15:14: Counseling is remedial discipleship and involves one-on-one use of the Scripture to lay or place on someone God's truth in order to bring about change.
4. Ephesians 4:15, 25: OAN requires speaking the truth in love—be graciously and courageously honest and humbly approachable with the goal to grow up into one body because we are all members of that body. OAN fosters a foretaste of heaven.

Eight: Believers are to have a servant's heart and a learner's spirit. OAN involves Right Action.

1. Romans 1:12: Paul encouraged mutual ministry so that: *you and I may be mutually encouraged by each other's faith*: faithful people proving faithful to each other's faith within the body. That is a goal of OAN.
2. Romans 12:3-8: Each believer is to do a self-inventory in order to think correctly about self, to make a sober judgment, and to keep the unity of the body in the forefront of his thinking in terms of the use of different gifts.
3. Ephesians 5:1-2: OAN-ers are lovers, "welcomers," and "acceptors." They are to be imitators, as dearly loved children. The body of Christ is family, and family life is to be patterned after Christ's love. When you see a OAN-er, you see Christ.

4. 1 John 3:11-18: I have paraphrased these verses that address some aspects of *how* believers are to act within the body. I think it is an accurate summary of body life and OAN.

It was given to a congregation for the purpose of assurance: so they may know they have eternal life—which starts her locally at home and at Church (5:13) Read them and write out the principles of OAN and write how you and your church are doing in applying them.

> Verse 11: *love one another.*
>
> Verse 12: *don't act like Cain who was a murderer. It was his legacy from Satan.*
>
> Verse 13: *The world (that system and those opposed to God in Christ) hates you as it did Jesus—John 15:18-21. Christians need to help one another.*
>
> Verse 14: *love is the sign of a radical and supernatural family and kingdom transfer. Members in the new family and kingdom look away from self to God and others.*
>
> Verse 15: *hate is murder and is the sign of membership in Satan's kingdom and his influence. It looks toward self.*

Verse 16: *love is demonstrated: laying down one's life for your brother.* What does it mean to "lay down one's life"? (John 10:14-18 and 13:1-17).

Verse 17: *helping those in need: material possessions* (Matthew 25:31-46).

Verse 18: *Love and wisdom are shown by words and deeds* (James 3:13-4:3).

Also by Dr. Jim Halla and Ambassador International

Being Christian in Your Medical Practice

Depression Through A Biblical Lens: A Whole-Person Approach

Endurance: What It Is and How It Looks in a Believer's Life

How to Be a God-Pleasing Patient: A Biblical Approach to Receiving Medical Care

Joy in Grief: God's Answer for Hard Times

Pain: The Plight of Fallen Man

The Book of Job: God's Faithfulness in Troubled Times

Out of the Maze: A Covenantal View of Hope

For more information about
Dr. Jim Halla
&
Out of the Maze
please visit:

www.jimhalla.com
www.facebook.com/jimhalla
jimhalla@yahoo.com

For more information about
AMBASSADOR INTERNATIONAL
please visit:

www.ambassador-international.com
@AmbassadorIntl
www.facebook.com/AmbassadorIntl

www.ingramcontent.com/pod-product-compliance
Lightning Source LLC
Chambersburg PA
CBHW070553090426
42735CB00031B/1997